1000 QUESTIONS AND ANSWERS

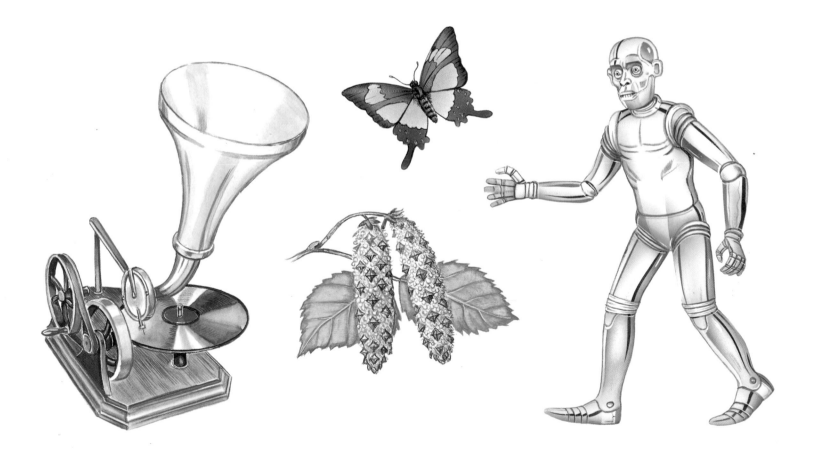

ARMADILLO

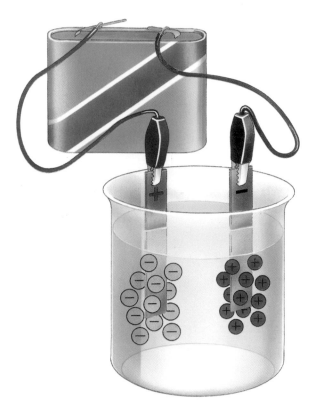

Text: Nicola Baxter
Design: Amanda Hawkes
Editorial consultant: Ronne Randall

Illustrations: Kim Broe-Ward (Linden Artists), Peter Bull Art Studio,
Rob Chapman (Linden Artists), Duncan Gutteridge,
Deborah Kindred (Linden Artists), Terry Pastor,
Steve Weston (Linden Artists)
Photographs: Corel Professional Photos

First published in 1997 by Armadillo Books
An imprint of Bookmart Limited
Desford Road, Enderby
Leicester LE9 5AD, England

ISBN 1-90046-503-5

Reprinted 1998 (three times)
Reprinted 1999

Printed in Italy

CONTENTS

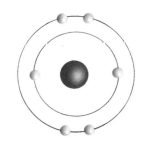

HOW THINGS WORK

 CONTENTS

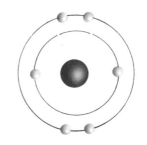

HOW THINGS WORK

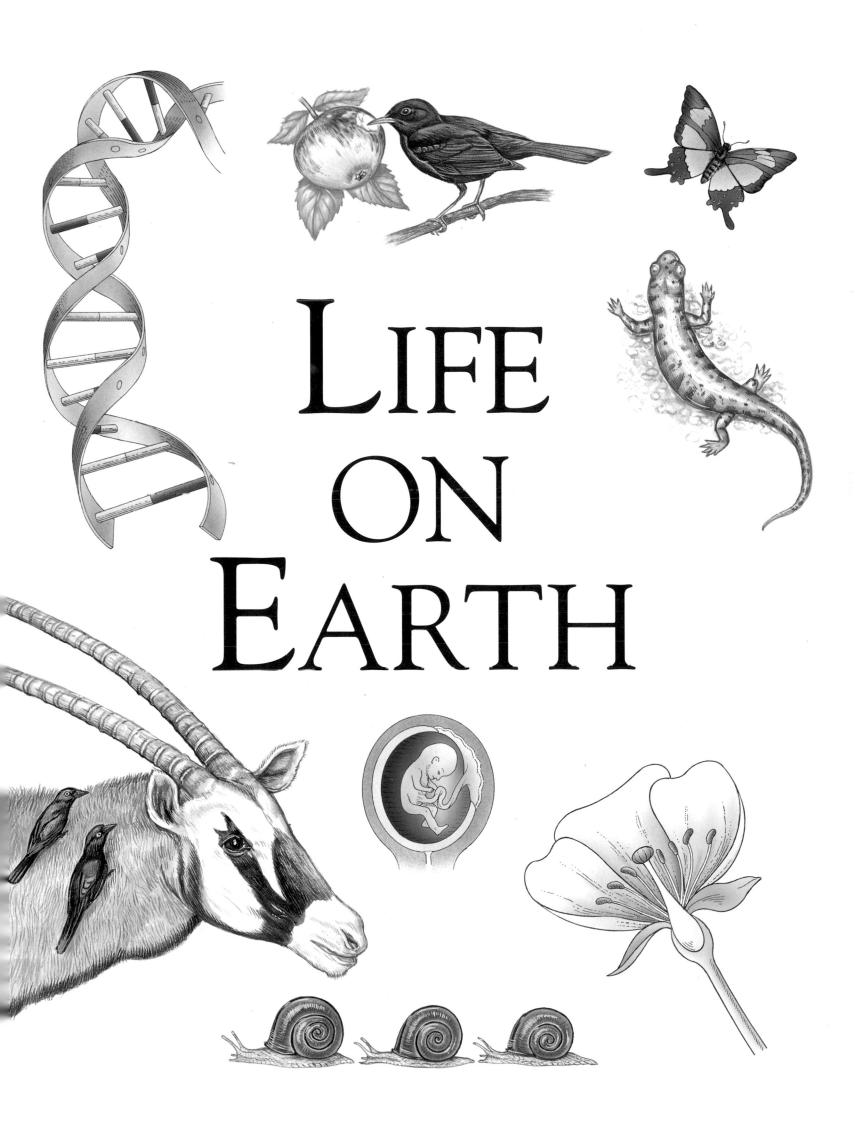

LIFE ON EARTH

WHERE IN THE UNIVERSE ARE WE?

The universe is the name we give to all of space. Astronomers use huge telescopes, both on Earth and in space, to measure light, x-rays and radio waves from objects that are billions of light years away. Earth is one of the nine planets that orbit our Sun. It is part of the Milky Way Galaxy, one of billions of galaxies in the universe.

WHICH IS THE NEAREST STAR?

THE SUN is our nearest star. It is 149.6 million km (92.9 million miles) away from Earth. Stars are massive nuclear reactors,

generating energy in their cores. It is the heat and light from the Sun that makes life on Earth possible. The huge gravity pull of the Sun keeps the planets of our Solar System orbiting around it.

WHAT ARE THE PLANETS OF THE SOLAR SYSTEM?

THE FIRST FOUR planets are known as the Inner Planets. The remaining five are the Outer Planets.

Planet	Diameter	Length of year	No. of moons
Mercury	4878km	88 Earth days	0
Venus	12,103km	225 Earth days	0
Earth	12,756km	365 Earth days	1
Mars	6794km	687 Earth days	2
Jupiter	142,800km	11.9 Earth years	16
Saturn	120,000km	29.5 Earth years	18
Uranus	52,400km	84.0 Earth years	15
Neptune	49,400km	164.8 Earth years	8
Pluto	1100km	248.5 Earth years	1

WHAT IS A GALAXY?

A GALAXY is an enormous group of stars held together by gravity. Our galaxy, the Milky Way, is in the shape of a spiral. Other galaxies are elliptical or irregular. There may be 100 billion galaxies in the universe. Many of them are grouped together in clusters, with huge areas of space in between.

spiral galaxy   elliptical galaxy   irregular galaxy

WHY DO CONSTELLATIONS HAVE SUCH STRANGE NAMES?

HUMAN BEINGS have always tried to see pictures in the patterns the stars make. The names given to those pictures by European scholars in medieval times and earlier are often used by astronomers today. Most of them are in Latin as that was the language of scholarship in Europe for hundreds of years.

Aquila (the eagle)   *Scorpius* (the scorpion)

IS THERE LIFE ELSEWHERE IN THE UNIVERSE?

As there are so many billions of planets in the universe, it may be that life exists on some of them. In 1996 scientists believed they had discovered signs of fossilized life in a meteorite that landed on Earth from Mars.

WHAT ARE SHOOTING STARS?

Shooting stars are meteors, made of particles of rock and dust, that shine brightly as they burn up in the Earth's upper atmosphere.

WHY IS IT SOMETIMES HARD TO SEE THE STARS?

The stars are still there! It may be that cloud is covering the night sky. Also, there is so much artificial light at night now, from homes and street lighting, that it is often not dark enough to see the stars.

WHAT IS AN ECLIPSE?

Eclipses happen for a brief period when the Moon, Earth and Sun are in line. A lunar eclipse happens when the Earth lies between the Moon and the Sun, blocking off the light to the Moon, so that the Moon seems to vanish. A solar eclipse is when the Moon blocks the Sun's light from the Earth, so that the Sun seems to disappear.

Space travel gave human beings their first opportunity to see the Earth from outside the Earth's atmosphere.

WHEN DID SPACE EXPLORATION BEGIN?

THE FIRST ARTIFICIAL SATELLITE, *Sputnik 1*, was launched by the USSR in October 1957. The same year, a dog called Laika was the first living creature to travel in space in *Sputnik 2*. It was the USSR again that put the first human in space in 1961, when Yuri Gagarin travelled in *Vostok 1*. In 1969, US astronauts were the first to land on the Moon in *Apollo 11*.

As there is no wind or weather on the Moon to erase them, the footprints left by astronauts are still there!

WHY DOES THE MOON CHANGE SHAPE EACH MONTH?

OF COURSE, the Moon does not really change shape – it just seems as though it does. The Moon orbits the Earth once every 27.3 days. It has no light of its own, but as it moves around, it is lit by the Sun. Only the part of the Moon that is both turned towards the Earth and lit by the Sun is visible on Earth. The amount of the Moon's surface that can be seen changes as the Moon's position changes.

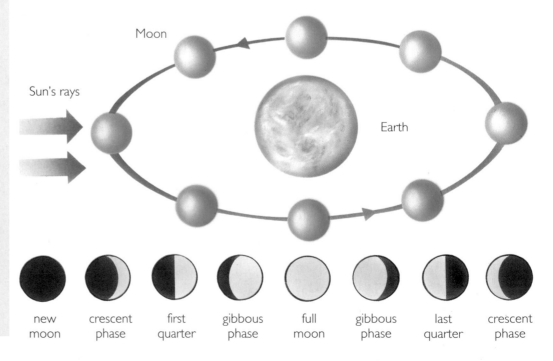

Moon

Sun's rays

Earth

new moon | crescent phase | first quarter | gibbous phase | full moon | gibbous phase | last quarter | crescent phase

WHAT IS INSIDE THE EARTH?

Beneath the land and water that cover the Earth's surface lie layers of rock and metal at very high temperatures. The deepest mines ever dug have not reached the bottom of the outer layer, called the crust. Under the crust, a layer called the mantle is thought to be made partly of solid and partly of molten rock. At the centre of the Earth, there is an outer core of molten metal and an inner core of solid metal, probably largely iron.

crust
between 5 and 80km
(3 and 50 miles) thick

mantle
2900km (1800 miles)
thick

HOW ARE EARTHQUAKES MEASURED?

THE SIZE of the shock waves from an earthquake is measured on the Richter scale. No earthquake has ever measured more than 9 on this scale. However, the size of the shock waves cannot tell us how much damage the earthquake has done. That depends on many factors, such as the kind of soil on which buildings are constructed, how they are built and so on. The effects of earthquakes are measured on the Modified Mercalli scale. The highest point on this scale is 12, which describes the total destruction of all buildings but has luckily rarely been used.

outer core
2255km (1400 miles) thick

inner core
1200km (745 miles) thick

WHAT CAUSES EARTHQUAKES?

THE EARTH'S CRUST is made up of 15 pieces or "plates", which float on the molten rock below. The places where these plates meet are called faults. Along the lines of faults, the plates move and push against each other. Sometimes this causes a violent shock, with waves of tremors moving out and shaking the Earth's surface.

The San Andreas fault runs along the west coast of the United States of America. Most older houses in San Francisco, which lies near the fault, are built of wood. They do not collapse as easily as brick buildings if the ground shakes.

CAN ANY BUILDING WITHSTAND AN EARTHQUAKE?

NO STRUCTURE can withstand very large earthquakes, but by using reinforced materials and foundations that allow for movement, architects have been able to design buildings able to survive even quite strong shocks.

In Tokyo new buildings are designed to withstand most earth tremors.

WHAT IS A GEYSER?

IN SOME AREAS, underground lakes, rivers and springs are heated by molten rocks below. The hot water bubbles to the surface in springs and forms pools, or it may shoot upwards under great pressure, forming a geyser.

This famous geyser in Yellowstone National Park, USA, is known as "Old Faithful".

WHY DO VOLCANOES ERUPT?

LIKE EARTHQUAKES, volcanoes mainly occur along fault lines. Molten rock, gases and ash are forced out through a gap in the Earth's crust to release the pressure beneath. Over thousands of years, cooled rock sometimes builds up around the fissure in the ground to form the familiar conical shape of a volcano.

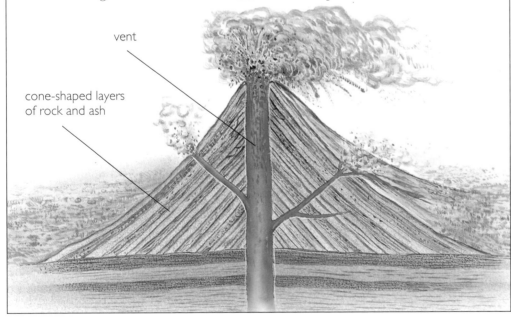

vent

cone-shaped layers of rock and ash

WHAT CAN VOLCANOES TELL US?

ONE interesting aspect of volcanic eruptions is that surrounding areas are covered rapidly in molten rock or ash, sometimes preserving the animals, plants and structures underneath. Archaeologists have been able to study life in Roman times, for example, by examining the remains of Pompeii, in Italy, buried when Vesuvius erupted in AD 79.

fast facts

CAN EARTHQUAKES BE PREDICTED?

Not very well. Scientific instruments attempt to detect early signs, and the behaviour of birds and animals may give warning of a shock, but none of these methods is currently foolproof.

WHAT IS THE EPICENTRE OF AN EARTHQUAKE?

The epicentre is the point on the Earth's surface directly above where the earthquake occurs. Shock waves move out from the epicentre to surrounding areas.

WHAT IS A TSUNAMI?

A tsunami is a huge tidal wave, caused by an undersea earthquake. It is dangerous to shipping and can also cause damage on land when it breaks over the coast.

ARE THERE VOLCANOES UNDER THE SEA?

Most active volcanoes *are* under the sea! Their effects are usually not noticed on land.

WHAT IS A DORMANT VOLCANO?

Dormant means "sleeping". A dormant volcano might erupt in the future. An *extinct* volcano, on the other hand, will not become active again.

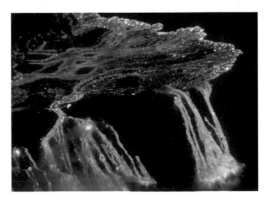

The lava flow from a volcano can be spectacular, as this photograph of Kilauea Volcano, Hawaii, shows.

WHEN DID LIFE BEGIN ON EARTH?

The Earth began to be formed over 4.5 billion years ago, but for millions of years nothing could live here. Gradually, the Earth's crust and the atmosphere formed. The simplest forms of life, bacteria and algae, probably began to grow less than four billion years ago. Human beings did not appear until about two million years ago.

On the coast of Western Australia, strange formations called stromatolites have been found. They are formed of layers of fossils of blue-green algae and may be over three billion years old.

WHAT WERE THE FIRST LIVING THINGS ON EARTH?

ALTHOUGH VIRUSES are the simplest living things, they need to live and reproduce themselves inside a larger organism, so they are unlikely to have been the first living things on Earth. The earliest evidence of life that has been found is tiny fossils of primitive bacteria in rocks about 3800 million years old. Later, blue-green algae evolved. They could use energy from the Sun and in so doing gave off oxygen. Modern plants and animals share these simple organisms as ancestors.

HOW DO WE KNOW ABOUT PREHISTORY?

ALMOST EVERYTHING that we know about the living things on Earth before humans evolved has been learnt from fossils. Fossils are the remains of dead animals and plants that have been turned to stone over millions of years.

An animal dies and is covered by sediment washed on top of it.

Under great pressure, the sediment slowly solidifies into rock.

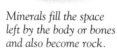

Minerals fill the space left by the body or bones and also become rock.

Over thousands of years, weather and the Earth's movement may bring the fossil to the surface.

HOW ARE PREHISTORIC TIMES DESCRIBED?

THE PERIODS when the Earth was forming and early kinds of life were developing have been given names. There is also a short way of saying "55 million years ago": 55mya.

WHEN DID THE EARTH BEGIN TO LOOK AS IT DOES TODAY ?

THE SURFACE of the Earth is changing all the time. When living things first began to evolve on Earth, there was just one huge continent. Over millions of years, this continent broke up and moved to become the land masses we recognize today. This is why similar dinosaur fossils have been found in very different parts of the world, although dinosaurs were land creatures and could not cross the oceans.

PRECAMBRIAN 4600–590mya	PALEOZOIC 590–248mya						MESOZOIC 248–65mya		
	Cambrian	Ordovician	Silurian	Devonian	Carboniferous	Permian	Triassic	Jurassic	Cretaceous

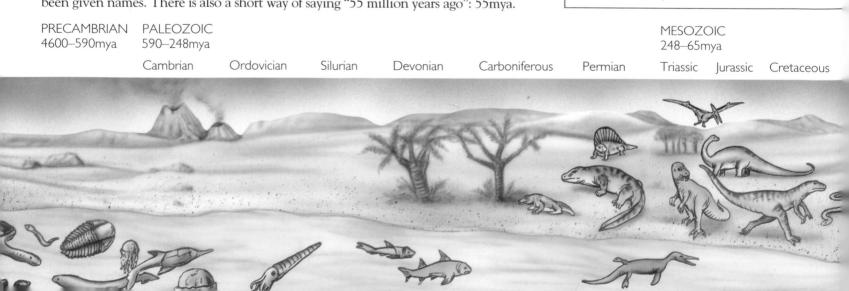

fast facts

WHAT IS PREHISTORY?

Prehistory is what we call the time before written records.

CAN WE SEE EVOLUTION HAPPENING?

It takes many, many generations for evolutionary changes to take place, so we cannot usually see them happening. But as some insects live for a day or less, scientists can trace changes in them in only a few years.

WHAT IS PALAEONTOLOGY?

Palaeontology is simply the scientific name for the study of fossils.

ARE NEW FOSSILS STILL BEING FOUND?

Every year fossils are found that add to our knowledge of prehistoric life. Very often they are discovered by ordinary people walking in the countryside. Places where soil is frequently being washed away from rocks, such as at the bottom of cliffs, are good places to look.

WHAT IS EVOLUTION?

LIVING THINGS inherit characteristics from the generations that have gone before, but each individual is slightly different. Over many generations, the differences that are more successful survive, so that the species gradually adapts. In time, these changes, called evolution, can lead to major adaptations and even new species. All living things have evolved from the simple organisms that began to grow in the Earth's waters. Many of these, such as the dinosaurs, have since become extinct, although they may have lived successfully on Earth for millions of years.

WHEN WERE FOSSILS DISCOVERED?

EVER SINCE HUMAN BEINGS first lived on Earth they have been finding fossilized remains. But it was really only in the nineteenth century that scientific study of the fossils took place. Until then, people believed that the fossils came from dragons, giants or even unicorns!

There are large gaps in the fossil record that have puzzled scientists. That is why there was once talk of "missing links" – living things that had evolved to a point between early fossil forms and modern creatures and plants. Although some modern reptiles look as ancient as dinosaurs, they are not directly descended from them, but they may share a common ancestor.

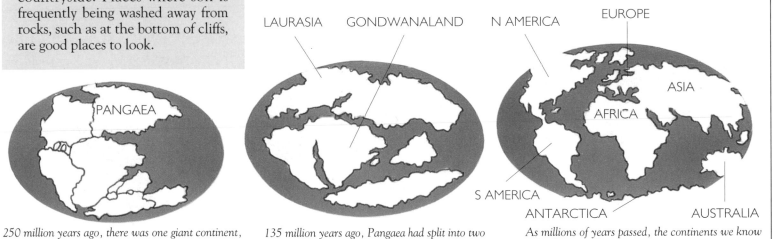

250 million years ago, there was one giant continent, now named Pangaea.

135 million years ago, Pangaea had split into two main continents: Laurasia and Gondwanaland.

As millions of years passed, the continents we know today began to form.

CENOZOIC
65mya–today

Tertiary   Quaternary

DID DINOSAURS RULE THE EARTH?

During the 150 million years that they lived on Earth, dinosaurs certainly included the largest creatures to live on land and the fiercest hunters. But they were not the only animals to live successfully on Earth by any means. There were many species of insect and the earliest winged animals could be seen in the skies. The seas were teeming with fish and other sea-life. The first mammals were also thriving, ready to become the dominant creatures when the dinosaurs became extinct.

WHAT COLOUR WERE DINOSAURS?

DINOSAUR FOSSILS, even when they show the skin of the animal, cannot show us what colour it was. Dinosaurs may have been green and brown in colour, camouflaging them amongst the leaves and rocks. It is also possible that some of them were very brightly coloured, just as some tropical lizards are today.

This scene shows what the landscape may have looked like during the Cretaceous period. In many parts of the world there were plentiful streams and rivers, with marshy plains in between. Lush vegetation allowed the plant-eating dinosaurs to grow even larger.

Iguanodon was a plant-eater, tearing leaves from high branches.

Baryonyx had sharp claws and teeth. It is likely that it ate fish from streams and lakes.

Polacanthus was a plant-eating dinosaur, browsing near the ground. Its spines helped to protect it from attack.

Fossil footprints show that some dinosaurs, such as *Hypsilophodon*, seem to have moved in groups. As with herds of browsing animals today, this meant that they were safer from predators.

ARE FOSSILS THE ONLY EVIDENCE OF LIFE IN PREHISTORIC TIMES?

OVER TIME, the remains of plants and animals decay. Fossilization is one way in which their forms have survived to give us information about prehistoric times. Since the time of the dinosaurs, however, the climate of parts of the Earth has cooled. In recent years, frozen remains of mammoths and even humans have been found, preserved in the ice of polar or mountainous regions.

Another source of information about prehistoric life is cave painting. In several parts of the world, early paintings have been found on rocks, often hidden from view for thousands of years. Viewed by the flickering light of torches, as they would have been when first painted, the animals almost seem to move.

WHAT HAPPENED TO THE DINOSAURS?

ONE THEORY is that climate changes gradually led to a drop in dinosaur numbers. Another is that a huge meteorite hit the Earth, throwing up a massive dust cloud. Mammals managed to survive the climate change, but dinosaurs did not.

WHO WERE THE FIRST HUMANS?

SCIENTISTS believe that humans and apes had a common ancestor. About five million years ago in Africa, some hominids (early humans) began to walk on two legs. Over millions of years, they developed bigger brains and began to spread out to other parts of the world. Later hominids began to make tools, develop language, use fire and wear clothes. The scientific name for modern people is *Homo sapiens sapiens*. They invented farming about 9000 years ago. Their early settlements led to the first civilizations.

Homo habilis made stone tools.

Homo erectus used fire and could live in cooler climates.

Homo sapiens neanderthalensis lived in Europe and had burial ceremonies.

Homo sapiens sapiens, modern man, does not seem to have evolved from Homo sapiens neanderthalensis.

HOW ARE LIVING THINGS CLASSIFIED?

Living things are classified in groups that have certain characteristics in common. The largest groups are called kingdoms. All living things can be classified as belonging to one of the five kingdoms: animals, plants, fungi, protists and monerans. Kingdoms can be divided into phyla (singular: phylum) or divisions and subphyla, which in turn can be separated into classes. Classes are divided into orders and suborders. These are separated into families and then into genera (singular: genus). Finally, each genus contains a number of species.

WHICH ARE THE SIMPLEST LIVING THINGS?

MEMBERS of the moneran and protist families are the simplest organisms. Individuals are much too small to be seen without a microscope.

HOW IS A LION CLASSIFIED?

LIONS belong to the:

Animal (*Animalia*) kingdom
Chordate (*Chordata*) phylum
Mammal (*Mammalia*) class
Carnivore (*Carnivora*) order
Cat (*Felidae*) family
Big cat (*Panthera*) genus
Lion (*leo*) species

The scientific name for lions is *Panthera leo*, the last two divisions.

WHICH IS THE LARGEST GROUP OF LIVING THINGS?

THE CLASS of insects is the largest class of living things, containing over one million different species.

WHY DO LIVING THINGS HAVE LATIN NAMES?

THE SYSTEM of classifying living things was invented by a Swedish botanist called Carolus Linnaeus (1707–78). Latin was traditionally the language used by scholars, so the classifications have Latin names. This also means that living things can be identified by scientists in every country, no matter what the local name for a species might be.

Classifying millions of living things is very complicated. This chart has been simplified to include the main groups of plants and animals.

KEY

KINGDOM

phylum

class

MONERANS

single-celled organisms without a cell nucleus, such as bacteria

PROTISTS

single-celled organisms with a cell nucleus, such as amoebas and diatoms

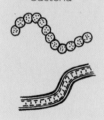

FUNGI

organisms with bodies made of a mass of threads, feeding on plants and animals, such as moulds, mildews and mushrooms

PLANTS

have cell walls of cellulose, and most make their food from sunlight by photosynthesis

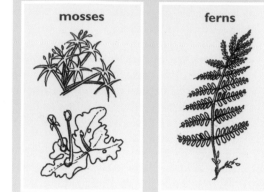

mosses

ferns

ANIMALS

can move for at least part of their lives, feeding on plant or animal matter

sponges

molluscs

sea anemones, jellyfish, corals

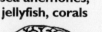

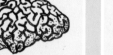

flatworms, tapeworms

star fish, sea urchins

roundworms

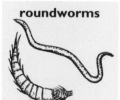

leeches, worms

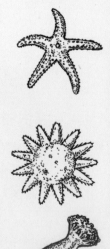

conifers

flowering plants

monocotyledons
have seeds with only one seed-leaf (cotyledon)

dicotyledons
have seeds with two seed-leaves

chordates
have a backbone (vertebrates) or stiff spinal cord

fish

amphibians

reptiles

birds

mammals

arthropods
have jointed bodies, divided into segments, with an external skeleton

horseshoe crabs

millipedes

centipedes

scorpions, spiders

insects

crabs, lobsters, shrimps

fast facts

ARE NEW SPECIES STILL BEING DISCOVERED?

There are many parts of the Earth where new species are still being discovered, including the rainforests, which are teeming with living things, and the oceans, still the least explored part of our planet.

HOW ARE NEW SPECIES NAMED?

Usually new species can be fitted into an existing genus. The species name may describe a characteristic of the new discovery or show where it was found, or it may be named after the person who found it.

WHAT IS AN EXTINCT SPECIES?

An extinct species is one where there are no more living examples on Earth.

HOW MANY SPECIES HAVE BECOME EXTINCT?

Species are evolving all the time. The climate, new predators, or the success of other species may cause them to become extinct. It is thought that as many as 95% of the species that have ever lived on Earth are now extinct.

DOES THE CLASSIFICATION OF LIVING THINGS EVER CHANGE?

When Linnaeus first proposed his system of classification, he based his decisions mainly on the appearance of the living things. Since then, scientists have been able to study the physical and chemical structures of organisms and form views on how they evolved historically. This has meant that some living things have been reclassified as more is known about them.

HOW DO PLANTS LIVE?

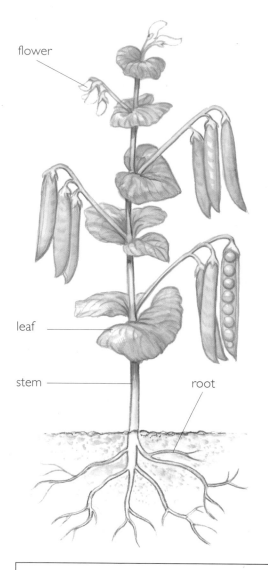

flower

leaf

stem

root

Like animals, plants need food for energy to survive and grow, but while animals can move about to catch their food or find new areas of vegetation, plants are usually rooted to one spot. But plants can do something that no animal can do. They can make energy from sunlight. This process is called photosynthesis. As well as light, plants also need water and nutrients.

HOW DOES PHOTOSYNTHESIS WORK?

A PLANT'S LEAVES contain a green substance called chlorophyll. The chlorophyll enables chemical reactions to take place. These use energy from the Sun and carbon dioxide gas from the air to make food for the plant to live and grow. As photosynthesis happens, oxygen is given off into the air.

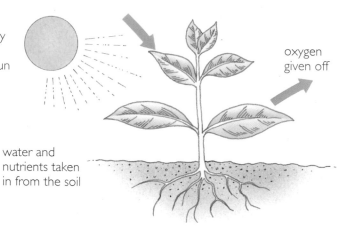

carbon dioxide from the air

light energy from the Sun

oxygen given off

water and nutrients taken in from the soil

WHAT ARE PLANTS USED FOR APART FROM FOOD?

OVER THOUSANDS OF YEARS, human beings have found many uses for plants. Some of the most common ones are shown here.

Both linen and cotton threads, used to make fabric, come from plants.

Most paper is made from the cellulose fibres found in wood pulp.

Rubber comes from the sap of a tropical tree.

Sisal and hemp are tough plant fibres used for ropes and matting.

Many objects, including buildings, are made from wood.

Plant extracts are used in perfumes and many cosmetic and cleaning preparations.

WHY ARE PLANTS IMPORTANT?

IF THERE WERE NO PLANTS, there could not be animal life on Earth. All animals either eat plants or eat other animals that in turn eat plants themselves. In this way, every living thing on Earth indirectly gets its energy from the Sun, although only plants can convert the Sun's light into a usable form.

Humans use milk and meat from cows for energy. Cows take in energy from plants. Plants convert energy from the Sun. This is called a food chain.

HOW DO PLANTS REPRODUCE?

THERE ARE TWO MAIN WAYS in which plants reproduce. In sexual reproduction, pollen is transferred by insects or the wind from one part of a flower to another, in such a way that fertilization can take place. Seeds are then formed. These seeds in turn are distributed in different ways to a spot where they can germinate and grow.

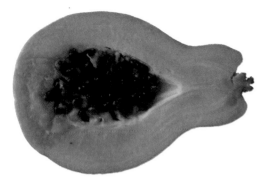

Seeds may be surrounded by fleshy fruit. Some fruits, such as cherries, contain just one seed. Others, like this papaya, have many seeds inside.

This popular houseplant produces small plants at the end of stems. If put in soil, these will grow and can be separated from the parent plant.

In asexual reproduction, a plant can reproduce without fertilization taking place. It may, for example, reproduce by sending out runners from its roots or by growing new plants on the tips of its leaves or branches.

DO PLANTS REALLY EAT INSECTS?

SOME PLANTS do gain extra minerals and other nutrients by trapping and "eating" insects. They are usually found in areas where there are not enough nutrients in the soil for healthy growth.

When an insect lands on tiny hairs on the Venus' flytrap's sensitive leaf tips, the pairs of leaves snap shut, trapping the insect inside.

HOW HAVE HUMANS CHANGED PLANTS?

ABOUT 9000 years ago, human beings invented farming. Since then, they have carefully selected the crops that give the best harvests under different conditions. Particularly in the last two hundred years, selective plant breeding has developed the characteristics that farmers and consumers require. Now that machines are used to pick most crops, and large stores prefer to package fruits and vegetables in regular sizes, many commercial varieties have been bred to produce even fruits that ripen together.

In the wild, flowers appear over a period of weeks. Commercial growers have bred varieties that will flower and can be picked all at one time.

DO ALL PLANTS HAVE FLOWERS?

Flowering plants are known as angiosperms. Although there are plenty of plants that do not have flowers, such as mosses, ferns, algae and conifers, the majority of plants on Earth are flowering ones. That does not mean that they are what we generally think of as flowers – colourful blooms that can be presented in bouquets. Most trees and grasses, for example, are flowering plants, but their flowers may be so small that they usually go unnoticed.

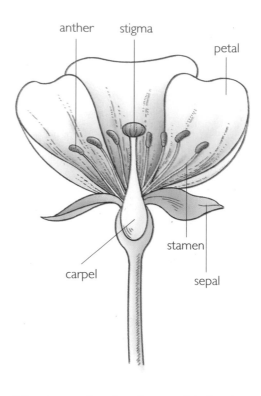

WHAT ARE FLOWERS FOR?

FLOWERS are the reproductive parts of a plant. Usually, one flower has both male and female parts. The male parts are the stamens, which consist of filaments and anthers. Filaments are like little stalks that support the anthers. Anthers produce tiny dust-like grains called pollen. The female part of a flower is called the carpel. This consists of an ovary, ovules, a style and a stigma. The ovary is hidden in a bulb-shaped receptacle at the base of the flower. Inside the ovary are one or more ovules, which become seeds if the flower is fertilized. Rising from the ovary is a small, sticky stem called the style, the tip of which is the stigma. In order for a flower to be fertilized, pollen must be transferred from the male stamen to the female stigma.

Although many plants have flowers with both male and female parts, as in this cross-section, some have male and female flowers on the same plant, and some have only male or only female flowers. Holly trees are an example of this. In order for a female holly to produce berries, it must be fertilized by a nearby male holly, which will never produce berries.

WHY ARE THERE SO MANY FLOWER SHAPES?

THE DIFFERENT SHAPES of flowers help to ensure that they are fertilized. Flowers that rely on insects for pollination must make sure that the insect is carrying pollen from the same kind of plant. The shape of the flower ensures that only certain kinds of insect can pollinate it. Flat flowers, such as daisies and sunflowers, can be visited by hoverflies and some bees. Flowers that are formed into tubes only attract insects that have long tongues. As flowers bloom at different times of the year, there are usually only a few different species available to each insect at any one time, so the chances of pollination are increased.

The ancestors of these garden flowers developed different formations of petals, stamens and carpels. Over the centuries, horticulturists have developed these shapes further by selective breeding.

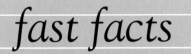
fast facts

WHICH IS THE LARGEST FLOWER?

The largest flower in the world is *Rafflesia arnoldii*, from Asia. Its flowers can measure over 1m (3ft) across.

WHAT ARE PERENNIALS, BIENNIALS AND ANNUALS?

Some plants grow from a seed, flower, produce their own seeds and die all in one year. They are called annuals. Those taking two years to complete their life cycle are called biennials. Plants that live for several years, even if they die down in the winter, are called perennials.

WHAT IS POT-POURRI?

This fragrant mixture is usually made from dried flower petals, spices and sweet-smelling oils. It was very useful in the days when rooms – and people – were dirtier and smellier than we would like today, but pot-pourri is still popular for its sweet scent.

WHAT IS THE LANGUAGE OF FLOWERS?

From early times, flowers have been thought to have a special meaning when presented to a loved one. The Victorians developed this to a fine art. An admirer sending a red rose to signify "pure love" might receive the reply of a Michaelmas daisy, meaning "farewell"!

HOW HAVE FLOWERS HELPED HISTORIANS?

Flowers seem very delicate, but parts of them last almost indefinitely in the right conditions. This is particularly true of pollen, which can still be recognized long after it was part of a growing plant. Historians have been able to tell which plants grew in ancient times by examining the pollen found in tombs and graves thousands of years old.

HOW ARE FLOWERING PLANTS FERTILIZED?

THE POLLEN that fertilizes the stigma may come from the same flower or from a nearby flower. Many flowers are fertilized (or pollinated) by insects. The flowers produce drops of a sweet liquid called nectar at the base of their petals. When insects visit the flower to drink the nectar, pollen from the anthers rubs off onto their wings, bodies and legs. When the insect visits another flower, the pollen is deposited on its sticky stigma.

Some plants, such as willows and hazels, have long dangling flowers called catkins. The wind is their pollinator, as great clouds of pollen blow off in the breeze and find their way to neighbouring catkins.

HOW ARE SEEDS DISPERSED?

WHEN THE FLOWER has been fertilized, the ovary swells to form a fruit, inside which one or more seeds will grow. These seeds may simply fall to the ground below, or the plant may have methods of ensuring that its offspring grow much further away.

Some seeds in fruits and berries have tough outer cases with fleshy fruits around them. The seeds can pass through the digestive system of birds and grow wherever the birds' droppings fall.

Dandelion seeds are dispersed by the wind. Each seed has a hairy parachute that can carry it for many metres.

Some trees rely on animals to carry their seeds far away. Squirrels, for example, collect acorns and nuts and may bury them to eat later. Often these stores are forgotten, and the seeds grow where they were buried.

HOW ARE NEW FLOWERS BRED?

FLOWERS that are closely related often cross-pollinate in the wild, creating a variety of flower shades and shapes. Under controlled conditions, plant breeders ensure that their parent plants are not pollinated naturally. They then transfer pollen from a selected "father" plant to the stigma of the "mother" plant and wait for seeds to form. These are sown to see what kind of flowers result. It may be years before the results are known and even then only a few of the plants will prove to be different and attractive enough to be launched as new varieties.

WHICH ARE THE BIGGEST PLANTS?

Trees are the largest plants on Earth and play a very important part on the planet. They cover almost a quarter of the Earth, helping to stabilize the atmosphere by taking in huge amounts of carbon dioxide from the air and giving off oxygen. In addition, tree roots help to retain fertile soil and stop the rain from washing it down hillsides, while the huge amount of water vapour given off by trees has an important effect on the weather.

WHY ARE TREES IMPORTANT?

As well as directly affecting the environment, trees supply homes and food for millions of other living creatures, including people. They are also the source of wood, which is used in buildings and for making such essential items as furniture and paper.

DO TREES HAVE FLOWERS?

Trees can be divided into two groups. Broad-leaved trees, which may also be deciduous, meaning that they drop their leaves in winter, are flowering plants. Sometimes their flowers are very small and difficult to spot. Conifers, most of which are evergreen, retaining their leaves all year round, are cone-bearers. They have small male cones and larger female cones instead of flowers.

apple-tree flowers

cone

The trunk, branches, leaves and roots of this tree provide food and shelter for many insects, birds and animals. Some plants, too, grow on these much larger plants.

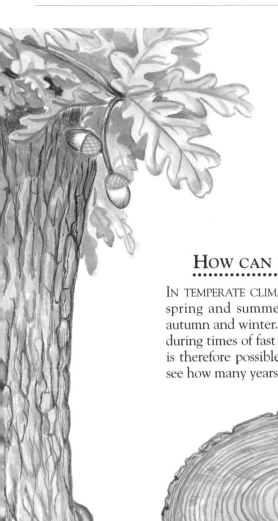

HOW ARE YOUNG TREES PRODUCED?

TREES PRODUCE SEEDS just as smaller plants do. Their flowers or cones are fertilized by the wind, or insects or birds. But a parent tree takes up large amounts of water from the area around it, and its leaves prevent sunlight from reaching the ground beneath, so it is important that all the seeds do not fall directly beneath the tree. Some trees produce fruits that are eaten by birds or animals and carried far away in their digestive systems. Others bear seeds that have "wings" and can be blown far away by the wind.

HOW CAN YOU TELL HOW OLD A TREE IS?

IN TEMPERATE CLIMATES, a tree makes rapid growth in the warm spring and summer months and much slower growth in the autumn and winter. This growth shows in the trunk as a light ring during times of fast growth and a darker ring for slower growth. It is therefore possible to count the pairs of light and dark rings to see how many years the tree has been growing.

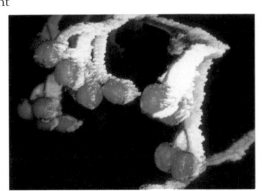

Hawthorn berries pass through the digestive system of birds before the seeds germinate. In winter, birds are glad of fruits to eat, as insects are hard to find.

Counting the rings of some ancient trees shows that they were growing when the pharaohs ruled Egypt.

HOW CAN YOU IDENTIFY A TREE?

OFTEN the easiest way to identify a deciduous tree is to look at the shape of its leaves. The general shape of the tree, the way in which the branches join and the pattern of the bark also give clues, especially in winter when the leaves have fallen.

fast facts

WHAT IS THE TALLEST TREE IN THE WORLD?

The giant sequoia is not only the tallest tree in the world but the tallest living thing of any kind. It can reach over 90m (270ft).

WHICH TREES LIVE THE LONGEST?

Yew trees can live to a very great age, but the oldest living tree is probably a bristlecone pine, in the western United States, which is over 4300 years old.

HOW MANY SPECIES OF TREE ARE THERE?

There are thought to be about 40,000 species of tree, of which about 700 are conifers.

WHAT WERE THE FIRST TREES LIKE?

Trees have been on Earth longer than many animals. The first trees were cone-bearing.

DO ALL TREES GROW TALL?

The dwarf willow, which grows in the Scottish highlands, reaches only 2.5cm (1 inch) in height.

WHAT IS AN INVERTEBRATE?

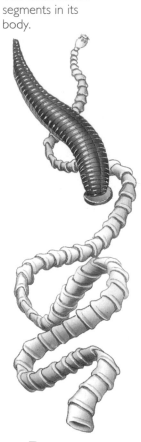

The leech has 33 segments in its body.

An invertebrate is an animal without a backbone. More than 90% of all animals are invertebrates. Insects form the largest group of invertebrates. Like millipedes and centipedes, crustaceans and spiders, they are arthropods, with jointed bodies and an outer protective casing. There are also many soft-bodied creatures, such as worms and jellyfish, often living in water or damp areas where sun and air will not dry out their bodies. Molluscs are also soft-bodied, but many of them are protected by an outer shell.

WHICH INVERTEBRATES CAN BE MISTAKEN FOR PLANTS?

CNIDARIANS are invertebrates, mainly living in the sea, that have a single space inside them where food is digested. A mouth leads from the outside to the space, which is called the coelenteron. Often the mouth is surrounded by tentacles, which help to catch food and pass it into the coelenteron. Corals, sea anemones and jellyfish are all cnidarians. Both corals and sea anemones can look like plants at first sight.

Brightly coloured sea anemones look like exotic flowers but are in fact made of jelly. Their waving tentacles have stinging cells to attack any small fish that swims through them. The tentacles then shorten to draw the fish into the body of the anemone, where it is slowly digested.

The coral reefs to be found in tropical waters are made from millions of little creatures, rather like sea anemones, called polyps. They live in colonies begun by just one polyp that "buds" and produces new polyps. Each polyp builds a hard skeleton around itself. When the polyps die, their skeletons remain.

HOW MANY DIFFERENT KINDS OF WORM ARE THERE?

THERE ARE well over fifty thousand different kinds of worm, divided into three main groups. The annelids have bodies that are divided into segments. They include earthworms and leeches. Roundworms, also known as nematodes, do not have segments. Many of these are crop pests, eating plants and making crops prone to diseases. Others are parasites, living on or in other animals, some causing serious diseases in humans. Finally, flatworms also include several parasites, including some with a complicated life cycle that involves them living in two different animal hosts one after the other.

Tapeworms are flatworms that live and lay eggs inside an animal. The eggs are passed out in the animal's waste matter and can then infect another host.

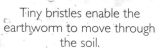

Tiny bristles enable the earthworm to move through the soil.

Earthworms improve the quality of the soil by mixing up different layers as they burrow and allowing water to drain freely through the soil.

Earthworms "eat" soil and digest small pieces of plant material in it as it passes through their bodies. Undigested soil is passed out of the other end of the worm to form wormcasts on the surface.

How does a man o' war catch its food?

ALTHOUGH at first sight the man o' war appears to be a jellyfish, in fact it is made up of a whole colony of polyps, each of which has a particular job to do. Some form stinging tentacles; others digest food; and one large polyp is filled with gas to form the "sail" that allows the man o' war to float, powered by the wind.

fast facts

Do you share your bath with an invertebrate?

Sponges are invertebrates! Natural sponges are the bodies of sea-dwelling animals. When alive, the sponge draws water through its holes to trap tiny food particles, which are then absorbed.

How have leeches been used by doctors?

Leeches are segmented worms with a sucker at each end. Some leeches attach themselves to animals and suck their blood. In the past, doctors used leeches to "bleed" a patient, thinking that they could draw out sickness that way. Today scientists are looking at the leech's ability to produce a chemical that stops blood from clotting, to see how this could help human beings.

Which animals have their skeletons on the outside?

ARTHROPODS have skeletons on the outside, which give them several advantages over soft-bodied animals. The skeleton forms a waterproof casing, preventing the body from drying out and allowing the animal to live outside water or damp places. In addition, skeletons on the outside, just like those on the inside, give muscles a firm anchoring point, so that the animal is often stronger than soft-bodied creatures of a similar size.

Which is the largest invertebrate?

The largest invertebrate is a mollusc, the giant Atlantic squid (*Archteuthis*), which can reach 20m (66ft).

How do centipedes and millipedes differ?

Centipedes are meat-eaters with only one pair of legs on each body segment. Vegetarian millipedes, however, have two pairs of legs on each segment.

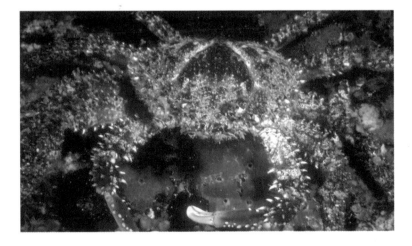

Centipedes, millipedes, spiders, insects and crustaceans are all arthropods. Some crustaceans, such as many crabs and lobsters, have particularly hard outer casings. Shrimps and barnacles are also crustaceans.

How common is the common earthworm?

Earthworms live in soil in which there is at least some plant material for them to eat. There can be well over seven million earthworms in every hectare of topsoil (over 17 million per acre).

What is a mollusc?

AFTER INSECTS, molluscs form the largest group of animals. Molluscs have soft, muscular bodies, often covered by a protective shell. Some, such as snails, move on a muscular foot, which can be withdrawn into the shell for protection. Other, sea-dwelling molluscs, such as squid and scallops, take in water and squirt it out to jet-propel themselves along.

CAN ALL INSECTS FLY?

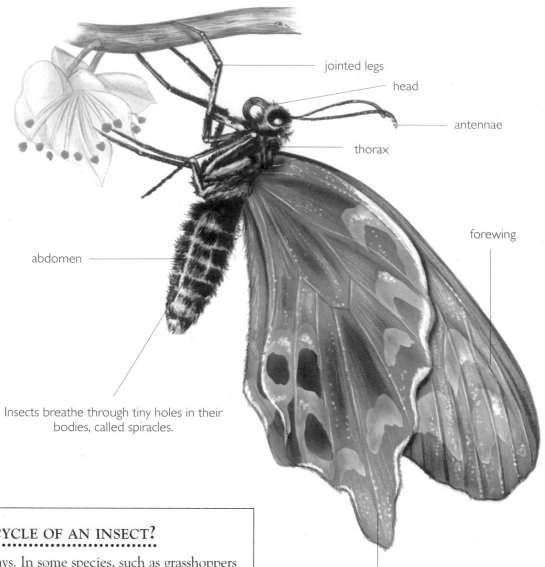

Most insects have wings at one time or another in their lives, although a very few species, such as fleas, silverfish, firebrats and springtails, do not. Flying insects have two pairs of wings – forewings and hindwings – although not all of them use both pairs for flying. All insects have a tough outer skeleton, six legs and bodies divided into three distinct parts, but there is enormous variation between insect species.

jointed legs

head

antennae

thorax

forewing

abdomen

Insects breathe through tiny holes in their bodies, called spiracles.

hindwing

WHAT IS THE LIFE CYCLE OF AN INSECT?

YOUNG INSECTS develop in two main ways. In some species, such as grasshoppers and locusts, the young that hatch from eggs look rather like small adults, and are called nymphs. As they grow, the nymphs shed their skins, looking more and more like adults each time.

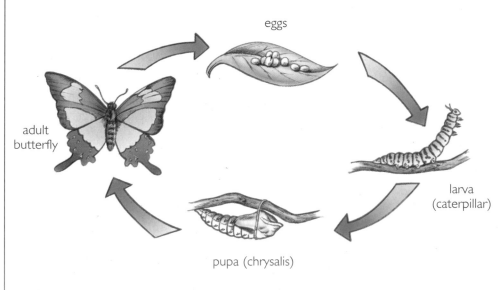

eggs

adult butterfly

larva (caterpillar)

pupa (chrysalis)

Other insects, such as butterflies, bees and beetles, go through a process called metamorphosis. Their eggs hatch into larvae or caterpillars. Later these become a pupa or chrysalis, within which an imago, or adult insect, develops. The larvae may live in a different habitat from the adult and require different foods.

ARE SPIDERS INSECTS?

SPIDERS belong to the class of arachnids, which also includes scorpions, ticks and mites. None of these are insects. They have eight legs, and their bodies are divided into two parts, not three.

Although they are not insects themselves, spiders are meat-eaters, feeding on insects – and other spiders.

WHICH INSECTS LIVE IN COLONIES?

WASPS, bees, ants and termites live in large social groups, in which individual insects each have their part to play in the success of the whole colony. These colonies are built around a single egg-laying female, called the queen. The colonies often build large and elaborate homes. Bees make structures containing six-sided cells in which eggs and honey can be safely stored. Ants and termites often build huge mounds, with tunnels and galleries inside, to house the colony.

Honey bees are able to tell other colony members where good sources of food can be found by performing a special dance on their return to the hive.

DO INSECTS HAVE EYES?

INSECTS' extraordinary compound eyes are made up of hundreds of tiny lenses. The images from all the lenses are made sense of by the insect's brain. Like us, insects can see colour, although in a different way. Flowers that seem dull to us may seem very bright to an insect. As well as having good vision, many insects have sensitive hearing and an acute sense of smell. A female moth, for example, gives off a smell that can be detected by male moths several kilometres away.

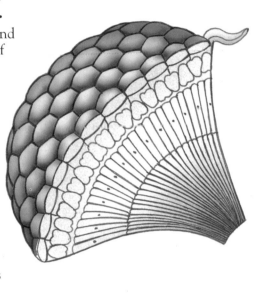

HOW DO INSECTS PROTECT THEMSELVES?

THERE ARE almost as many different ways in which insects protect themselves from enemies as there are different insects. Some insects, such as wasps and ants, have powerful stings or are able to shower their attackers with poisonous fluid. The hoverfly does not sting, but its colouring is so like that of a wasp or bee that enemies are very wary of it! Other insects, such as stick insects and praying mantises use camouflage. They look like the leaves and twigs among which they feed.

fast facts

WHICH IS THE BIGGEST INSECT?

The goliath beetle (*Goliathus*) can weigh well over 100g (3.5oz).

ARE THERE STILL INSECTS TO BE DISCOVERED?

Well over a million species of insect are known, yet many hundreds of previously unknown insects are discovered each year.

DO INSECTS HAVE BLOOD?

Insects do have blood, but it may be blue, yellow or green!

HOW CAN TINY INSECTS BE DANGEROUS TO HUMANS?

Insects are very helpful to humans. While searching for food, they help to pollinate crops. By eating dead plant and animal material, they help to clean up the environment. But insects are also pests, sometimes devouring whole fields of crops in a matter of hours. They also carry diseases to plants, animals and humans. Finally, some insects have painful or deadly bites and stings.

HOW DO INSECTS HELP TO CATCH MURDERERS?

Very soon after death, bodies begin to break down. This process is helped by a number of insects that feed or lay their eggs on the body. Scientists have found that these insects appear in a particular order. Examining the insects found in a body can help to pinpoint the time of death, and in many cases this has helped the police to find a killer.

The leaf katydid of Borneo is wonderfully camouflaged amongst leaves and branches. It is only when it begins to move that predators take a closer look. The burying beetle, found in the deserts of Arizona, has colouring that warns enemies that it may be poisonous.

HOW DO FISH BREATHE?

Fish are the oldest vertebrates on Earth. They are cold blooded and spend all their lives in water. They breathe by taking in oxygen dissolved in the water. Most fish breathe by using gills. They gulp in water through their mouths and pass it out through the gills, which are rich in blood and extract oxygen from the water as it passes through them.

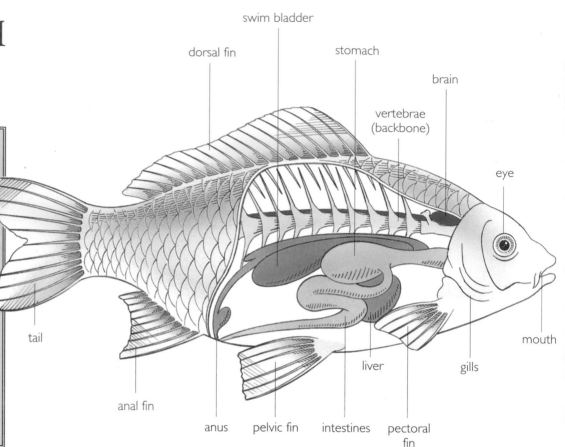

The illustration of the fish above shows features shared by all teleosts. Fish scales may be silvery or, in the tropics, glowing in bright rainbow colours.

HOW DO BONY FISH AND CARTILAGINOUS FISH DIFFER?

THE LARGEST GROUP of fish are bony fish. Most of these, making up 95% of fish species, are known as *teleosts*. They have skeletons made of bone and are usually covered with small overlapping bony plates called scales. They also have swim bladders, filled with gas, to help them remain buoyant. Cartilaginous fish include sharks, skates and rays. Their skeletons are made of flexible cartilage but, as they do not have swim bladders, they must keep moving all the time to keep their position in the water. They usually have tough, leathery skins and fleshy fins.

WHICH FISH TRAVEL THE LONGEST DISTANCES?

THE SALMON hatches in freshwater streams and rivers but then begins an incredible journey of up to 5000km (3000 miles), first to the open sea and then to return to the same river in which it was spawned in order to breed. The salmon only makes the journey once – after spawning, it dies. The European eel makes the reverse journey. It spawns in the Sargasso Sea, in the western Atlantic, and its tiny larvae swim to the shores of Europe and North America, becoming elvers (small eels) on the journey. They then spend several years in freshwater rivers and lakes before returning to the Sargasso Sea to breed. Whales also travel huge distances, this time in search of food. The tiny plankton that they eat are found more abundantly in certain areas during the year.

During its journey upstream to breed, the salmon may leap over rocks and up small waterfalls. In North America, bears wade into the river to catch some of the fish making their annual migration.

IS IT TRUE THAT MALE SEAHORSES BECOME MOTHERS?

OF COURSE, it is the female seahorse that is the real mother, producing and laying eggs. The difference is that she lays the eggs in a special pouch on the male seahorse's body. The babies develop inside the pouch and emerge when they are fully developed. As they emerge, it looks as though they are being born from the male seahorse.

It is easy to see that the seahorse was so named because of the shape of its head. In order not to be swept along by the current, the seahorse can grasp the fronds of seaweeds with its tail.

ARE ALL SHARKS DANGEROUS TO HUMANS?

ALL SHARKS are carnivorous (meat-eaters), and a few species, such as the white shark, which can grow to 9m (30ft), have been known to attack humans or even boats. But 90% of all shark species are not dangerous to humans at all.

The shark's streamlined shape and muscular body enables it to move at great speed through the water. Its keen sense of smell means that it can locate and devour living or dead animals with ease. The shark's teeth are serrated, so that it can saw at the flesh of its victims.

WHAT IS A "MERMAID'S PURSE"?

A VERY FEW FISH give birth to live young, but most lay their eggs in the water, which is called spawning. A fish may lay millions of eggs, only a small proportion of which will grow into adults. A few fish, such as salmon and sticklebacks, build nests underwater to protect their eggs. They lay fewer eggs because more young survive. Dogfish and skates protect their eggs in black capsules. The empty capsules are often washed up on the beach, and it is these that are known as "mermaid's purses".

fast facts

WHICH FISH HAVE NO JAWS?

Lampreys and hagfish do not have jaws, but they do have teeth. Some of them are parasites, attaching themselves to other fish and feeding on their blood and flesh.

HOW DO SOME FISH USE ELECTRICITY?

Some fish, such as the Atlantic torpedo, the African electric catfish and the electric eel, can store electrical charges in their muscles – sometimes up to 500 volts. They may ward off attackers with electric shocks or use this extraordinary ability when catching food or attracting a mate.

WHAT IS A COELACANTH?

The coelacanth is often called a living fossil. It was known only from fossil examples until a live fish was caught off the coast of Madagascar. Coelacanths have hardly changed in the last 90 million years. They use their fins alternately, like legs, instead of together.

ARE THERE REALLY FLYING FISH?

The flying fish (*Cypselurus heterurus*) has large fins that it can spread out. When escaping its enemies, it can launch itself from the water and glide up to 100m (330ft) through the air.

HOW FAST CAN FISH SWIM?

The marlin can reach speeds of 80km/h (50mph).

WHICH IS THE SMALLEST FISH?

The dwarf goby (*Pandaka pygmaea*), which is also the smallest vertebrate, is a freshwater fish that never reaches more than 1.25cm (0.5 inches) in length.

CAN ALL AMPHIBIANS LIVE BOTH ON LAND AND IN WATER?

Amphibians have different life cycles. Many live mainly on land, but most of them spend at least some of their lives in water. Frogs, toads, newts and salamanders are all amphibians. Frogs and salamanders are able to breathe through their damp skins to a certain extent, both in the water and on land, but toads must rely largely on their lungs and cannot remain in water for long.

WHAT IS THE LIFE CYCLE OF AN AMPHIBIAN?

MOST AMPHIBIANS lay their eggs in water. Frogs' eggs are called spawn. They are protected from predators by a thick layer of jelly. Inside this a tadpole develops. When it hatches out, it is able to swim, using its long tail, and breathes through gills. As the tadpole grows, first hind legs and then fore legs begin to grow. Lungs develop, and the young frog is able to begin to breathe with its head above water. Gradually, the tail shortens until the young frog resembles its adult parents.

HOW DO FROGS AND TOADS DIFFER?

TOADS AND FROGS are similar in many ways, although toads usually have rougher, drier skins and may waddle rather than hopping as frogs do. Some toad spawn is produced in strings, like necklaces, rather than the mass of eggs laid by a frog.

Toads are often well camouflaged, easily blending into a stony or leafy background.

Adult frogs often return to the pond in which they hatched to breed.

Frog spawn hatches into larvae called tadpoles after about a week.

By 16 weeks, the froglet has four legs and almost no tail. Lungs have taken over from the gills.

By about ten weeks, the tadpole has hind legs, internal gills, and can eat small insects, worms and its smaller brothers and sisters.

At first tadpoles feed on algae and breathe through feathery gills.

HOW CAN A TREE FROG CLIMB TREES?

THE RED-EYED TREE FROG lives in the rain-forests of South America. Although it can swim, it spends much of its life out of water, among the leaves of trees where there are plentiful insects for food. The tree frog's toes have sticky pads that enable it to grip branches as it climbs.

Some tree frogs, living high in the Amazon rainforest, use the pools of water in the centre of certain tropical plants. They lay their eggs among the leaves and carry their tadpoles to water on their backs.

WHAT IS THE LEGEND OF THE SALAMANDER?

IN ANCIENT TIMES, it was believed that salamanders could live in the middle of fires, as the cold of their bodies extinguished the flames around them. Of course, this is quite untrue, but the story may have come about because salamanders were often seen to run out of logs thrown onto the fire.

Salamanders and newts, unlike frogs and toads, have distinct necks and long tails in adulthood. Their bright colours warn of their poisonous skin.

HOW DO AMPHIBIANS DEFEND THEMSELVES?

AMPHIBIANS have a wide range of ways of protecting themselves. Some brightly coloured amphibians produce poisons in glands on their skins. The bright colours warn birds and animals not to attempt to eat them. Others use camouflage, blending with their surroundings, to prevent enemies from spotting them. Some frogs and toads puff themselves up or stand on tiptoes to look larger than they really are!

fast facts

WHICH IS THE LARGEST AMPHIBIAN?

The Chinese giant salamander grows up to 1.8m (6ft) long.

DO ALL AMPHIBIANS HAVE LEGS?

Caecilians are amphibians that look rather like worms. They are adapted for a life burrowing in soil or underwater. They have no legs and are practically blind, but they feel by means of tiny tentacles on their cheeks.

WHAT IS AN AXOLOTL?

Axolotls are a kind of salamander found in Mexico. Like other amphibians, they begin life as tadpoles, breathing through gills, but they never develop further and breed in the water without ever changing into an adult form.

HOW DO SOME FROGS USE A KIND OF ANTIFREEZE?

In North America, some frogs build up chemicals in their blood at the onset of cold weather. These act as a kind of antifreeze, allowing the frog to survive temperatures as low as –8°C (18°F) without freezing.

WHAT IS SPECIAL ABOUT THE MIDWIFE TOAD?

The midwife toad has a special way of hatching its eggs. The male wraps the string of eggs around its body and back legs, where they remain until they hatch.

These frogs have skins that are coloured and speckled to blend perfectly with the background of their habitats. Camouflage is their best protection from predators.

HOW MANY DIFFERENT KINDS OF REPTILE ARE THERE?

There are four orders of reptile, by far the largest of which is the order of lizards and snakes. There are nearly 6000 different species of these. The other orders are much smaller. There are about 200 species of turtles, tortoises and terrapins, and only just over 20 species of crocodiles and alligators. Rarest of all is the tuatara, which forms an order all by itself.

WHAT ARE THE SPECIAL CHARACTERISTICS OF REPTILES?

REPTILES are cold blooded, so must gain warmth from their surroundings. This means that they can be found anywhere except in the very coldest regions of the Earth. Those that live in cooler areas usually spend the winter hibernating. Most reptiles lay eggs with hard or leathery shells. Their young hatch into miniature versions of their parents, but as reptiles can continue to grow after they are mature, some reach an enormous size.

The giant dome-shaped tortoise of the Galapagos Islands can live to a great age and considerable size.

Alligators (and crocodiles) are more closely related to dinosaurs than to other living reptiles.

Crocodiles can reach up to 7m (22ft) in length.

HOW CAN YOU TELL A CROCODILE FROM AN ALLIGATOR?

BOTH CROCODILES AND ALLIGATORS spend most of their lives in swamps and rivers in warm climates, although they breathe air through nostrils on the top of their snouts, closing these off when they dive. Caymans and gavials are relatives of crocodiles and alligators. The simple way of telling them apart is that crocodiles show the fourth tooth in their lower jaw when their mouths are closed, while alligators do not. It is probably not wise to go near enough to a live crocodilian to find out, however, as they have been known to attack humans!

The sharp teeth of crocodiles and alligators enable them to grip larger prey and drag them down under the water, where they drown. They have been known to kill farm animals in this way.

HOW DOES A CHAMELEON CHANGE COLOUR?

THE CHAMELEON is able to change colour to match its surroundings by releasing or tightening special cells on its skin. As well as this remarkable ability, chameleons are amazing in other ways. They are able to grip very strongly with their toes and tails to balance on precarious branches. Their extraordinary tongues, which are able to shoot out as far as the chameleon's body length, are sticky and able to scoop back prey like a piece of elastic. Finally, the chameleon's eyes are bulging and can move in any direction, protected by an eyelid that is fused all round the eye, leaving only a tiny hole in the middle. Even stranger, the chameleon can move each of its eyes in a different direction at the same time!

Some snakes kill or immobilize their prey by injecting it with poison from their fangs. Some cobras are particularly dangerous, as they can spit their venom several feet. Other snakes squeeze their prey to death in their muscular coils.

Snakes that eat fairly large prey have flexible joints in their jaws, enabling them to open their mouths incredibly wide to swallow the prey whole.

HOW DO SNAKES MOVE?

MANY SNAKES throw themselves along the ground in waves that pass from head to tail. They have hundreds of pairs of ribs and strong muscles to enable them to do this, while their scales grip the ground. North American sidewinders, however, move as their name suggests, by throwing their coils sideways along the ground.

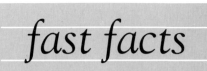

WHICH IS THE LONGEST LIVING REPTILE?

The giant tortoise can live for up to 150 years.

ARE THERE ANY VEGETARIAN SNAKES?

All snakes are carnivores, eating anything from insects to small mammals.

CAN LIZARDS REALLY GROW A NEW TAIL?

If they are in serious danger from a predator, some lizards are able to discard part of their tails. The tail continues to wriggle while the lizard escapes. Within a few months, the soft part of the tail will be regrown, although it will not have bones inside it as the original tail had.

WHICH IS THE WORLD'S LARGEST SNAKE?

The anaconda and the reticulated python can both grow to over 9m (30ft) in length.

WHICH SNAKE IS THE DEADLIEST?

Up to a hundred thousand people die each year from snake bites. The snake responsible for more human deaths than any other is the Asian cobra, which is very common on the Indian subcontinent.

DO SNAKES HAVE A SENSE OF SMELL?

Strangely enough, snakes smell by using their tongues! By flicking their tongues in and out, snakes carry air to a special "smelling" gland in their mouths.

HOW DO BIRDS AND MAMMALS DIFFER?

It is likely that birds evolved from reptiles. Like reptiles but unlike most mammals, they lay eggs that hatch outside the mother. All adult birds have feathers, rather than fur or scales, and most can fly. However, birds are similar to mammals in being warm blooded.

IS IT EASY TO TELL MALE AND FEMALE BIRDS APART?

SOME MALE AND FEMALE BIRDS of the same species have very different plumage, with the male usually being more brightly coloured to attract females. Other species show little or no difference between the sexes. As well as having different plumage, birds may make displays to each other during the breeding season. Some dance in elaborate curving patterns, spread their feathers and strut, or sing. Male birds may fight to defend their territories during nesting.

The peacock displays its magnificent tail to attract the much less showy peahen. Remarkably, despite the weight of its tail feathers, a peacock can still fly.

Both male and female flamingos have pink plumage in their native habitats in Africa. They live in colonies and have long legs for wading in shallow waters.

WHAT DO BIRDS EAT?

DIFFERENT SPECIES of birds have different diets, just as mammals do. Some are vegetarian, eating fruits and seeds. Others feed on insects and other invertebrates, such as worms. Birds' beaks are adapted to the kind of food they need. The beaks of meat-eaters are often hooked and sharp, ideal for tearing flesh from carcases. Birds that search for food along the seashore or on mud banks often have long pointed beaks for burrowing into the soft ground.

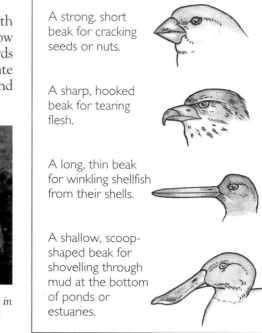

A strong, short beak for cracking seeds or nuts.

A sharp, hooked beak for tearing flesh.

A long, thin beak for winkling shellfish from their shells.

A shallow, scoop-shaped beak for shovelling through mud at the bottom of ponds or estuaries.

HOW DO BIRDS FLY?

BIRDS are specially adapted for flight, whether skimming short distances between branches or flying for weeks at a time above the oceans. The shape of their wings gives a clue to the kinds of flight they make. Birds' bodies need to be light enough for flight. The large surface area of their wings pushes air downwards as they flap to lift the bird. At the same time, birds need immensely powerful chest muscles to move their wings. Feathers are the ideal covering – they are light but strong and flexible. In flight, they can lie flat against the bird's body to reduce wind resistance.

The structure of a bird's legs and wings has much in common with that of the legs and arms of humans, but they are specially adapted for flight and the bird's habitat. Swimming birds, for example, have webbed feet to help propel them through the water.

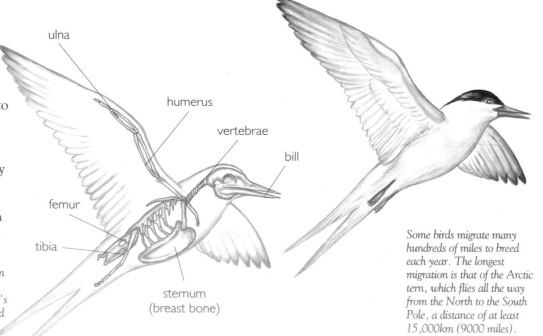

ulna

humerus

vertebrae

bill

femur

tibia

sternum (breast bone)

Some birds migrate many hundreds of miles to breed each year. The longest migration is that of the Arctic tern, which flies all the way from the North to the South Pole, a distance of at least 15,000km (9000 miles).

WHAT ARE FLEDGLINGS?

WHEN THEY FIRST HATCH from the egg, baby birds are called nestlings. At this stage, many of them have no feathers. Blind and helpless, they are completely dependent on their parents for food and protection. As their feathers grow, they become fledglings, with open eyes and hearty appetites. When the fledglings have all their feathers and are strong enough, they are ready to learn to fly and begin to be independent.

WHAT KINDS OF HOMES DO BIRDS MAKE?

BIRDS show extraordinary variety and ingenuity in the nests they build. An untidy mound of sticks, simply dropped on top of one another, is all that a mute swan requires. House martins, on the other hand, literally build their homes. They skim over puddles and ponds, picking up little pieces of mud, which are built up into round-walled structures on the sides of buildings. Cuckoos, of course, are renowned for the fact that they use other birds' nests in which to lay their eggs. They are able to mimic the size, shape and colour of the host-bird's eggs to some extent, so that the additional egg is not immediately obvious.

Skilfully built, this mud nest becomes a strong structure in which several nestlings can be raised.

Dried grass, twigs, moss and feathers are easy to find for nest-building and also help to camouflage the nest.

WHICH IS THE LARGEST BIRD?

THE OSTRICH, running in herds in southern Africa, is the largest bird in the world. It can stand more than 2m (7ft) high. As well as being able to run at enormous speed from danger, the ostrich has powerful legs and sharp claws, which can deliver a kick hard enough to kill many predators.

CAN ALL BIRDS FLY?

MOST BIRDS can fly, but there are also some flightless species. These all have other ways of escaping from predators. The larger flightless birds, such as ostriches and emus, can run very fast. Penguins cannot fly but can swim and dive at great speed, using their wings as flippers to power them through the water.

fast facts

WHAT ARE FEATHERS MADE OF?

Feathers are made of keratin, which is a protein. Hair, hoofs and finger-nails also contain keratin.

WHY ARE SOME BIRDS' BONES HOLLOW?

Hollow bones are strong but also help birds to be light enough to fly.

WHICH IS THE SMALLEST BIRD?

The bee hummingbird (*Mellisuga helenae*) is just 5.7cm (2.24 inches) long and weighs only about 1.6g (0.056oz).

HOW FAST CAN BIRDS FLY?

The white-throated spine-tail swift (*Hirundapus caudacutus*) can fly at over 170km/h (105mph).

HOW MANY FEATHERS DO BIRDS HAVE?

It varies, but some birds have more than 25,000 feathers.

WHAT IS SPECIAL ABOUT MAMMALS?

There are around 4000 species of mammal. Some spend their whole lives swimming in the ocean, while others never venture into the water. Most have fur or hair on their bodies at some time in their lives. Some walk on two legs and some on four. What all mammals have in common, however, is that they are warm blooded and breathe air. Mammal mothers feed their young on milk from their mammary glands. Mammals also have lungs, a heart with four chambers and well-developed brains.

WHY IS IT AN ADVANTAGE TO HAVE WARM BLOOD?

WARM-BLOODED ANIMALS are able to control their internal temperature to a greater degree than cold-blooded animals, so that they are less dependent on the temperature of their surroundings. While reptiles slow down when the weather is cold, mammals are able to lead an active life. Mammals have adapted to life in all parts of the world where there is food for them to eat.

WHY ARE SOME MAMMALS' BABIES ABLE TO RUN ALMOST AS SOON AS THEY ARE BORN?

ALMOST ALL MAMMAL BABIES grow inside their mother until they are able to breathe and feed outside, but mammal babies differ very much in the kind of help they need after birth. Human babies, for example, need the attention of their parents for many years before they are able to fend for themselves completely. Most grazing animals, on the other hand, have adapted to life on wide, open grasslands, where they are constantly at risk from attack by predators. It is important that these animals give birth to young that can stand on their own feet and run from danger almost immediately.

Mammal mothers produce milk for their offspring from mammary glands. The babies are able to suck the milk from nipples on their mother's stomach or chest. Usually, animals that have many babies at one time have several nipples. The mother's milk is a complete food for the babies, until they are weaned. This means introducing them to the foods they will eat as adults.

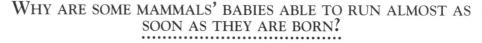

Many mammals sweat or pant to lose heat if they become warm. Dogs, for example, are able to lose heat through their tongues. If the temperature becomes too cold, blood vessels contract, causing goosebumps, and muscles cause shivering in order to warm up the body with movement. Human beings, of course, can also regulate their heat by changing their clothing so that it is suitable for the conditions they meet.

DO ALL MAMMALS GIVE BIRTH TO LIVE YOUNG?

MOST MAMMAL BABIES develop inside their mothers until they are ready to be born. The exceptions are the monotremes, a small group of mammals found in Australia. Like most reptiles, they lay eggs rather than giving birth to live young. Perhaps the best known of these is the duck-billed platypus.

Although the young of the duck-billed platypus hatch from eggs, they are mammals, so they still receive nourishment from their mother's milk. The eggs are laid underground in burrows, where the mother cares for her young until they are able to swim and forage for themselves.

WHICH MAMMAL IS THE FASTEST?

THE CHEETAH (*Acinonyx jubatus*) can reach 105km/h (65mph) when sprinting over a short distance.

WHAT IS A MARSUPIAL?

A marsupial is a very special kind of mammal. Although it does give birth to live young, they are very immature when born. Their mothers have a pouch on their abdomens, where the babies are protected and can drink milk until they are ready to survive in the open.

Female kangaroos have the extraordinary ability to keep an embryo in the womb in a state of suspended animation for several years until conditions are right for a baby (called a joey) to be born.

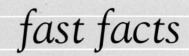

fast facts

WHICH IS THE LARGEST LAND MAMMAL?

The largest mammal on Earth is not a land mammal at all, but the blue whale (*Balaenoptera musculus*). The largest land mammal is the African elephant (*Loxodonta africana*), which can weigh up to 7 tonnes (6.9 tons).

CAN MAMMALS FLY?

Nowadays human beings can fly, of course, but only with the help of machines. The only mammals that can really fly are bats, which have flaps of skin between their front and hind legs, acting as wings. Other mammals, such as some possums and squirrels, can spread out their bodies and glide through the air, but they do not truly fly.

WHICH IS THE LARGEST ORDER OF MAMMALS?

There are over 1600 species of rodent, making them the largest order of mammals. Rodents have chisel-shaped front teeth, called incisors, that can be used for gnawing food. Most rodents, such as rats and mice, are quite small, but the capybara of South America can grow over a metre (3ft) long.

WHAT IS A PANGOLIN?

The pangolin is an extraordinary mammal that is covered with scales rather than fur. The pangolin eats ants, and the scales protect its body from the bites of these insects.

WHICH IS THE SMALLEST MAMMAL?

Savi's pygmy shrew (*Suncus etruscus*) weighs less than 3g (0.1oz).

WHICH ARE THE MOST NUMEROUS PRIMATES?

There are about 180 different species of primate, most of them living in the tropical regions of the world. The exception, and also the most numerous primate, is Homo sapiens – human beings. All primates have fairly large brains and forward-facing eyes that enable them to judge distances accurately. Instead of claws or hoofs, like other mammals, they have fingers and toes with soft, sensitive tips. They also have the ability to grasp with their fingers, thumbs and toes. The order of primates can be divided into prosimians, also known as primitive primates, and anthropoids, the higher primates, which include marmosets, monkeys, apes and, of course, human beings.

The ring-tailed lemur has a very long tail, like many of its relatives.

WHAT ARE PROSIMIANS?

THE PROSIMIANS include lemurs, the aye-aye, lorises and tarsiers. Lemurs live in the forests of Madagascar and nearby islands, where they eat insects, small vertebrates, shoots and leaves. They spend their time mainly in the trees, coming to the ground occasionally to feed. Most of them have long tails and many are nocturnal. Lorises come from Africa and southern Asia. They have huge, round eyes and eat insects. Tarsiers, living in the forests of Indonesia and the Philippines, also have huge eyes. Although they do not grow to more than 16cm (6.5 inches), they can leap over 1.8m (6ft) from tree to tree.

HOW DO OLD WORLD AND NEW WORLD MONKEYS DIFFER?

THE MONKEYS of the American continent, the "New" World, differ in several ways from those of Africa and Asia. New World monkeys, such as capuchins, spider monkeys, howler monkeys and woolly monkeys, have flat noses and widely spaced eyes. They live in family groups and spend much of their time in the trees, feeding mainly on fruit and leaves. Most of them have long tails, which they can use like an extra arm or leg to cling to branches. Old World monkeys live in a wide variety of habitats. They walk on all fours and, although they may sleep in trees, some species live mainly on the ground. They have narrow noses, and their nostrils face forward. Old World monkeys include macaques, mandrills and mangabeys.

The mandrill is one of the largest of the Old World monkeys. It can weigh as much as 20kg (44lb).

The cotton-top tamarin is a New World monkey, living in the forests of South America.

HOW DO PRIMATES COMMUNICATE?

PRIMATES other than humans communicate with each other in a number of ways. Many primates use touch to establish relationships, grooming each other to show friendship and to remove insects. Howler monkeys, living in the tropical forests of South America, make very loud calls. The male calls to mark his territory and can often be heard over 3km (almost 2 miles) away. Male gibbons, too, have loud calls, used for communicating with family members and to warn off other males. Some Old World monkeys have brightly coloured faces and bottoms, which the males use in courting displays and to frighten off enemies and rivals. Gorillas thump on the ground to warn off rival males, or beat their chests and roar to demonstrate their strength and power. Chimpanzees communicate with each other by using sounds and gestures.

WHICH ANIMALS ARE HUMAN BEINGS' NEAREST LIVING RELATIVES?

THE GREAT APES are the nearest living relatives to *Homo sapiens*. There are four species of great ape: the orang-utan, chimpanzee, gorilla and gibbon. Both orang-utans and gibbons spend most of their time in the trees, where they are very agile, swinging from branch to branch. Gorillas live in family groups, led by a large male, and feed mainly on the ground. The dominant male is often called a "silverback" – like humans, their hair becomes grey with age. Chimpanzees are very intelligent. They can use tools and solve puzzles. Their gestures and expressions often make them seem uncannily like humans.

All primates, including humans, take care of their young for a long time before they become adults. Apes look after their young for up to five years. Usually only one baby is born at a time.

fast facts

DO ALL PRIMATES LIVE IN GROUPS?

Most primates do live in family groups, but the orang-utan often lives alone, joining other orang-utans only to mate.

HOW DO HUMAN FEET DIFFER FROM THOSE OF OTHER PRIMATES?

All primates have opposable thumbs – their thumbs can swivel to be used with the fingers to grip and grasp objects. Most primates have this ability with their feet as well – humans are the only primates that do not have opposable big toes.

WHICH IS THE LARGEST PRIMATE?

The gorilla (*Gorilla gorilla*) is the largest primate. A male can weigh up to 275kg (605lb) – as much as three heavyweight boxers!

WHICH IS THE SMALLEST PRIMATE?

The mouse lemur (*Cheirogaleidae*) has a head and body length of 12.5cm (6 inches).

WHAT IS BIG FOOT?

There is a legend that an apelike animal, behaving like a human being, lives in the forests of North America. No such creature has ever been captured, although many hunters and hikers claim to have seen it or its tracks, which is why it is called Big Foot. Similar tales are told of the yeti of the Himalayas.

ARE ALL PRIMATES VEGETARIANS?

Many humans, of course, eat foods from both animals and plants. Most other primates are mainly vegetarian, but some, like chimpanzees, also eat insects, birds' eggs and small vertebrates at times.

HOW HAVE HUMAN BEINGS CHANGED THE EARTH?

There have been living things on the Earth for thousands of millions of years. It is only during the last million years that one animal has become dominant. In that time, human beings have brought huge changes to the planet, so that today there are very few places untouched by human activity. In fact, many scientists would say that our actions have had such an enormous effect that the climate of the globe has been altered, with serious consequences for every living thing that shares our Earth.

WHAT ARE THE EFFECTS OF FARMING ON THE WORLD'S WILDLIFE?

ONCE HUMAN BEINGS lived a nomadic life, hunting and gathering food as they travelled. Their lives had little effect on the ecosystems of the planet. Gradually, some nomadic peoples began to domesticate animals such as goats and sheep. By taking animals with them on their travels, they ensured a constant supply of milk, meat, skins and wool. But it was when they began to grow crops and settle in one place that humans really began to change the face of the Earth.

In huge areas of the world, natural vegetation has been ploughed up so that crops can be grown. Vast European forests were cleared for farming hundreds of years ago. Large areas of the prairies of America have been cultivated within the last two hundred years. Today the clearance still goes on as rainforests are felled. Even where land has not been ploughed, overgrazing by cattle can destroy grasslands.

Large fields without hedges can suffer from soil erosion as winds sweep across them, blowing away the topsoil.

Pesticides enter the food chain when affected insects or small animals are eaten by birds and other creatures. These in turn feed larger birds and mammals, which may be taking in harmful or even fatal amounts of chemicals.

Large fields are easier for machinery but mean that hedgerows and the habitats they provide are destroyed.

Modern intensive farming relies on chemicals to put nutrients back into the soil and kill pests. These chemicals can seep into river systems, polluting the water and damaging the habitats of many living things.

fast facts

WHY DO LIVING THINGS BECOME EXTINCT?

Living things usually become extinct because of a change in their environment. Attack by a predator, destruction of habitats or food sources and climate change can all be fatal. Humans are only a recent cause of some extinctions.

WHY IS IT IMPORTANT TO SAVE ENDANGERED SPECIES?

Living things depend on each other in complicated ways. The loss of one species may change the balance of a habitat, leading to the loss of other living things. And once a plant, for example, is extinct, it is too late to find out that it might have supplied a life-saving drug or helped to feed people or animals.

CAN THE EARTH FEED EVERYONE?

The Earth is able to produce enough food for everyone on it, but billions of people go hungry each year because they do not have access to the planet's produce.

ARE HUMANS THE BIGGEST THREAT TO LIVING THINGS?

All living things may be attacked by predators or disease, but usually a whole species is not wiped out in this way. Natural disasters, such as volcanic eruptions, fires and floods also have a local effect on wildlife. But humans can affect habitats for a long time and over a huge area.

HOW FAST IS THE WORLD'S HUMAN POPULATION GROWING?

Two hundred years ago the population of the world was around one billion (1,000,000,000). Today it is about six billion. The growth may slow in the twenty-first century, but the population is still likely to reach 10 billion before the year 2100.

WHAT IS ACID RAIN?

WHEN FOSSIL FUELS are burnt, nitrogen oxide and sulphur dioxide are given off. These substances dissolve into the moisture in the air and rise into clouds. These are blown along by the wind and fall as rain, sometimes hundreds of kilometres away. This "acid rain" kills vegetation and the living things that feed on it. It can be difficult to find the source of the problem because of its distance from the damage being done.

WHAT IS GLOBAL WARMING?

BURNING COAL AND OIL gives off carbon dioxide and other gases. At the same time, cutting down forests means that less carbon dioxide is used by plants for photosynthesis. In the modern industrial world, more and more carbon dioxide is being produced. This and other gases are known as greenhouse gases. They are held in the atmosphere of the planet and prevent heat from escaping, so warming the Earth by means of the "greenhouse effect".

CAN CITIES PROVIDE HABITATS FOR LIVING THINGS?

WHEN TOWNS AND CITIES are built, the habitats of the living things in the area are destroyed. Gradually, however, other plants and animals find a foothold in the urban environment, while a few of the original species adapt to the new conditions. Even in the largest cities there are parks, gardens and tree-lined roads. Human beings throw away an enormous amount of food, which can provide nourishment for insects, birds and animals.

At first sight a city such as New York does not appear to be an ideal habitat for wildlife, but even the largest city can provide food and homes for a wide variety of living things. Not all of these are welcomed by the city's human residents, however.

ARE WEATHER AND CLIMATE THE SAME THING?

The lower levels of the Earth's atmosphere are in constant motion. As the atmosphere heats and cools, it expands and contracts, causing changes in pressure and air movement. These changes cause the weather that we experience on Earth. The daily occurrence of sunshine, rain, hail, snow, fog or wind is what we call weather. Climate is the overall weather in a particular area over a longer period of time.

HOW DO WE DESCRIBE THE WIND?

KNOWING THE DIRECTION of the wind is not always enough. People on land and sea also need a way of describing the strength of the wind. In 1805, a British admiral called Beaufort devised the scale that still bears his name.

0	**Calm**	Smoke rises straight upwards
1	**Light air**	Smoke slowly drifts
2	**Light breeze**	Tree leaves rustle
3	**Gentle breeze**	Flags flutter
4	**Moderate wind**	Branches wave
5	**Fresh wind**	Small trees sway
6	**Strong wind**	Umbrellas misbehave!
7	**Near gale**	Large trees bend
8	**Gale**	Small branches break
9	**Severe gale**	Roof tiles dislodge
10	**Storm**	Trees blown over
11	**Severe storm**	Buildings damaged
12	**Hurricane**	Major structural damage

WHAT CAUSES LIGHTNING?

THE WATER DROPLETS in clouds have a positive electrical charge at the top of the cloud and a negative charge at the bottom. When the negative charge comes near enough to an attracting positive charge on the Earth below or on another cloud, the electrical energy is released in a flash of light. There may also be a loud bang, called thunder, at the same time. However, as light travels faster through the air than sound, we see the lightning flash before hearing the thunder.

WHAT IS THE WATER CYCLE?

WATER ON EARTH is constantly recycled. Water evaporates into the air from rivers, lakes and oceans. As it rises into the air, the vapour is cooled and condenses into clouds. The wind blows the clouds along until eventually precipitation – rain, snow or hail – results. The precipitation falls to Earth, where it runs through the soil to join rivers, lakes, oceans and underground reservoirs. Without water, there could be no life on Earth.

Water falls back to the ground as rain, snow or hail.

Water vapour forms clouds.

Water vapour rises.

Water rises by evaporation from rivers, lakes and oceans.

Water runs from rivers into the sea.

cirrus

cumulonimbus

cirrocumulus

altostratus

cumulus

stratocumulus

nimbostratus

stratus

WHAT ARE THE DIFFERENT KINDS OF CLOUD?

MOST OF THE NAMES given to different kinds of cloud simply describe their shapes and positions or give a clue about what we can expect from them. *Cirro* means "curled"; *cumulo* means "piled up"; *nimbo* means "rain"; *strato* means "in layers or sheets" and *alto* means "high". Higher levels of cloud are made of ice crystals. As you might expect, it is the clouds with the word *nimbus* or *nimbo* in their names that bring rain, hail or snow. The very lowest clouds drift over high ground as fog.

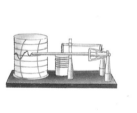

An anemometer measures wind speed.

A simple weather vane is effective for measuring wind direction.

A barograph charts air pressure.

A thermometer measures air temperature.

HOW DO METEOROLOGISTS FORECAST THE WEATHER?

AS EVERYONE KNOWS, predicting the weather can often be difficult. Professional weather forecasters, called meteorologists, use information collected by weather stations on land, at sea and on satellites in space. Rainfall, sunshine and wind speed can all be measured fairly easily, but they only tell us what the weather is like *now*. A better gauge of future weather is to study air pressure and cloud formation. Today's meteorologists use computers to help make sense of all the information received and to predict, based on past events, the weather of the future.

Some people feel that age-old methods are just as effective as computers in predicting the weather. "Red sky at night, shepherd's delight, red sky in the morning, shepherd's warning" is a traditional saying.

fast facts

WHICH IS THE WINDIEST PLACE IN THE WORLD?

Antarctica holds the record for being the windiest place on Earth. Although higher wind speeds have been recorded for short periods elsewhere, Port Martin regularly has winds of over 100km/h (65mph).

WHICH IS THE DRIEST PLACE IN THE WORLD?

The Atacama Desert, in Chile, is the driest place in the world. Parts of it have never had rain since records have been kept.

WHAT CAUSES THE SEASONS?

As it moves around the Sun on its yearly orbit, the Earth is slightly tilted, so that at different times of the year the northern and southern hemispheres may be slightly nearer or slightly further from the Sun. This is what causes the differences in temperature and weather that we call seasons. The equator is always about the same distance from the Sun, so its climate is the same all the year round.

WHAT IS A TORNADO?

A tornado is a wind that twists violently to form a funnel. Rising air within the funnel can literally suck objects, including buildings and people, into the air. Tornadoes are particularly dangerous because they move at high speed and can change direction very rapidly.

ARE SNOWFLAKES REALLY ALL DIFFERENT?

Examined under a microscope, all snowflakes are made up of six-sided shapes that appear to be different from each other. The problem is that no one can look at all the millions of snow crystals that form to check that there really are not two the same!

WHAT IS AN ECOSYSTEM?

Different parts of the world vary enormously in the kinds of plant and animal life they can support. This is mainly caused by the climate in each place, which allows different kinds of living things to thrive. The climate itself is influenced by the physical characteristics of a region – whether it is mountainous or near the sea, for example – and its position on the Earth – how near to the equator it is. Different parts of the world can share similar conditions, even if they are thousands of miles apart. Each area contains communities of millions of living things that rely on each other for survival. These communities are called ecosystems.

DO ECOSYSTEMS CHANGE?

OVER TIME, ecosystems can alter a great deal. The climate of the Earth has gradually changed many times even within the time when records have been kept. Before that we know that parts of the world experienced Ice Ages, which had huge effects on the environments of living things. Human beings also alter ecosystems, often without realizing the possible results of their actions. Once large areas of North America and Europe were covered with deciduous woodland. Over hundreds of years, trees have been cut down for building, to supply fuel and to clear land for farming, so that remaining areas of woodland are comparatively small.

Human beings have also altered ecosystems by introducing plants and animals from other parts of the world. European settlers in Australia, for example, took rabbits with them, which have bred in the wild and become serious pests, ousting native species.

WHERE ARE THE MAIN ECOSYSTEMS OF THE WORLD?

THE MAP BELOW shows the main ways in which the Earth can be divided into different ecosystems. These are based mainly on the kind of plants that grow in an area, as all other living things rely directly or indirectly on plants for their food. Of course, there are many smaller ecosystems within these broad divisions.

KEY

ice and tundra

coniferous forest

deciduous woodland

Mediterranean

grassland

savannah

tropical rainforest

desert

HOW DO THE MAIN ECOSYSTEMS DIFFER?

Ice and tundra
In the cold conditions of the Poles, very few species can survive, but during the summer the ice around the Arctic and Antarctic Circles melts to reveal tundra, on which sparse vegetation can live.

Coniferous forest
The coniferous forests that stretch across northern Europe, Asia and America are called the taiga. Most of the trees are evergreen, offering food and shelter to animals all the year round.

Deciduous woodland
Deciduous woodlands occur in temperate parts of the world, where the climate is fairly mild for part of the year and there is plenty of rainfall.

Mediterranean
The area around the Mediterranean Sea is known for its long, hot summers and cooler winters. Parts of Australia and North America also have this ecosystem.

Grassland
These areas are too dry to support large plants such as trees but have a variety of grasses and smaller plants on which grazing animals can feed.

Savannah
This is also grassland but it is found in tropical regions. Rainfall usually happens once a year, when grasses can grow up to 3m (10ft) tall.

Tropical rainforest
Rainforests, with their warm, moist climate, support an extraordinary variety of living things.

Desert
Desert areas have little or no rainfall. Plants and animals here have adapted to conserve every drop of available water.

HOW DO LIVING THINGS SURVIVE TOGETHER?

All living things are linked in complicated food webs, relying on each other for nourishment, but some animals and plants have very special relationships, where a partnership may benefit one partner or both.

WHAT IS SYMBIOSIS?

WHEN BOTH PARTNERS benefit equally from a partnership, they are said to be in a symbiotic relationship. There are many such relationships in the natural world. For example, when a bee goes to a flower to collect nectar, it also brings about pollination by carrying pollen on its furry body from one flower to the next. Both the bee and the flower benefit.

Symbiosis can sometimes help to kill parasites. Small birds called oxpeckers peck parasites from the skins of antelopes on the African savannah.

HOW DO CLOWNFISH AND SEA ANEMONES LIVE TOGETHER?

IN TROPICAL WATERS, clownfish have a symbiotic relationship with sea anemones. They live among the anemone's tentacles, unharmed by its stings but enjoying protection from predators.

In turn, the clownfish seem to protect the anemone from some predators too. They may even lure fish into the anemone's tentacles, where they can be caught and digested.

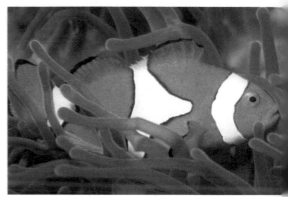

HOW DO CUCKOOS FOOL OTHER BIRDS INTO BECOMING BABYSITTERS?

CUCKOOS do not raise their own young. They are said to be brood parasites. They lay a single egg in a nest that already contains several eggs while the parent bird is away. Although cuckoo eggs are often slightly bigger than the other eggs, the female cuckoo has the extraordinary ability partially to match the colour of her egg to the others. The eggs are hatched by the host bird. The young cuckoo is bigger and stronger than the other nestlings and demands more food. To ensure that it receives all the food brought to the nest by the foster parents, it pushes the other young birds out of the nest.

Lichens are plant-like growths that result from the symbiotic relationship of fungi and algae. The fungi form the "body" while the algae enable the lichen to use photosynthesis.

WHY DO SOME DISEASES NEED ANIMAL AND HUMAN HOSTS?

EVEN THE TINIEST living things may be parasites. The micro organisms that cause malaria and sleeping sickness, for example, are parasites that need more than one host to complete their life cycles. The diseases are spread by infected insects, which bite human beings to feed on their blood and in so doing pass on the infection. The organisms multiply in the person's body, causing illness. The cycle is completed when an infection-free insect bites the person and in its turn becomes a carrier of the disease.

A parasite is a living thing that benefits from a relationship with another species but actually causes harm to that species. Some fungi are found on dying birch trees and can also live for a while on the wood after the tree has died.

HOW HAS DOMESTICATING ANIMALS HELPED HUMANS?

BY DOMESTICATING goats, cattle, sheep, pigs and poultry, humans have been able to ensure that food is always available. Horses, mules and camels have been used to carry people and goods over long distances. Pets provide companionship but can also be very useful. Sheepdogs help farmers to round up their flocks. Guide dogs for the blind and hearing dogs for the deaf help their owners to lead full lives. Animals are also used to guard property, perform rescues and carry messages.

Until the introduction of machinery, many tasks on the farm were done using the strength of horses.

Near the Arctic Circle, dogs have traditionally been used to pull sleds. They are able to withstand the very cold conditions and move quickly over the snow.

Camels are used as beasts of burden in parts of the world where there are often dry conditions.

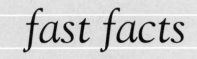

fast facts

WHAT IS COMMENSALISM?

Commensalism is a relationship where one partner gains a benefit but the other is not affected at all.

WHICH WERE THE FIRST PETS?

Dogs were probably the first animals to be domesticated, perhaps to help with hunting. All modern dogs are related to wolves (*Canis lupus*).

WHY CAN IT BE A MISTAKE TO KILL PESTS?

A pest, such as an aphid attacking plants in the garden, may be food to an insect such as a ladybird. If all the aphids are destroyed, the ladybirds will die out too. They will then not be available to go into action if another colony of aphids arrives. Links like this between living things are happening all the time, in complicated relationships. Killing pests can affect the whole balance of an ecosystem.

ARE BACTERIA ALWAYS HARMFUL?

The human body is host to millions of bacteria. Many of these are useful, helping us to digest our food. In fact, some of the foods we eat, such as yoghurt and blue cheese, are made by allowing certain kinds of bacteria to breed in them.

WHY DO SOME ANIMALS HAVE HUNDREDS OF YOUNG AND SOME ONLY ONE?

All animals want to make sure that at least some of their young reach adulthood and reproduce themselves. Some animals do this by looking after a few babies until they can fend for themselves. Other animals produce hundreds of eggs, which they leave to develop by themselves. Most of them will die, but a few will survive, just as in smaller families.

HOW CAN GRASSLANDS SUPPORT SO MANY ANIMALS?

When not shaded by larger plants, grasses grow very quickly, especially if frequently nibbled or cut, as anyone who has to help mow a lawn knows. Up to 30% (almost a third) of the Earth's land is covered by grassland. Grass plants can survive fire, which spreads rapidly across the land but burns for only a short time, as there is little to fuel it. Flash floods are also not a problem, as the shallow, dense roots of the grasses prevent the soil from being washed away.

WHY ARE THERE VERY FEW TREES ON VAST STRETCHES OF GRASSLAND?

IT WAS ONCE THOUGHT that large areas of grassland did not have enough rainfall or had soil that was too poor for trees to grow. Now it is also thought that they may have lost trees through fire. When grazing animals pass frequently over newly growing forest, young trees are soon killed by nibbling and trampling, so that the trees would never have a chance to become established again.

giraffe

Grant's gazelle

hyena

vulture

DO GRASSLANDS ALL OVER THE WORLD HAVE SIMILAR CLIMATES?

THE CLIMATES of the world's grasslands vary a great deal. In Africa there are huge areas of grassland called savannah. These are warm all year round with summer rains. They support large populations of seed-eating birds and grazing animals, which in turn provide food for large meat-eating animals, such as lions, leopards, cheetahs, hyenas and jackals. The North American prairies and Russian steppes are similar in having hot summers but very cold winters. Great herds of bison once roamed the North American "sea of grass", but early settlers killed enormous numbers of them for food and sport. Now the bison is a protected species. South American grasslands, called pampas, and the South African veld have sparser tussocks of grass.

Before hunting severely reduced the numbers of bison on the American prairie, it was said that a herd could take many days to pass.

How do grasses keep growing if they are constantly eaten?

GRASSES are well suited to being grazed. Although many will grow to more than two metres (over six feet) if left undisturbed, they do not need to reach this height to reproduce. Even if a flower and seed head are never allowed to form, the plant can reproduce by sending out runners underground, from which new daughter plants can grow. As well as being able to grow upwards from their central stem, grasses also have lower growing points from which new stalks can grow if the central one is cut. In fact, by this means grasses grow more thickly than ever, giving more food for grazing animals to eat.

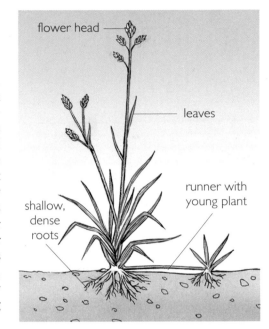

flower head

leaves

shallow, dense roots

runner with young plant

What defences do grazing animals have against predators?

FOR MOST GRAZING ANIMALS, being part of a herd is their best defence against attack. Although individual animals, especially young, old or sick ones, may be picked off by predators, most animals will be safe. There are also more animals to watch out for danger while the rest graze. When attacked, the best defence of an antelope or zebra is its speed. At least over short distances, it can usually outrun its attackers. Wildebeest and some other heavier animals also have a powerful kick, which can break the bones of a lion or hyena if well aimed.

zebra

lion

What is a herbivorous animal?

Herbivorous animals are plant-eaters, unlike carnivorous animals, which eat meat. Omnivorous animals, like most human beings, eat almost anything!

How many vertebrae does a giraffe have?

Despite its extraordinarily long neck, a giraffe has exactly the same number of vertebrae as a human being – just 24.

Do male or female lions hunt for food?

It is usually the females in a pride, or group of lions, that hunt for food.

What are scavengers?

Scavengers are carnivores that feed on meat that is already dead. They steal meat from the kills of other animals or "clean up" when a larger animal has eaten its fill.

How have human beings changed grassland wildlife?

Big-game hunters have almost wiped out some kinds of grassland wildlife. Now most larger game is protected by law, but illegal poaching still goes on. In temperate areas, such as Russia and North America, large areas of natural grassland have been ploughed and used for growing crops. Although the soil is very fertile, crops often need more water and protection from the wind than grasses, which can cause problems for farmers.

Are there also animals living under grasslands?

AS GRASSLANDS usually have few trees or rocks to offer cover to smaller animals, many of them live in burrows underground. In North America, prairie dogs (*Cynomys ludovicianus*) live in huge numbers in connected burrows, sometimes causing the ground to cave in. The South American pampas also has many burrowing animals, including viscachas (*Lagostomus maximus*) and cavies (*Cavia aperea*), related to guinea pigs.

WHY ARE RAINFORESTS SO RICH IN LIVING THINGS?

> *Rainforests are tropical evergreen forests. They have at least 4000mm (156 inches) of rain each year. The climate is warm and moist all year round, giving conditions in which green plants can produce huge amounts of vegetation, flowers and fruit. There is always plenty to eat for insects and the animals that, in turn, feed on them. The rainforest also offers an extraordinarily wide range of habitats for living things.*

WHERE ARE THE WORLD'S RAINFORESTS?

STRICTLY SPEAKING, tropical rainforests should fall within the *tropics* – between the Tropic of Capricorn and the Tropic of Cancer. In fact, most are found even nearer to the equator. South America, Africa and Asia have large areas of rainforest.

WHAT IS THE DIFFERENCE BETWEEN A LEOPARD AND A JAGUAR?

RAINFORESTS in different parts of the world often have similar species, but because they have developed separately for thousands of years, they each have their own characteristics. Both South American jaguars and African leopards have spotted skins that camouflage them in the dappled light of the forest floor. Like leopards, jaguars have rings of black spots on their coats, but they also have smaller spots within those rings.

Leopards are often nocturnal, hunting by night when lions and other predators are not active. They are also excellent climbers.

Jaguars, the largest wild cats on the American continent, prowl the forest floors of South America in search of prey.

WHY ARE RAINFORESTS IN DANGER?

RAINFORESTS are being cut down at an alarming rate for two main reasons. Both large commercial farming companies and individual families clear the forest to gain land to cultivate and graze animals, although the rainforest soil is not suitable for this use. Secondly, forests have been felled to supply tropical hardwoods for furniture-making and building. Woods such as mahogany have been highly prized in wealthy countries for hundreds of years.

ARE ALL RAINFOREST ANIMALS BRIGHTLY COLOURED?

As in most other habitats, the colouring of animals in the rainforest is very varied. Some are brilliantly coloured, to attract mates or to warn predators that they are poisonous. Other creatures have green or dark colouring to camouflage them amongst the vegetation. This hides them from their enemies and enables them to creep up on their prey unseen.

The scarlet macaw is the largest parrot in South America. Its powerful beak can crack open seeds and nuts – even Brazil nuts.

WHAT DIFFERENT HABITAT LAYERS ARE FOUND IN A RAINFOREST?

THE MANY HABITATS to be found in rainforests can be thought of as layers. In real forests, of course, these layers overlap each other a good deal.

The *emergent layer* consists of the tallest trees, with umbrella-like branches poking through the mass of leaves below. In this layer live free-flying birds and bats, including birds of prey.

The *tree canopy* consists of the leaves of mature trees. Their tops spread out to reach as much of the light as possible. As well as birds and fruit bats, monkeys and squirrels live in this layer, feeding on the fruits, nuts and leaves of the trees in the canopy.

Very little light filters through the leaves of the canopy. In the *mid-zone*, creepers called lianas hang in great ropes among the trees. Here there are monkeys, squirrels, birds and bats again, but also some snakes and tree frogs.

The *forest floor* is very dark. Larger mammals, such as deer, tapirs, elephants, jaguars and bush pigs, forage among the fallen leaves or prey on each other or smaller animals.

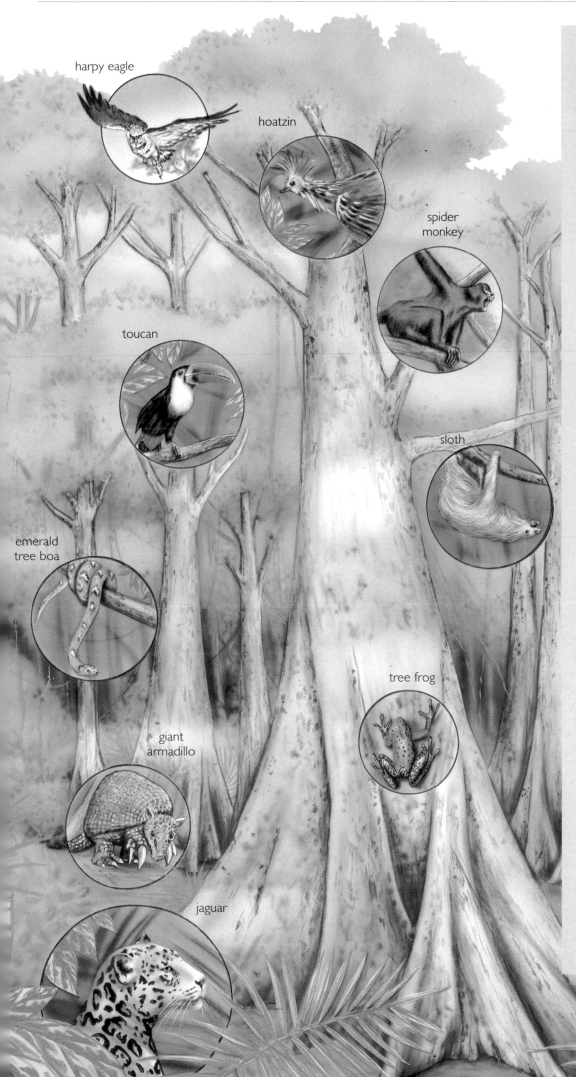

harpy eagle

hoatzin

spider monkey

toucan

sloth

emerald tree boa

giant armadillo

tree frog

jaguar

fast facts

HOW DO PLANTS HIGH IN THE TREES GET WATER?

Some plants, called bromeliads, collect water in their cup-shaped leaves. Insects and even frogs may be found living in the tiny pool.

IS THE SOIL OF RAINFORESTS PARTICULARLY FERTILE?

The hot, moist climate of rainforests means that fallen leaves decay extremely quickly and their nutrients are taken up by the roots of plants almost at once. Nutrients are not held in the soil as happens in other environments. If the rainforest is cut down, the soil is not fertile enough for farming.

ARE SLOTHS SLOTHFUL?

Sloths are tree-dwelling mammals from South America. They hang from branches and eat leaves. It would not be fair to say that sloths are slothful, or lazy, but they do move very slowly. In fact, tiny plants called algae grow on their coats, giving them green fur!

HOW MANY SPECIES LIVE IN RAINFORESTS?

It is estimated that over two million different species of plant and animal thrive in rainforests. So far, only a small proportion of these have been discovered by humans.

WHICH RAINFOREST BIRD HAS CLAWS ON ITS WINGS?

Like many birds that live among the rainforest trees, the South American hoatzin can only fly for short distances – after all, there are too many branches in the way for long flights. Instead it climbs through the branches. Young hoatzins are helped to clamber around by tiny claws on their wings.

CAN LIVING THINGS SURVIVE WITHOUT WATER?

No plants or animals can survive if they have no water at all for a long period, but in the desert regions of the world many living things have adapted so that they can thrive with very little water. Deserts are places with very little rainfall, but they are not always hot. Some are very cold at night or in the winter. Animals and plants have to be able to deal with extreme temperatures as well as a lack of water.

HOW ARE CAMELS ADAPTED TO DESERT CONDITIONS?

CAMELS are among the largest desert animals, but they are so well adapted to dry conditions that they have been domesticated for thousands of years by people living in desert areas. They are kept mainly as beasts of burden but are also eaten and used as racing animals! Camels' feet are able to splay out to prevent them from sinking into loose sand. They are able to close their nostrils to keep out sand, and their eyes are also protected by long eyelashes. The fat in their humps is a food store. Camels very rarely sweat, so they are able to conserve the water in their bodies much more efficiently than human beings.

Camels were taken to Australia during the 1800s to enable settlers to travel across the large deserts of the interior. There are now several herds that have returned to the wild.

HOW MUCH OF THE EARTH IS DESERT?

More than a third of the Earth's land is covered by desert, but very little of it has the sandy appearance that we usually think of when deserts are mentioned. Most of the world's deserts are barren, stony places.

Like most of the world's deserts, this one in Arizona has a surface of weathered rocks, rather than sand.

Although only 15cm (6 inches) long, the jerboa has enormously strong back legs and can jump well over 2m (6ft) in one leap. Its very long tail helps it to keep its balance.

How do animals survive in the desert?

IN DESERT REGIONS all over the world, animals have developed similar ways to make the best use they can of the little water that is available. Some creatures stay in burrows underground during the heat of the day, only venturing out during the night, when it is cooler. Many desert animals do not have sweat glands, and their kidneys are able to remove most of the water from their urine. Several animals have ways of storing food as fat, for use when their normal food is scarce. As well as camels, these include lizards that have fat stores in their tails.

What are succulent plants?

THE CACTI of American deserts are probably the best known examples of these plants. They store water in their fat, fleshy stems, so that they can survive in times of very little rain. Their leaves are reduced to narrow spines, so that they have a very small surface area from which to give off water by evaporation.

The fennec fox has large ears, which allow heat to escape from its body. They are also very sensitive, allowing the fox to detect the movements of its prey.

The spiny-tailed agama is a lizard that can store fat in its tail for times when food is scarce.

fast facts

What is aestivation?

Aestivation is the opposite of hibernation. While some animals avoid the harsh conditions of winter by hibernating, or sleeping through the coldest months, a few desert creatures sleep underground during the hottest summer months. In other words, they aestivate!

Do deserts grow?

At the moment it certainly seems as if many of the world's deserts are getting larger. This has often been caused by the actions of human beings in cutting down vegetation or over-cultivating or overgrazing the lands on the edges of deserts. Once the natural ecosystem of such an area has been destroyed, it is very difficult to repair the damage.

Are there some animals that never drink?

It seems that some desert animals do not drink at all. The kangaroo rat of North America and the jerboa of the Sahara seem to get all the moisture they need from the food they eat.

Is all of the Sahara covered with sand?

As well as mile after mile of sand dunes, the Sahara has rocky outcrops and several mountainous regions, where very little can survive.

Are some desert animals poisonous?

In desert areas, where food for all is very scarce, animals need a quick method of killing their prey and of protecting themselves, so it is not surprising that some use poison. Among these creatures are the western diamondback rattlesnake and desert tarantula of North America and the desert scorpion of the Sahara.

WHAT CAN LIVE IN THE COLDEST PLACES ON EARTH?

As in other extreme climates, only specially adapted plants and animals can live in the coldest parts of the world. In fact, at the North and South Poles, almost nothing can survive, but around the edges of the Arctic and Antarctic there are seas rich in plant and animal life. This means that larger animals, living on the edge of the ice, can find food in the teeming waters.

HOW DO THE ARCTIC AND ANTARCTIC DIFFER?

AT THE North and South Poles there are areas that are covered by thick layers of snow and ice all year round, but the two areas are very different. The Antarctic region, around the South Pole, has land far under the ice. The Arctic region, around the North Pole, is actually frozen sea. It is possible for a submarine to travel right under the North Pole. Because in polar regions the sea is warmer than the land or ice, the Arctic, with more sea, is not as cold as the Antarctic.

DO THE POLAR REGIONS HAVE SEASONS?

THERE ARE SEASONAL VARIATIONS at the Poles, but these are much more noticeable in the Arctic than in the Antarctic. During the Arctic summer the sea ice begins to melt and break away in large icebergs. Although the area around the North Pole is always covered by ice, the snow melts around the edges of the Arctic Circle so that Arctic animals can browse on the sparse vegetation. One result of this is that some Arctic mammals, who need camouflage to keep them safe from predators, change the colour of their coats from white in the winter to brown in the summer months.

Arctic hares turn white in the winter. In summer they moult to reveal brown coats that camouflage them against the tundra.

HOW DO POLAR ANIMALS KEEP WARM?

IN VERY COLD CLIMATES, animals need excellent insulation to stop their body heat from escaping. This may be on the outside, in the form of dense hair, fur or feathers, or on the inside, in the form of a thick layer of fat or blubber.

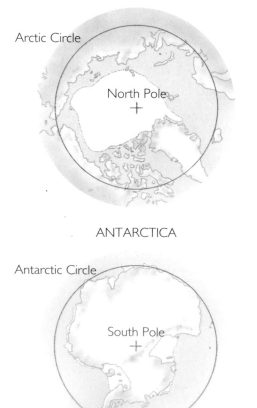

THE ARCTIC

Arctic Circle

North Pole
+

ANTARCTICA

Antarctic Circle

South Pole
+

Many kinds of seal live in the Arctic Ocean, feeding on fish and shellfish. They come out of the water to give birth to their pups.

HOW DO PENGUINS KEEP THEIR EGGS WARM?

PENGUINS are only found in the southern hemisphere, not in the Arctic. Many penguins lay only one egg during the dark days of winter. One penguin "sits" on the egg, holding it off the ice with its feet, until it hatches two months later.

The macaroni penguin huddles over its egg, keeping it warm and protecting it from predators.

HOW DOES THE WALRUS USE ITS TUSKS?

DURING THE BREEDING SEASON, walruses gather on the Arctic ice. The males fight each other for the females, often causing serious wounds with their long tusks. But the main reason for these impressive extended teeth is for digging up shellfish from the ocean floor.

Polar bears are fierce predators. They wait by holes in the ice to catch seals that come up for air. Although they are large, polar bears are very fast and excellent swimmers.

No one is quite sure why the narwhal has such a long tusk. It is a mammal, giving birth to live young underwater.

fast facts

WHERE IS THE COLDEST PLACE ON EARTH?

The average temperature at the South Pole is around –50°C (–58°F), although temperatures 40°C (104°F) lower have been recorded.

WHAT IS THE ARCTIC UNICORN?

Some people believe that stories of unicorns came about because sailors found the horns of narwhals and did not know that they came from a sea mammal.

WHICH IS THE LARGEST POLAR MAMMAL?

Although polar bears in the Arctic are very large, the biggest polar mammal does not live on land at all. It is the blue whale, which swims around the Antarctic Circle and is the largest mammal ever to have lived on Earth. Despite its huge size, the blue whale survives by eating tiny shrimp-like creatures called krill (*Euphausia superba*).

HOW DO POLAR BEARS AVOID SLIPPING ON THE ICE?

Polar bears have very hairy feet! These help them to grip the ice, and their sharp claws enable them to take a firmer grip still.

WHAT IS TUNDRA?

Tundra is the name given to the bleak land of the Arctic that is only covered by ice and snow in the winter. During the summer, many species of plant grow there, but the earth is too cold for their roots to reach down far. Grazing animals, such as reindeer and the musk ox, feed on the low-growing plants.

The Arctic Ocean is rich in fish, shellfish and krill, which are tiny shrimp-like animals. These in turn feed on microscopic plant life.

IS THERE LIFE IN THE DEEPEST OCEANS?

It is likely that life on our planet began in the oceans. As much more of the Earth is covered with water than with land, and the sea can be thousands of metres deep, there is simply more space for living things in the oceans. However, the conditions that they experience there are not so varied, so there are fewer different species than there are on land. Well over 90% of the living things that thrive in the oceans are found in the fairly shallow waters around the continents. However, scientists have found that there is life even in the deepest oceans, although it is not easy to study wildlife in such remote areas.

WHAT IS A CONTINENTAL SHELF?

AROUND THE CONTINENTS of the world there are areas of fairly shallow sea called continental shelves. Here the sea bed is quite flat and only about 130m (430ft) below the surface. There is usually plenty of marine life in these areas. Beyond the shelf, the sea floor drops, so that the sea is much deeper further from shore. In the middle of the oceans, however, the sea bed rises into a ridge, where the plates of the Earth's crust meet.

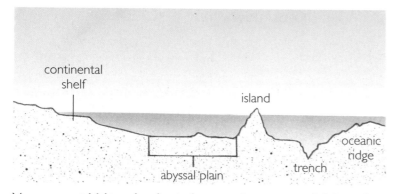

Most commercial fishing takes place in the waters above continental shelves. The deepest ocean is found in trenches where the sea floor plunges hundreds of metres.

HOW DO OYSTERS MAKE PEARLS?

PEARL OYSTERS are molluscs. Their soft bodies are protected by a tough outer shell, hinged at one side. When a piece of grit becomes embedded in the soft body of the oyster, it protects itself by building up layers of a shiny, shell-like material around the foreign body. This happens naturally, but today many pearls are cultivated in oyster farms, where "seeds" are injected into the oysters so that they will form pearls.

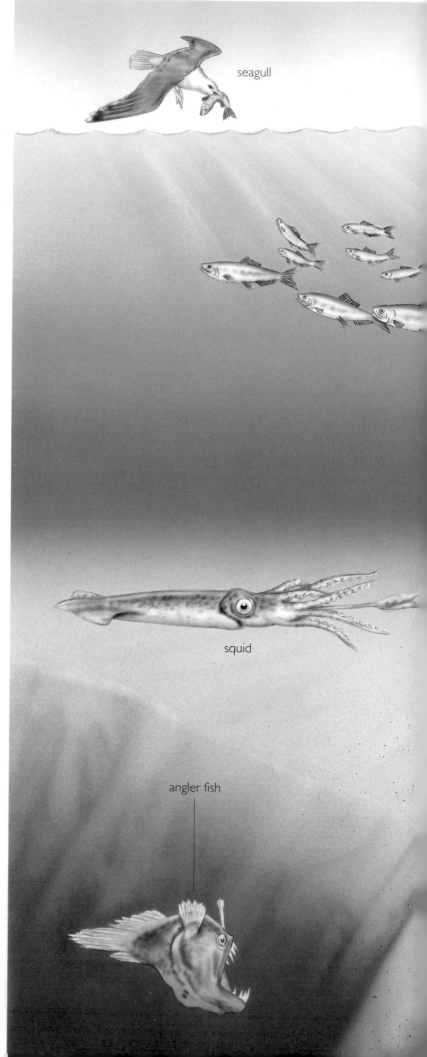

shoal of mackerel

ray

plaice

HOW DO SCIENTISTS INVESTIGATE OCEAN LIFE?

BY CARRYING OXYGEN TANKS, divers can examine the wildlife of the top few metres of the oceans, but for deeper investigations, where the water pressure is higher, they need diving suits or specially adapted submersibles. Mechanical arms can be operated from within the sub to retrieve samples of plants, animals and minerals.

Fortunately, most ocean life is within reach of divers carrying oxygen. Coral reefs are particularly rich in living things.

WHY DO SOME FISH HAVE BOTH EYES ON THE SAME SIDE?

WHILE MANY FISH swim in shoals, eating plankton as they flash through the water, others spend most of their time on the ocean bed. As the fish evolved, their eyes developed on the same side, so that both can see into the water above.

Some fish use camouflage just as land animals do. While they are not moving, it can be very difficult to see them among the sand and stones of the sea bed.

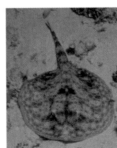

fast facts

HOW MUCH OF THE EARTH'S SURFACE IS COVERED BY SEA?

Over two-thirds (71%) of the Earth's surface is covered by the oceans.

WHAT IS PLANKTON?

Plankton is the millions of tiny plants and animals, too small to see without a microscope, that live in huge numbers in the oceans. They are food for many species, including some of the largest ones – whales.

WHY IS THE SEA SALTY?

The sea is salty because chemicals from rocks and soil have been dissolved in it. These include sodium, chlorine (which together make the salt we put on our food), magnesium, calcium and potassium.

HOW DEEP IS THE DEEPEST OCEAN?

The deepest ocean known is in the western Pacific. It is called the Marianas Trench and is about 11,000m (36,000ft) deep. Mount Everest could be placed in it and there would still be thousands of metres of water above it.

WHICH IS THE FURTHEST MAMMAL MIGRATION?

The longest mammal migration takes place in the oceans. The blue whale travels up to 20,000km (12,500 miles) each year.

CAN DEEP-SEA CREATURES SEE IN THE DARK?

OCEANS offer various habitats at different depths below the surface. These are called zones. The euphotic zone is at the top, ending at a depth of about 200m (660ft). Below this, very little light from the Sun can reach. The bathypelagic zone below is totally dark, so no plants can live there, but a number of fish, squid and crustaceans do make this zone their home, feeding on waste material that sinks down from above and on each other. Deep-sea creatures cannot see in total darkness, but their other senses help them to find food. Some, such as angler fish, carry their own lights. They are not bright enough to search for food by, but they may lure other fish towards them and help fish of the same species to recognize each other.

HOW DO FRESHWATER ECOSYSTEMS OPERATE?

Freshwater habitats include both still and moving water. Living things within rivers and streams can travel through the water to different areas. Many underwater inhabitants of ponds and lakes, however, cannot escape from what may be quite a small area of water. However, even a tiny pool may have a complete, self-contained ecosystem. As well as plants and fish, freshwater ecosystems support living things that visit the water but spend part of their lives on land, such as amphibians, birds and insects. Many mammals also spend time in and around the water. Finally, the kinds of wildlife found in freshwater ecosystems will be affected by the climate and landscape around it. For example, the crocodile may be the fiercest predator in an African river, but its place may be taken by an otter in a European stream.

The wildlife to be found in fresh water varies a great deal, depending on whether the water is still or moving and on the climate of the surrounding countryside. In the Brazilian rainforest, the Amazon is as teeming with life as the forest itself. The giant water lily is the largest in the world. The leaves are strong enough to support a small child!

WHERE DOES THE WATER IN PONDS AND RIVERS COME FROM?

PONDS AND RIVERS are part of the water cycle – the water that is constantly evaporating from the Earth, forming clouds and coming back to Earth as rain or snow. Some of this water seeps into underground streams and pools, which in turn may feed a spring that is the source of a river. Other rivers are fed by melting glaciers or very large lakes.

Although many parts of the world appear to have plenty of surface fresh water, in fact most of the world's fresh water is held underground or as ice. Less than 0.5% is to be found in rivers, lakes and the atmosphere.

DO FISH BUILD HOMES?

ALTHOUGH they often lay hundreds or even thousands of eggs, some fish do build nests to protect their young. The stickleback, found in European ponds and rivers, builds a nest of plant fibres in which the male guards the eggs until they have hatched, chasing away even the female that laid them.

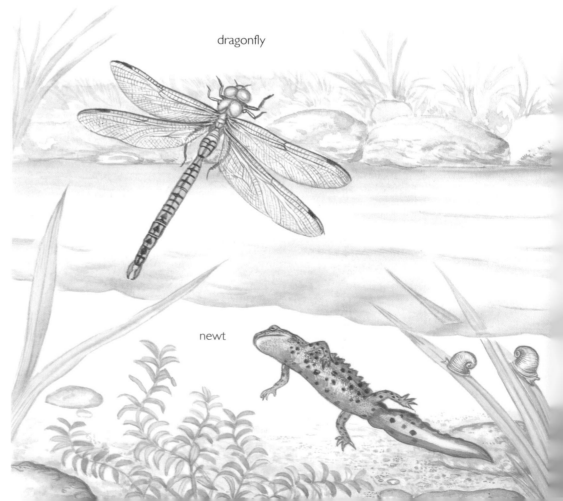

dragonfly

newt

HOW IS AN OXBOW LAKE FORMED?

AS A RIVER FLOWS through countryside, it rarely follows a straight line, but bends and twists following the natural contours of the ground and washing away the softest soil. Water flows fastest on the outer side of the bends, causing that bank to wash away further. In the meantime, soil being carried along in the river water, called silt, is deposited on the opposite bank. Over time, especially if there is flooding, the river may cut across the neck of the bend, creating an oxbow lake beside the river.

The river meanders as it crosses flat ground.

The river's current causes the bend to become greater and silt to be deposited on the bank opposite.

The river breaks through the neck of the bend and leaves an oxbow lake to one side.

WHY DO BEAVERS BUILD DAMS?

BEAVERS are rodents with very long, sharp front teeth. They use their teeth to gnaw down small trees for use in dam building or for food. Beavers build dams of sticks and mud across a river. This makes a calm pool the other side of the dam in which the beaver can build its home, or lodge. The inside of the lodge is reached by means of underwater tunnels. This keeps the beaver safe from predators such as wolves, even when the surface of the water is frozen in winter.

The beaver's thick fur keeps it warm in wet and icy conditions. In the past it also attracted fur trappers.

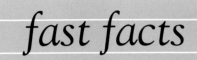

WHICH IS THE LARGEST FRESHWATER LAKE?

Lake Superior, one of the Great Lakes on the border between the United States and Canada, is 82,409sq km (31,820sq miles) in area. It is the largest freshwater lake in the world.

WHICH IS THE WORLD'S LONGEST RIVER?

The River Nile in Africa and the River Amazon in South America are similar lengths. The Nile is 6670km (4145 miles) long, while the Amazon stretches to 6437km (4000 miles).

WHICH IS THE HIGHEST WATERFALL?

The Angel Falls in Venezuela is the highest waterfall in the world at 979m (3212ft).

WHY ARE SOME LAKES SALTY ALTHOUGH CUT OFF FROM THE SEA?

Some lakes are salty because minerals from the surrounding soil are dissolved in their water.

WHAT IS AN ESTUARY?

An estuary is the mouth of a large river, where it flows into the sea. The river is often wide and shallow at this point and its mixture of salt and fresh water provides a habitat with its own distinct range of wildlife.

HOW DOES WATER FLOW EFFECT FRESHWATER WILDLIFE?

A FAST-FLOWING RIVER sweeps soil from the riverbed so that plants cannot grow there. On the other hand, there is more oxygen dissolved in the water, so that fish such as salmon thrive. Rivers in areas where the soil is peaty often have very little wildlife, because acid from the soil washes into the water.

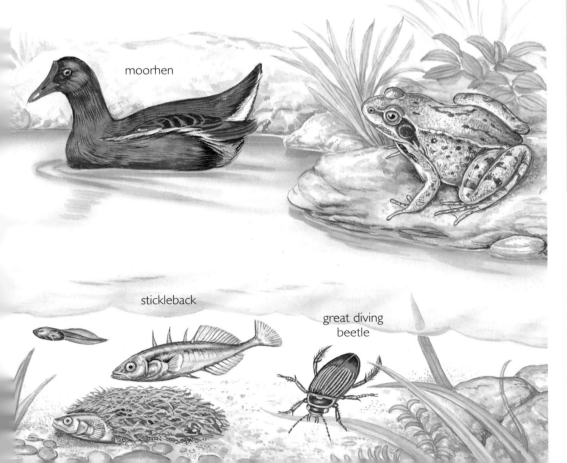

moorhen

stickleback

great diving beetle

WHAT ARE LIVING THINGS MADE OF?

Everything in the universe is made of atoms, arranged in different ways. But living things, unlike rocks or metal, have larger building blocks called cells. Some living things have only one cell, while others contain millions. Each cell has a job to do, but they all work together to make a living organism.

WHAT IS A CELL?

CELLS certainly are the building blocks of life, but they are very busy building blocks! Inside each cell thousands of chemical reactions are going on, so that the cell can carry out its tasks. A typical cell has a cell wall or membrane surrounding a kind of watery jelly called cytoplasm. Within the cell there are a number of parts called organelles. These do all the work that the cell is designed to do. The nucleus is a particularly important organelle. It controls all the activities of the cell.

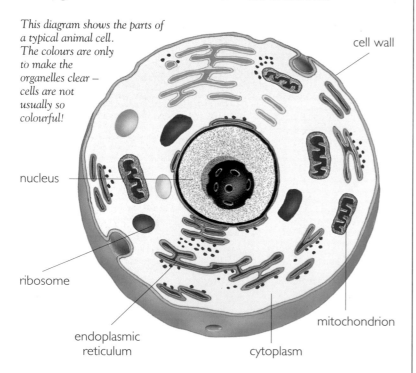

This diagram shows the parts of a typical animal cell. The colours are only to make the organelles clear – cells are not usually so colourful!

cell wall

nucleus

ribosome

endoplasmic reticulum

cytoplasm

mitochondrion

WHAT ARE MITOCHONDRIA?

MITOCHONDRIA are organelles that break up food materials to make energy. Other important organelles are ribosomes, which make proteins, and endoplasmic reticulum. This is a structure, made of double membranes, that is linked to the nucleus and to the cell wall, so that chemicals can be carried around the cell. The cell wall itself is said to be semi-permeable. That means that some chemicals can pass through it into the cell but none can pass out.

WHAT DO ALL LIVING THINGS HAVE IN COMMON?

LIVING THINGS are said to be animate. Inanimate things are not living. Metal, plastic and glass, for example, are inanimate. All animate things are able to do six things that inanimate things cannot.

1. They can feed, taking in nutrients that can be used for energy or to build or renew body parts.

The bodies of living things are adapted to help them find and eat food.

2. They can grow. They may stay the same shape and simply become larger, or they may take on various forms during their life cycle.

Living things may grow to enormous size over hundreds of years.

3. They can respire, taking in gases from the air and using them as part of the process of converting food into energy.

Fish respire by taking in oxygen dissolved in the water through their gills.

4. They can excrete, getting rid of waste material through their surfaces or by means of special parts of the organism.

Some animals, such as rhinos, use excretions to mark their territory.

5. They are sensitive, reacting to stimuli from outside.

Horses can be trained to respond to the most delicate touch of a rider.

6. They can reproduce, creating new versions of themselves in order that the species will not die out.

Most larger mammals produce only one or two offspring at a time.

All animals and many plants are also able to move. Plants cannot move their whole bodies in search of food, shelter or a mate, as most animals can, but many can move in a very small way, bending towards light, for example.

HOW DO PLANT CELLS DIFFER FROM ANIMAL CELLS?

ALL CELLS have a cell wall, but in plant cells this is made of a stiff, tough layer of cellulose. Cellulose is made of tiny fibres, layered together to form a strong sheet. Most plant cells also contain organelles called chloroplasts. It is in these that photosynthesis takes place.

Plants do not have skeletons to form a rigid framework for their bodies. Instead, stiff cell walls hold them up.

WHAT IS DNA?

DNA IS AN ABBREVIATION of the name of a chemical: deoxyribonucleic acid. It is DNA that contains the instructions for making and controlling every living thing. Inside the nucleus of a cell, the DNA forms chromosomes. Living things have different numbers of chromosomes. Human beings have 46, arranged in 23 pairs. Each of us has inherited one half of each chromosome pair from our father and the other half from our mother. A gene is a small part of the DNA molecule that can make one of the proteins that the living organism needs.

fast facts

WHO DISCOVERED CELLS?

Robert Hooke (1635–1703), an English scientist, first noted shapes that he called "cells" when he looked at pieces of plant material through a microscope.

WHAT IS THE LARGEST KNOWN CELL?

The largest single cell is an ostrich egg. It is about 20cm (8 inches) long.

WHAT IS THE SMALLEST KNOWN CELL?

The smallest cells existing individually are called mycoplasmas. They are a kind of bacteria, measuring only about one ten-thousandth of a millimetre across.

WHO DISCOVERED DNA?

The structure of DNA was discovered in 1953 by the American scientist James Watson and Francis Crick, a British bio-physicist. The work of Rosalind Franklin, another British scientist, had helped them to make this discovery.

DO ALL CELLS HAVE NUCLEI?

The simplest forms of life, such as viruses and bacteria, do not have nuclei. They have only strings of DNA with a cell wall around them.

The molecules of DNA are in the form of a spiral, making a shape called a double helix.

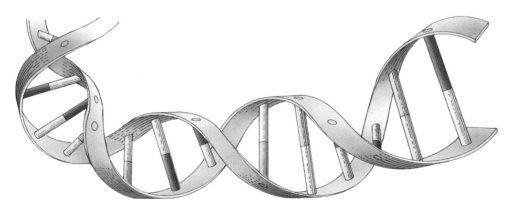

HOW DO LIVING THINGS GROW AND AGE?

Two things affect the way in which living things grow and age. The first is their genetic make-up – the genes that they have inherited from their parents. The DNA in their chromosomes controls the way that cells divide to cause the growth of the young organism, its coming to maturity and its aging. The other important factor is the environment and conditions that the organism experiences – how much of the right kind of food it eats, where it lives, the climate and the kinds of events and accidents that happen to it.

WHAT ARE THE LONGEST ANIMAL LIFE SPANS?

HUMAN BEINGS are far from being the longest-living animals. The giant tortoise can reach 150 years, while several aquatic creatures, such as the killer whale and some species of sea anemone, can survive for well over 80 years. At the other end of the scale, the adult mayfly lives for less than two days. The plant kingdom has far longer-living species. Several trees, such as the yew and giant sequoia, live for thousands of years.

WHAT IS GESTATION?

GESTATION is the length of time between conception – the fertilization of an egg by a sperm – and the birth of the baby that grows from the fertilized egg. The length of gestation varies according to the species.

Asian elephant : 660 days

cow: 278 days

human being: 267 days

cat: 61 days

dog: 63 days

mouse: 20 days

These are average gestation periods. The birth can be several days earlier or later than the average.

HOW ARE CHARACTERISTICS PASSED FROM ONE GENERATION TO THE NEXT?

THE CHARACTERISTICS of individual human beings are passed from one generation to the next in their chromosomes. Each of our parents gives us 23 chromosomes, making 46 in all. That means that we have two versions of each of our genes, but one is often dominant. We see the effect of the dominant gene, but the other (recessive) gene is still there and can be passed to our children.

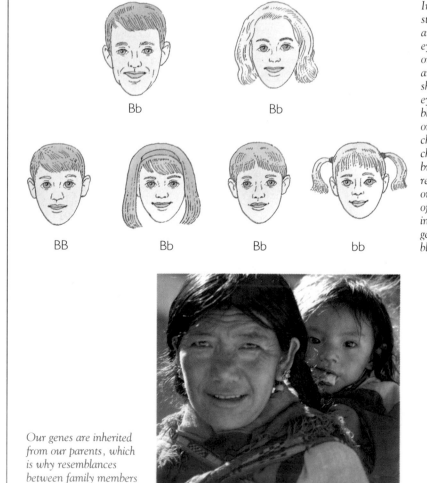

Bb   Bb

BB   Bb   Bb   bb

*In this diagram, **B** stands for brown eyes and **b** stands for blue eyes. If a child inherits one brown-eyes gene and one blue-eyes gene, she will have brown eyes, but she still has a blue-eyes gene to pass on to half of her own children. If her children's father also has brown eyes but a recessive blue-eyes gene, on average one in four of her children will inherit two blue-eyes genes and therefore have blue eyes.*

Our genes are inherited from our parents, which is why resemblances between family members can often be seen.

HOW DO HUMAN BABIES DEVELOP?

Human beings are mammals, which means that their young develop inside the mother until they are ready to be born. This development takes place inside the womb or uterus, where the baby gains the nutrients and oxygen it needs for growth from its mother's own blood, supplied through the umbilical cord.

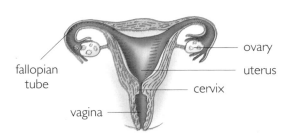

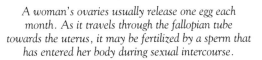

A woman's ovaries usually release one egg each month. As it travels through the fallopian tube towards the uterus, it may be fertilized by a sperm that has entered her body during sexual intercourse.

As soon as it is fertilized, the egg cell begins to divide, until it becomes a ball of cells called a blastocyst. This ball then implants itself in the wall of the uterus.

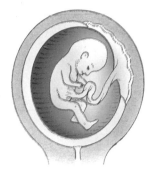

After four weeks, the blastocyst has become an embryo. Its brain, spine and limbs are already forming and its heart will soon begin to beat.

At 12 weeks, the embryo is now called a foetus. All its organs are formed. For the rest of the time before it is born, it simply has to grow.

From 38 weeks onwards, the baby is ready to be born. It moves down into the pelvis. At birth, the cervix gradually opens and the baby is born through the vagina.

Although human babies are quite helpless at birth, by nine months most are on the move by crawling or sliding along, and within a year they will be able to eat solid food, walk and begin to understand language.

HOW MUCH LONGER ARE PEOPLE LIVING NOW THAN IN THE PAST?

In many parts of the world, life expectancy – the number of years that a person can expect to live – is increasing. A thousand years ago, 40 might have seemed a good age for an adult to reach. Now we expect to live twice as long. Of course, these are just averages. Since records began there have been exceptional people who lived to 80 and beyond, but for most people, the dangers of dying of disease, accident, war or starvation were very high. Childhood in particular was a dangerous time. A woman might give birth to more than 10 children, none of them living to adulthood. We must not forget that there are parts of the world where this is still true, and billions of people still die each year from lack of food or medical care.

HAVE ALL HUMAN POPULATIONS INCREASING NUMBERS OF OLDER PEOPLE?

In the developed world, populations are aging, as better health care means that more people are living longer, while younger people are having fewer children. But in developing countries, where recent improvements in medical attention mean that fewer babies die in their early years, there are far more young people, under the age of 20, in the population than any other group.

WHY DOES SKIN WRINKLE WITH AGE?

As we get older, our skin becomes less elastic. We also tend to become thinner, so there is less fat beneath the skin to plump it out.

WHY CAN'T PEOPLE LIVE FOR EVER?

Every living thing has a natural lifespan. Gradually, the parts of the body do not repair and maintain themselves so effectively and most processes become weaker, until one breaks down and the organism dies. However, as scientists learn more about aging, it may be that the human lifespan can be lengthened.

DO HUMAN BEINGS SHED THEIR SKIN?

Human beings shed tiny particles of skin all the time. In fact, a large proportion of house dust is made up of human skin!

DO PEOPLE REALLY BECOME SHORTER AS THEY AGE?

In old age, our muscles weaken and there is a tendency to stoop, making us look shorter. In addition, the cartilage between the bones of our spine becomes thinner, reducing our height.

WILL LIFE ON EARTH GO ON FOR EVER?

Life on Earth cannot go on for ever because it depends on the Sun and, like all stars, our Sun will eventually die. However, that will happen billions of years in the future. In the meantime, we need to be concerned about the way in which we are using our planet now, so that it will continue to provide a home for all the living things that share it with us in the next century and beyond.

Pylons carrying electricity cables are such a familiar sight that it is hard to remember that two hundred years ago no one had any electrical appliances, lighting or heating.

WHAT ARE NON-RENEWABLE RESOURCES?

LIVING THINGS can grow and reproduce themselves. Given the right conditions, they can continue to do this for millions of years. But some of the Earth's resources cannot renew themselves. When they have been used up, there will be no more. Perhaps the most important of these non-renewable resources are what are known as fossil fuels. Both oil and coal were made millions of years ago when the bodies of prehistoric plants and animals were crushed under enormous pressure beneath moving rock. There is a limited supply of these fuels, making it necessary for us to develop energy sources that cannot run out.

WHICH KINDS OF ENERGY WILL NOT RUN OUT?

WIND, moving water and sunshine are always to be found somewhere on the Earth. All of these can be harnessed to provide energy. Wind farms, consisting of fields of enormous windmills, have been set up in many parts of the world to capture the wind's energy. Hydroelectric power uses the force of water hurtling over dams. Solar panels are warmed by the Sun and can be used to heat water and homes. At the moment, these methods are not able to produce all the energy that the world needs, but they hold out hope for the future.

wind farm

hydroelectric power station

Wood is a renewable resource as new trees can be planted, but it is not suitable for use as fuel on a large scale. After all, it takes only a few hours to burn a tree trunk but thirty years to grow another one.

solar panels

DOES THE PLANET HAVE ITS OWN RECYCLING SYSTEMS?

THE SAYING that there is nothing new under the Sun is strangely true. The stuff that makes up everything on Earth – animals, plants, rocks, water – cannot be destroyed, although it can be changed from one form to another. Living things are almost entirely made up of six elements: carbon, oxygen, hydrogen, nitrogen, phosphorous and sulphur. When a plant or animal dies, it decomposes. Gradually, its body breaks down, and the elements it was made of go back into the soil or water. These elements in time are taken up by new plants, which in turn are eaten by animals. This cycle of elements being released and re-used can take millions of years, but it is quite likely that within your body there are chemicals that were once part of a prehistoric plant – or even a dinosaur!

WHAT ARE THE MAIN PROBLEMS OF SPACE TRAVEL?

THE BIGGEST PROBLEMS of space travel all have to do with the enormous distances that are involved. Using today's technology, it would take years to reach even the nearest planets, and generations of space travellers would live and die on a journey to more distant ones. For this to happen, spacecraft will need to be self-supporting or able to travel faster than the speed of light.

COULD HUMANS FIND HOMES ELSEWHERE IN THE UNIVERSE?

AS THERE ARE BILLIONS of planets in our universe, it is likely that some of them could support life, but the vast distances that would have to be travelled to reach them are at present an immense problem. More possible is the idea that humans could build self-supporting communities on nearby planets. Ideally, these would need to be enclosed, containing their own atmosphere and able to support a variety of plant and animal life just as our planet does. Experiments are being made to see if it is possible to build artificial ecosystems like this here on Earth.

The Moon is so near that it would be possible to take day trips there! But it has no oxygen, so no living thing could survive there except inside a specially constructed building or suit.

COULD SCIENCE FICTION STORIES EVER COME TRUE?

SCIENCE FICTION STORIES do come true all the time. Less than a hundred years ago, space travel was a fantasy invented by storytellers such as H G Wells and Jules Verne. When we consider the extraordinary advances made in the fields of travel and communications in the past century, it is tempting to believe that *Star Trek* may in the future be nearer to reality than at present seems possible!

By studying the way in which the Earth's natural systems renew themselves, scientists hope to learn how to create successful ecosystems on other planets.

fast facts

HOW CAN HUMANS HELP WITH RECYCLING?

The first step is not to use too many of the Earth's resources in the first place. For example, we can try to use less fuel and buy fewer products that have a great deal of packaging. Many items that we need to use, however, can be recycled. Glass, paper, metals, plastics and even textiles can be recycled. Centres have been set up in many areas where household waste of this kind can be taken for recycling.

CAN OUR PLANET KEEP ITSELF IN BALANCE?

Some people believe that our planet is wiser than the people that live on it. They reason that life has continued on Earth for billions of years, despite natural "disasters" such as Ice Ages. The whole Earth (and the living things on it) is itself like a living organism, constantly adapting to the conditions in which it finds itself. This is a comforting thought, but it is wise to remember that we need the Earth much more than the Earth needs us. After all, life on Earth developed for millions of years before humans evolved.

HOW CAN POLLUTION BE REDUCED?

Pollution is the name we give to waste products that enter the air and soil and water but cannot be quickly broken down by natural processes. Instead, they affect the health of plants and animals, including humans, and the environments they live in. Controlling the emissions of factories and vehicles can help. It is also important, as far as possible, to use materials that can break down in the soil when they are thrown away. Such materials are said to be biodegradable.

GLOSSARY

Antifreeze A substance added to a liquid to raise the temperature at which it will freeze. Antifreeze added to the water in a car's radiator will prevent it from freezing except at very low temperatures.

Atmosphere The gases that form a layer around a planet.

Botanist A scientist who studies plants.

Camouflage The way in which the shape, colour or markings of a living thing can help it to blend into its surroundings and protect it from notice by its enemies.

Carnivorous Meat-eating. An animal that eats both plants and animals is said to be omnivorous.

Classification Organizing items into different classes or divisions. This helps scientists to describe them properly and to observe similarities and differences between them.

Condensation The changing of a gas or vapour into a liquid, often the result of cooling the gas or vapour.

Constellation Stars that appear to form a group or pattern when viewed from Earth.

Continent A very large body of land, surrounded by sea.

Environment The surroundings of a living thing.

Evaporation Molecules of a liquid escaping into the atmosphere to form vapour.

Hibernation Sleeping or greatly slowing down the body's functions during the winter.

Hominid A member of the primate family that walks on two legs, as people do.

Horticulturist A person concerned with growing and breeding plants, especially for gardens.

Life cycle The stages that a living thing normally goes through during its lifetime.

Metamorphosis Literally, changing form. The word is often used of the changing of a larva to a pupa in the insect world.

Nomad A person with no settled home, who moves about in search of food and shelter, often following the migrations of animals throughout the year.

Nutrient Something that gives nourishment. Part of the food of a living organism.

Orbit The path that a body takes as it circles another body, especially a planet or moon circling a star.

Organism A living thing, such as a plant or animal. Living things are made up of one or more cells.

Planet A large heavenly body that is in orbit around a star. A smaller body that is in orbit around a planet is called a moon.

Plankton Microscopic plants and animals that live near the surface of the sea and provide food for many sea creatures.

Predator An animal that hunts other animals for food.

Reproduction The creation of a new living thing similar to its parents. Sexual reproduction requires a male and female parent, while asexual reproduction can be achieved by a single organism.

Satellite Something that orbits a planet. This may be an artificial satellite, put into orbit by scientists, or a natural satellite, such as a moon.

Segment A section of the body of a plant or animal marked off by a clear line or division. Often such an organism has several similar segments making up its body.

Serrated With a saw-like edge.

Stimulus Something that prompts an organism or part of an organism into action or response.

Vegetation Plants of all kinds, especially those with abundant or large leaves.

SCIENCE

WHO WAS THE FIRST SCIENTIST?

Scientists study how and why things happen, or why they are as they are. They can use this knowledge in many different ways: to predict what will happen in certain circumstances, to understand why bodies and machines sometimes go wrong and to try to prevent this or put it right, and to develop inventions that will make a difference to the world. The first scientist was probably a very early human, or even human ancestor, who noticed something about the world, began to think about why this might be so and tried to test these ideas.

WHAT ARE THE MAIN FIELDS OF SCIENCE?

TRADITIONALLY, science has been divided into natural science, which deals with living things, and physical science, which is concerned with the matter that makes up the universe and how it behaves. Of course, these two fields overlap a great deal. There are also more detailed labels for different areas of scientific study.

Physics is the study of matter and energy and how they act on each other.

Biology is the study of living organisms.

Meteorology is the study of the weather and climates.

Botany is the study of plants.

Oceanography is the study of the world's oceans.

Chemistry is the study of the elements and how they join, and mix, and react with each other.

Biochemistry is the study of the chemistry of living organisms.

Astronomy is the study of the stars and other heavenly bodies.

Metallurgy is the study of metals.

There are many different ways of looking at the natural world. An engineer might be interested in the strength and structure of a honeycomb. A biochemist might want to look at the composition of the material from which the honeycomb is made. A naturalist might study whether bees learn to make these hexagonal chambers or hatch already possessing the skill.

HOW ARE EXPERIMENTS DESIGNED?

IN THE WORLD around us, nothing happens in isolation. One event affects another. The activity of one living thing changes the lives of other organisms. As the natural world is very complicated, it can be difficult to see clearly how and why things are happening. One of the most important factors in designing an experiment is to try to isolate the particular event or substance being studied, so that the results of the experiment are not influenced by other things. For example, to see if a plant needs sunlight to live, you can put it in the dark and watch what happens. But it is important to make sure that the plant still has the same soil, amount of water and temperature as before, so that you can be sure that any changes in the plant are a result of the lack of sunlight.

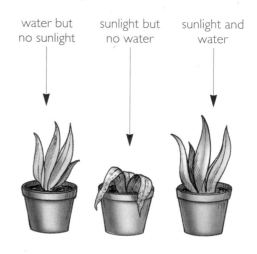

water but no sunlight   sunlight but no water   sunlight and water

Many experiments use something called a control. For example, to test a new drug, a hundred people may be given it and their health monitored very carefully. A hundred similar people may be given no drug or a harmless substance and their health monitored just as accurately. They are the control. It is the difference in results between the two groups of people that is important. The control group is designed to show what would have happened to the first group if it had received no drugs. Only then can scientists tell if the drug has had an effect.

WHAT IS A HYPOTHESIS?

ANYONE can make a guess, but scientists set about finding out if their ideas are true in an organized way. A hypothesis is a theory – an idea – about why something happens or what makes something work. A scientist will then try to think of a way of testing whether this idea is correct. Often this will mean designing a special experiment.

HOW HAVE COMPUTERS HELPED SCIENTISTS?

SCIENTIFIC STUDY relies on collecting and interpreting information (data). Sometimes thousands of different observations or measurements are made. Computers can help to collect and organize the data. For example, an astronomer might want to study the movement of a planet. A computer, attached to a radio telescope, can measure the position of the planet every five minutes for weeks – a task that would be very tedious for a scientist. Having collected the data, the computer can also process it and use it to predict future patterns of movement. Likewise, computers can perform very complex calculations at incredible speed, working out in less than a second something that a century ago might have taken a lifetime to calculate. Other computer programs can draw three-dimensional plans of objects as tiny as an atom or as large as a cathedral. These models can be turned on screen so that all sides can be viewed. Finally, scientists can search for information on the Internet, instead of visiting libraries that may be in other countries.

Without computers, space exploration would be impossible. Computers monitor all the astronauts' equipment and keep the ground crew informed of any problems before the astronauts are aware of them.

HOW IS SCIENTIFIC KNOWLEDGE PASSED ON?

IT IS INCREDIBLE to us now that five hundred years ago it was possible for a person to have a good understanding of every branch of science then known. Today there is so much information available that no one person can be informed about every area of science, and even specialists have difficulty in keeping up with new developments. There is a long established tradition that scientists who have made a new discovery publish a "paper" or article on the subject in scientific journals. People working in the same field can then read this to keep up to date with their subject. Some discoveries are so important or amazing that they reach the general public, through radio, television, books and newspapers.

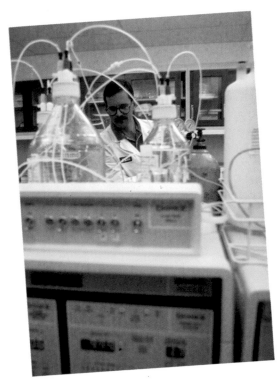

DO ALL SCIENTISTS WORK IN LABORATORIES?

SOME SCIENTISTS do wear white coats and work with test tubes, but many do most of their work in the world outside. A geologist, for example, may have to clamber a cliff face to obtain samples of rock.

Science is rarely easy, and scientists sometimes face dangerous situations where good preparation and equipment are vital. That is as true of a chemist dealing with dangerous chemicals in the laboratory as it is of a geologist looking for rock samples.

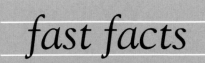

fast facts

HOW ARE IMPORTANT SCIENTIFIC DISCOVERIES MADE?

Scientific discoveries, like all great human achievements, are made by a combination of very hard work and luck. Although one person is often credited with an important discovery, it is likely that hundreds of other people also did work that made the discovery possible.

WHAT WERE THE FOUR ELEMENTS?

The ancient Greeks believed that everything was made from different proportions of four "elements": earth, water, air and fire.

WHAT WAS AN ALCHEMIST?

It is from the word *alchemy* that the modern word *chemistry* comes. Alchemists were early chemists, who discovered that metals could be extracted from minerals by heating them. The knowledge that one thing could apparently be changed into another led them to search for a way of changing "base" metals, such as copper, lead and iron, into gold. We know now that this is not possible, but while working on this problem, alchemists made other useful discoveries.

WHAT DOES THE WORD "LABORATORY" MEAN?

This word comes from the Latin word *laborare*, meaning "to work". So a laboratory is a place where scientific work is done.

WHAT IS MATTER?

Matter is the stuff that the universe is made of. The planets, this page, your body and the air that you breathe are all made of matter. Matter itself is made of very small particles called atoms, much too small to be seen with the naked eye or even with many microscopes. The kinds of atom that matter contains and the way in which they are joined together are what determine the kind of matter it is.

ARE ATOMS THE SMALLEST PARTICLES OF MATTER?

THE WORD "atom" comes from an ancient Greek word for a tiny piece of matter too small to be split up. Today we know that even atoms are made up of smaller parts, called subatomic particles. Protons and neutrons are the particles that make up the nucleus of an atom, while electrons can be thought of as circling around the nucleus like orbiting planets. However, these are not the only subatomic particles. Scientists have found hundreds more and are still discovering others by using a machine called a particle accelerator. Quarks, for example, form part of neutrons and protons.

WHAT IS THE STRUCTURE OF AN ATOM?

Each atom has a nucleus containing protons, and all except the hydrogen nucleus have neutrons as well. Neutrons have no electrical charge, but protons have a positive charge. Moving at high speed around the nucleus are little particles of energy called electrons, which have a negative charge. The number of protons and electrons in an atom is always the same. As opposite charges attract each other, the attraction between the protons and the electrons keeps the electrons around the nucleus, just as the force of gravity keeps the Moon circling around the Earth.

fast facts

WHAT IS AN ISOTOPE?

An element always has the same number of protons and electrons, but it may have different forms with different numbers of neutrons. These different forms are called isotopes. Chemically, the isotopes have the same properties, but physically they may differ.

HOW ARE NEW ATOMS NAMED?

Newly discovered atoms are often named in honour of a place or a famous scientist. For example, the element called curium is named after the chemists Marie and Pierre Curie. Marie Curie herself called an element that she discovered polonium, in honour of her native Poland.

WHICH IS THE MOST COMMON ELEMENT?

Hydrogen and helium are the most common elements by far in the universe, but the most common element in the Earth's crust is oxygen.

WHO WAS DIMITRI MENDELEYEV?

Dimitri Mendeleyev was a Russian scientist who, in 1869, suggested the method of setting out elements in a periodic table that we still use today. Mendeleyev was a far-sighted man. He even left gaps in his table for elements that he felt sure would be discovered in the future.

WHO DISCOVERED ATOMS?

The idea of atoms was first put forward by a Greek philosopher called Democritus about 400BC, but it was not until the beginning of the nineteenth century that an English chemist called John Dalton suggested that different atoms made different elements.

electron

proton

Although there may be many subatomic particles within an atom, most of the atom is empty space.

The electrons that move round the nucleus of an atom travel in different orbits, called shells. The number of electrons in each shell is limited. For example, there cannot be more than two electrons in the first shell, eight in the second shell, 18 in the third, and 32 in the fourth.

neutron

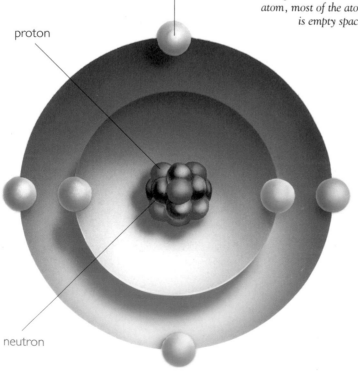

HOW MANY DIFFERENT ATOMS ARE THERE?

AN ELEMENT is a substance that is made up of only one kind of atom. The periodic table below shows all the elements currently known. However, there are more than 109 different atoms because some elements have more than one isotope.

The way that the periodic table is designed gives useful information about each element, depending on its position in the table. The elements are organized so that each has one more proton in the nucleus than the one before. The rows of the table are called periods. The elements in each period all have the same number of shells of electrons. The columns of the table are called groups. Each group has the same number of electrons in its outer shell. Elements in the first column have one, in the second two, and so on.

WHAT IS AN ATOMIC NUMBER?

THE ATOMIC NUMBER of an element is the number of protons it contains. For example, hydrogen has one proton, so its atomic number is one. Tin has an atomic number of 50 because it has 50 protons in its nucleus.

WHAT IS A MASS SPECTROMETER?

A MASS SPECTROMETER is a machine that can measure the mass of atoms and so identify them. In the table below, the relative atomic mass for radioactive elements is shown in parentheses: (242).

Key to example element:
- atomic number → 11
- chemical symbol → Na
- name → Sodium
- relative atomic mass (RAM) → 23.0

1 H Hydrogen 1.0																	2 He Helium 4.0
3 Li Lithium 6.9	4 Be Beryllium 9.0											5 B Boron 10.8	6 C Carbon 12.0	7 N Nitrogen 14.0	8 O Oxygen 16.0	9 F Fluorine 19.0	10 Ne Neon 20.2
11 Na Sodium 23.0	12 Mg Magnesium 24.3											13 Al Aluminium 27.0	14 Si Silicon 28.1	15 P Phosphorous 31.0	16 S Sulphur 32.1	17 Cl Chlorine 35.5	18 Ar Argon 39.9
19 K Potassium 39.1	20 Ca Calcium 40.1	21 Sc Scandium 45.0	22 Ti Titanium 47.9	23 V Vanadium 50.9	24 Cr Chromium 52.0	25 Mn Manganese 54.9	26 Fe Iron 55.9	27 Co Cobalt 58.9	28 Ni Nickel 58.7	29 Cu Copper 63.5	30 Zn Zinc 65.4	31 Ga Gallium 69.7	32 Ge Germanium 72.6	33 As Arsenic 74.9	34 Se Selenium 79.0	35 Br Bromine 79.9	36 Kr Krypton 83.8
37 Rb Rubidium 85.5	38 Sr Strontium 87.6	39 Y Yttrium 88.9	40 Zr Zirconium (91.2)	41 Nb Niobium 92.9	42 Mo Molybdenum 95.9	43 Tc Technetium (97.9)	44 Ru Ruthenium 101.1	45 Rh Rhodium 102.9	46 Pd Palladium 106.4	47 Ag Silver 107.9	48 Cd Cadmium 112.4	49 In Indium 114.8	50 Sn Tin 118.7	51 Sb Antimony 121.8	52 Te Tellurium 127.6	53 I Iodine 126.9	54 Xe Xenon 131.3
55 Cs Caesium 132.9	56 Ba Barium 137.3		72 Hf Hafnium 178.5	73 Ta Tantalum 181.0	74 W Tungsten 183.9	75 Re Rhenium 186.2	76 Os Osmium 190.2	77 Ir Iridium 192.2	78 Pt Platinum 195.1	79 Au Gold 197.0	80 Hg Mercury 200.6	81 Tl Thallium 204.4	82 Pb Lead 207.2	83 Bi Bismuth 209.0	84 Po Polonium (210)	85 At Astatine (210)	86 Rn Radon (222)
87 Fr Francium (223)	88 Ra Radium (226)		104 Db Dubnium (260)	105 Jl Joliotum (262)	106 Rf Rutherfordium (263)	107 Bh Bohrium (262)	108 Hn Hahnium (265)	109 Mt Meitnerium (266)									

57 La Lanthanum 138.9	58 Ce Cerium 140.1	59 Pr Praseodymium 140.9	60 Nd Neodymium 144.2	61 Pm Promethium (145)	62 Sm Samarium 150.4	63 Eu Europium 152.0	64 Gd Gadolinium 157.3	65 Tb Terbium 158.9	66 Dy Dysprosium 162.5	67 Ho Holmium 164.9	68 Er Erbium 167.3	69 Tm Thulium 168.9	70 Yb Ytterbium 173.0	71 Lu Lutetium 175.0
89 Ac Actinium (227)	90 Th Thorium (232.0)	91 Pa Protactinium (231)	92 U Uranium (238.1)	93 Np Neptunium (237)	94 Pu Plutonium (242)	95 Am Americium (243)	96 Cm Curium (247)	97 Bk Berkelium (245)	98 Cf Californium (251)	99 Es Einsteinium (254)	100 Fm Fermium (253)	101 Md Mendelevium (256)	102 No Nobelium (254)	103 Lr Lawrencium (257)

Key
- Alkali metals
- Transition metals
- Non-metals & semi-metals
- Lanthanides
- Alkaline-earth metals
- Poor metals
- Noble gases
- Actinides

WHAT IS RADIOACTIVITY?

Most elements do not change unless a force is applied to them that causes them to join with another element. They are said to be stable. But some elements are not stable. Their nuclei are constantly breaking down, or decaying, as they shed particles in an attempt to become stable. This is radioactivity, and the particles that are given off are known as radiation. Three types of particles are known to be emitted: alpha, beta and gamma rays.

α
β
γ

Radioactive radiation is named after three letters of the Greek alphabet: alpha, beta and gamma.

WHAT IS A NUCLEAR REACTION?

THERE ARE TWO KINDS of nuclear reaction, both of which give off huge amounts of energy. Nuclear fusion happens when two nuclei collide and combine to form one larger nucleus. This gives off enormous power. Nuclear fission happens when neutrons bombard the nucleus of an atom, causing the nucleus to split apart.

HOW DOES CARBON DATING WORK?

THE ISOTOPE called carbon-14 has a half-life of 5730 years. All living things on our planet contain this form of carbon, but they stop taking it in when they die. Scientists can examine ancient substances to see how much the carbon in it has decayed. They can then give a fairly accurate date for when the substance was alive. This is particularly useful for archaeologists and historians, who can date objects they find, helping to build up a picture of the past.

WHAT IS MEANT BY A HALF-LIFE?

THE HALF-LIFE of a radioactive substance is a measure of the rate at which the nuclei of its atoms are breaking up or decaying. It is the time it takes for half the atoms in a sample to decay. Thorium, for example, has a half-life of 24 days, while radium-221 has a half-life of only 30 seconds. Uranium has a half-life of 4.5 thousand million years. Of course, as each isotope of an element has a certain number of protons and neutrons in its nucleus, it changes as it decays, forming other elements. For example, plutonium-242 decays to become uranium-238, which in turn breaks down to become thorium-234.

Archaeologists use many clues to discover what happened in the past. Carbon dating is a useful tool to add to their skills.

WHEN WERE NUCLEAR WEAPONS FIRST USED?

NUCLEAR WEAPONS were first used in the Second World War. Two bombs were dropped on the Japanese cities of Nagasaki and Hiroshima, killing hundreds of thousands of people.

The mushroom shape of the cloud produced by a nuclear explosion is now a familiar image. With the development of nuclear weapons, human beings for the first time possessed the power to destroy the living world within seconds. Relationships between nations and the development of strategies for peace have never been so important.

This peace memorial park in Japan honours those who died when two nuclear bombs were dropped on the country in 1945.

fast facts

WHO DISCOVERED RADIOACTIVITY?

Antoine Becquerel (1852–1908) discovered "rays" coming from uranium. These were investigated by Marie and Pierre Curie, who later shared the Nobel Prize with Becquerel. Marie Curie may have died of cancer caused by radiation.

WHAT IS RADIOTHERAPY?

It is because radiation has an effect on the human body that it can be used for medical purposes. Radiotherapy involves directing radiation at harmful cells in the body, such as cancer cells, to kill them.

HOW ARE RADIOACTIVE MATERIALS HANDLED?

Exposure to radioactive radiation can be fatal to living organisms. For this reason, radioactive materials are carried in lead-lined containers and wherever possible robots rather than humans are used to deal with them. When people do need to handle such substances, they wear protective clothing and a meter that records the amount of exposure to radiation they are receiving.

HOW IS NUCLEAR POWER USED?

NUCLEAR FUSION releases so much energy that it is hard to control. At the moment, only nuclear fission is used to give nuclear power. In power stations with pressurized water reactors, a radioactive substance, such as uranium, is bombarded with neutrons so that its atoms split and release energy. This energy heats water. The resulting steam turns a turbine to create electricity. Nuclear power has also been used to power submarines. One problem with nuclear power is that the waste material left behind is still radioactive and must be disposed of safely.

WHAT DOES A GEIGER COUNTER MEASURE?

A Geiger counter measures the radiation being given off by a substance. It has both a dial, giving a reading, and a loudspeaker that transmits a regular clicking sound if radiation is detected. The faster the clicking, the more radiation there is.

WHO INVENTED THE GEIGER COUNTER?

Although the idea for the machine had already been suggested by other scientists, the Geiger counter was perfected by a German physicist called Hans Geiger (1882–1945).

This symbol on a container or building warns that there is radioactive material inside.

WHAT ARE MOLECULES?

In nature, it is rare to find one atom on its own. Atoms are usually grouped together in larger structures called molecules. A molecule is the smallest particle of a substance that can exist by itself. The atoms in a molecule are chemically bonded together. They may be atoms of the same element or they may be of different elements. A molecule of carbon dioxide, for example, has two atoms of oxygen and one of carbon.

HOW DO SOLIDS, LIQUIDS AND GASES DIFFER?

MANY SUBSTANCES can exist in three different states of matter: as solids, liquids and gases. In each state, the substance has the same chemical make-up – the elements in its molecules have not changed, but the way in which they are connected to each other has. Scientists think of all matter as being constantly in motion. The atoms and molecules of which it is made have energy, called kinetic energy.

In solids, the energy is not strong enough for the particles to break free of the attraction they have for each other. It is as though they are vibrating but not moving from their positions.

The molecules in a liquid have more energy and can move away from neighbouring molecules, so that a liquid will flow to cover as wide an area as it can.

The molecules of a gas have most kinetic energy. They will move apart from each other until they fill the space in which they are contained.

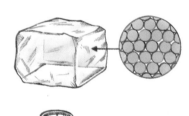
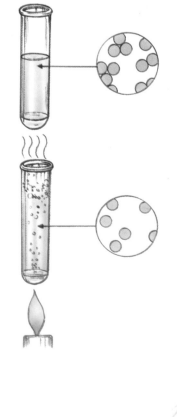

WHAT HAPPENS WHEN MOLECULES ARE HEATED?

WHEN MOLECULES are heated, they gain heat energy in addition to the kinetic energy they already have. If the molecules in a solid gain enough energy, they can break free of each other and become liquid. This is called melting. If they gain even more heat energy, the liquid becomes a gas.

Water freezes, or becomes solid, at temperatures of 0°C (32°F) or below. If the temperature outside drops to this level, the water on the surface of ponds and lakes will freeze, although the water below may hold enough heat to remain liquid.

When solid water (ice) is heated, it melts to become liquid. Generally speaking, we think of water as being liquid. That is because it is liquid at a "room temperature" of 20°C (68°F), or, in other words, under normal conditions. Copper, however, is a solid under such conditions, because it needs a temperature of 1083°C (1981°F) to melt into a liquid.

When water is heated and boils, it turns into a gas. We can see this when a kettle boils. In fact, it is not the billowing steam that is the gas – that is the water turning back into tiny droplets of liquid as it comes into contact with cool air. The real steam is invisible. It can be "seen" in the gap between the spout of the kettle and the visible vapour.

IS HEATING THE ONLY WAY TO CAUSE CHANGES OF STATE?

As well as heating or cooling, changing the pressure acting on a substance can also cause it to change state. If the pressure on the molecules in a substance is increased, it becomes harder for them to move apart from each other, so the temperature at which they become a liquid is increased. Similarly, at low pressure, changes happen at lower temperatures. It is impossible to make a good cup of tea or coffee at the top of Everest, for example, because water boils at a temperature almost 30°C (50°F) less than at sea level.

On top of a mountain, where the atmospheric pressure is less than at sea level, everything feels cold – not just the coffee!

WHAT IS MASS?

THE MASS of a substance is the amount of matter it contains. This is different from its weight, which is a measurement of the pull of gravity on this mass. For example, an astronaut would have the same mass on Earth as on the Moon, but his weight would be much less in the Moon's gravity than in the Earth's.

WHAT IS DENSITY?

THE AMOUNT of space that a substance takes up is called its volume. It is measured in cubic units. For example, a cube measuring one metre on each side has a volume of one cubic metre or $1m^3$. But a cubic metre of lead has a much greater mass than a cubic metre of wood. That is because the lead has a much higher density than the wood. Its particles are more tightly packed together. The density of an object is calculated by dividing its mass by its volume and is expressed as kilograms per cubic metre (kg/m^3) or pounds per cubic foot (lb/ft^3).

When water freezes, it expands. The water still has the same amount of matter in it when it is frozen – its mass is the same – but its volume has increased. This means that its density has decreased. Liquid water is denser than ice. That is why icebergs float in water.

fast facts

HOW BIG IS A MOLECULE?

Although it is larger than an atom, because it is made up of more than one atom, a molecule is still much too small to see with the naked eye.

WHAT IS SUBLIMATION?

A few substances pass from a solid state to a gas without beconring a liquid in between. This is known as sublimation.

WHAT IS IN A MOLECULE OF WATER?

A molecule of water contains two atoms of hydrogen and one atom of oxygen.

WHAT IS A CHEMICAL FORMULA?

A chemical formula is a short way of writing down the "recipe" for a molecule. It uses the chemical symbols from the periodic table for each atom, plus numbers to show how many atoms there are. The chemical formula for water is well known: H_2O. That is a short way of saying that there are two hydrogen atoms and one oxygen atom in a molecule of water.

HOW MANY DIFFERENT MOLECULES ARE THERE?

At present we know of more than a hundred different atoms, but these atoms can combine in millions of ways to form different molecules. So there are literally millions of different kinds of molecules.

Scientists often make models of molecules. Each coloured ball represents an atom. The picture below shows a molecule of water, which is quite simple, but for more complex molecules, hundreds of balls may need to be used.

hydrogen atoms   oxygen atom

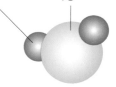

HOW DO ATOMS AND MOLECULES MIX AND JOIN?

Elements do not usually exist on their own. In the natural world, they are found in combination with other elements. By understanding how elements combine, scientists have been able to make new combinations, creating molecules that are not found in nature. These combinations are not made simply by mixing two or more substances together. Brown sugar and salt can be stirred together, for example, but this does not create a new substance. Each little particle is either a grain of sugar or a grain of salt – they have remained separate. Mixtures can usually be separated again, but when elements are chemically joined together, they are said to be bonded and have created a new substance.

HOW DOES BONDING WORK?

BONDING is caused by a chemical reaction. Most chemical reactions need some form of energy to start them. Usually, this energy is supplied in the form of heat. Many compounds are made by heating two or more substances together until their molecules are moving so fast that they react with each other.

When we cook food, chemical reactions take place as heat energy is supplied to the ingredients. New compounds are formed, so that the cooked dish usually has a different appearance, texture and taste from the mixed raw ingredients.

WHAT IS A COMPOUND?

A COMPOUND is a substance that is created when two or more elements are bonded by a chemical reaction. It is difficult to split a compound back into its original elements. Compounds do not necessarily take on the characteristics of the elements that form them. For example, sodium is a metal and chlorine is a gas. Together they form a compound called sodium chloride, which is not like either of them. In fact, sodium chloride is the chemical name for the salt that we put on our food.

WHAT IS MEANT BY VALENCY?

IT IS USEFUL to think of an atom as having electrons circling in layers around its nucleus. These layers are known as "shells". Each layer can only have a certain number of electrons before a new shell must be started. Atoms that have as many electrons as possible in the outer shell (or some other particular numbers) are said to be stable. They do not easily form bonds with other atoms. Atoms that are not stable try to become so by sharing electrons with, or borrowing electrons from, or giving electrons to, another atom. The number of electrons that an atom needs to give or gain to achieve a stable outer shell is called its valency.

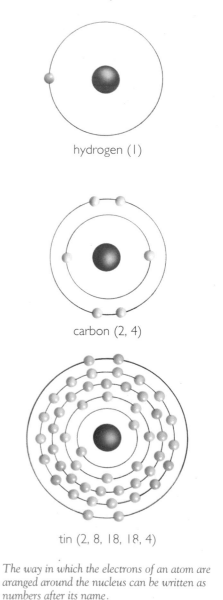

hydrogen (1)

carbon (2, 4)

tin (2, 8, 18, 18, 4)

The way in which the electrons of an atom are arranged around the nucleus can be written as numbers after its name.

WHAT IS A COVALENT BOND?

COVALENT BONDS usually take place between non-metals. Many substances made in this way are gases or liquids at room temperature. A covalent bond is one in which two atoms share one or more electrons in order to complete their outer shell of electrons. Water is an example of a covalent bond. A water molecule has two hydrogen atoms and one oxygen atom. The hydrogen atoms have one electron, while the oxygen atom has six electrons in its outer shell. By sharing the hydrogen electrons, the oxygen atom has eight electrons in its outer shell, creating a stable molecule.

When water freezes in the form of snow, it forms crystals with a regular, six-sided shape. The way in which hydrogen bonds with oxygen is responsible for these forms.

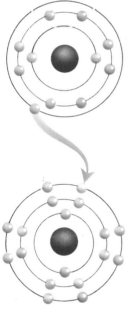

sodium (2, 8, 1)

chlorine (2, 8, 7)

When sodium and chlorine bond to make sodium chloride, the sodium atom gives the single atom from its outer shell to the chlorine atom, which then has eight electrons in its outer shell. This is an ionic bond.

Quartz crystals are made of silicon and oxygen. When an electric current is passed through them, they vibrate at a regular rate. This has meant that they can be used in clocks and watches to give very accurate timing.

WHAT IS AN IONIC BOND?

IONIC BONDS happen when one atom gains one or more electrons from another atom. The electrons in an atom have a negative charge and are equal in number to the positively charged protons in the nucleus. When an atom gains or loses electrons, the balance of charges is broken, so the atom becomes either positively or negatively charged. It is called an ion. An atom that has gained electrons has a negative charge and is called an anion. One that has lost electrons has a positive charge and is called a cation. As opposite charges attract each other, the two atoms that have gained and lost electrons are pulled together into a bond.

fast facts

WHAT IS A SALT?

A salt is a compound made when a metal and a non-metal are bonded together. Common salt, which contains the metal sodium and the non-metal chlorine, is one example. Chalk, plaster of Paris and copper sulphate are also salts.

WHAT IS STUDIED IN ORGANIC CHEMISTRY?

Organic chemistry is the study of organic compounds. These are compounds that contain carbon. Organic compounds are very important. All living things contain carbon compounds, as do fuels such as coal and oil.

WHAT IS A CRYSTAL?

A crystal is a solid substance that has a regular shape with straight edges and flat sides. Diamonds and other minerals are clearly crystals. So are many other solids – but their crystals are too small to see without a microscope.

HOW HAVE SYNTHETIC COMPOUNDS BEEN MADE?

Organic compounds that occur in nature can be duplicated in the laboratory. By studying these compounds, chemists have also been able to make new, synthetic compounds, such as plastics, paints and medicines.

WHAT IS HYDROGENATION?

Hydrogenation is a chemical reaction where hydrogen atoms are added to molecules of certain kinds of organic compounds. For example, unsaturated vegetable oils can be made into solid, saturated fats by hydrogenation.

HOW DO METALS AND NON-METALS DIFFER?

There are over 80 different metals. They tend to conduct heat and electricity well, and many of them can be shaped by pulling, beating, or melting and pouring into a mould. Metals with similar properties are often grouped together, although a metal may sometimes appear in more than one group, as these pages show. Unlike most non-metals, metals are shiny when cut. Metals have played an enormous part in the history of human activity, which is why some periods, such as the Iron Age and the Bronze Age, are known by the names of metals. Some people say that our present period should be called the Silicon Age. But silicon is what is known as a semi-metal, having some but not all of the properties of metals.

The chlorophyll in the leaves of this plant contains magnesium.

Lead is added to glass to make it soft enough to cut into intricate patterns.

WHAT IS REACTIVITY?

THE ABILITY of an element to take part in a chemical reaction is called reactivity. Metals vary in their reactivity. Some alkali metals, such as sodium and potassium, are so reactive that they have to be stored in oil. They would react strongly with the oxygen in air or water. The least reactive metal is gold.

The stainless steel used in this sink is an alloy of iron, chromium and nickel. The nickel stops the iron from corroding.

Tin cans are made of steel, not tin, but they do have a coating of tin to stop food inside corroding the steel. Drinks cans are often made of aluminium.

Another way to prevent steel from corroding is to galvanize it. That means giving it a coating of zinc.

Copper wires conduct electricity. They are usually wrapped in a non-conducting plastic covering for safety.

Three-quarters of all known elements are metals, so it is not surprising that metals are found in most everyday objects. Even the human body contains large amounts of calcium and trace amounts of iron and other metals.

The paint used on white electrical goods may contain compounds of titanium.

WHAT ARE THE NOBLE METALS?

NOBLE METALS are those that can be found in their pure state, not mixed with other substances. As might be expected, they are not very reactive, which is why they do not readily form compounds in their natural state. This also means that they do not corrode easily, making them traditionally suitable to be formed into coins or jewellery. Noble metals include gold, silver, platinum and copper.

WHAT ARE ALKALI METALS?

AN ALKALI METAL is one that reacts vigorously with water to make an alkaline solution. Lithium, sodium, potassium, rubidium, caesium and francium are all alkali metals. They appear in the first column, or group, of the periodic table. All alkali metals are soft enough to cut with an ordinary knife and are a whitish silvery colour.

Streetlights that give off a yellowish orange light have sodium vapour inside.

Gold is sometimes found in its pure state as nuggets in streams that pass over gold-bearing rocks. The great gold rushes of America and Australia saw many prospectors panning for gold.

WHY DO METALS CORRODE?

SOME METALS corrode badly on contact with air and water. This means that the surface of the metal reacts with oxygen to form an oxide. The metal loses its shine as a layer of oxide covers it. This is sometimes known as tarnishing. When a bowl covered with silver is cleaned, for example, what is really happening is that the layer of tarnish is being rubbed away. Over a long period of time, all the silver may be rubbed off. Iron corrodes in air and water to produce rust. Non-reactive metals are less likely to corrode than reactive ones.

The Golden Gate Bridge in San Francisco needs to be painted regularly to stop it from corroding.

WHAT KIND OF METAL IS CALCIUM?

CALCIUM is one of a group of metals called the alkaline-earth metals. They form alkaline solutions with water and are found in many natural substances. Calcium is an important constituent of bones, making them hard and stable. Magnesium is found in chlorophyll, the green part of plants that can make energy from sunlight by photosynthesis. Alkaline-earth metals form the second group of the periodic table.

Aluminium has a low density, so it is very light. That makes it ideal, mixed with other metals, for use in building aircraft, where weight must be controlled.

WHY IS ALUMINIUM KNOWN AS A POOR METAL?

POOR METALS have a low melting point and are quite soft, but they are still very useful. The seven metals that come to the right of the transition metals in the periodic table are known as poor metals. They are aluminium, gallium, indium, thallium, tin, lead and bismuth. Lead has a very high density, so radiation cannot easily pass through it. That is why radioactive materials are often carried in lead-lined containers and the operators of x-ray machines wear lead aprons. Poor metals may be combined with other metals to form useful alloys.

fast facts

WHAT IS MEANT BY A TRANSITION METAL?

Transition metals are those in groups three to 12 of the periodic table, including iron, chromium, nickel, copper, gold and silver. Transition metals have a high melting point and are not too reactive. They are easy to shape and have thousands of uses in industry.

WHAT IS BRONZE?

Bronze is an alloy of tin and copper. It was probably the first alloy made by humans, thousands of years ago.

WHAT IS A DUCTILE METAL?

A ductile metal can be drawn out into a wire. Copper, for example, can form very fine wire that conducts electricity efficiently.

WHAT DOES "MALLEABLE" MEAN?

The word "malleable" comes from a Latin word, *malleus*, meaning a hammer. Malleable metals can be beaten into very thin sheets. Gold, for example, may be beaten into gold leaf – a very, very thin layer that can be used to decorate picture frames and other ornaments.

WHAT IS SPECIAL ABOUT MERCURY?

Mercury is the only metal that is not solid at room temperature.

WHAT IS AN ACID?

The word "acid" comes from a Latin word meaning sour. Acids contain hydrogen and, when dissolved in water, produce positively charged hydrogen ions. Our tongues are able to detect acidic flavours, such as those of vinegar or citrus fruits, but these are very weak in comparison to some acids used in industry, such as sulphuric acid, which burns badly if it comes into contact with skin.

The juice of citrus fruits, such as lemons, limes and oranges, contains a weak acid called citric acid.

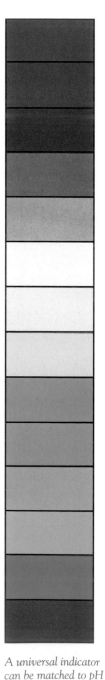

A universal indicator can be matched to pH numbers to measure a substance's acidity or alkalinity.

ARE BASES AND ALKALIS THE SAME THING?

A BASE is the opposite of an acid. Most soap and many household cleaners are bases. An alkali is a base that can be dissolved in water.

WHAT DOES A pH VALUE MEASURE?

THE ABBREVIATION pH stands for "power of hydrogen". It describes how concentrated the hydrogen ions in a substance are. A pH value below seven shows that the substance is acid. Above seven, it is an alkali.

WHAT IS AN INDICATOR?

AN INDICATOR is a substance that changes colour when it comes into contact with something acid or alkali. Several materials occuring in nature will do this, including litmus, which comes from lichen, and a substance in red cabbage. By using a range of different dyes, scientists make something called a universal indicator, which is able to show how acidic or alkali a substance is.

WHICH INTERNATIONAL SYMBOLS WARN ABOUT CHEMICALS INSIDE CONTAINERS?

INTERNATIONAL SYMBOLS warn people that the contents of containers are dangerous. The symbol on the left means "harmful chemical inside", while the other means "corrosive chemical inside".

HOW ARE ACIDS AND ALKALIS USED IN INDUSTRY?

MANY PRODUCTS and processes require the use of acids and alkalis. Here are just some of them.

Car batteries contain acid. Acids are also used to make fertilizer, paint, detergents, plastics, dyes and some artificial fabrics.

Alkalis are used in the manufacture of soap, floor cleaners, indigestion tablets and cement.

HOW DO ACID AND ALKALI SOILS DIFFER?

IT IS POSSIBLE to measure the acidity or alkalinity of soil. Acid soils are usually found in peaty or forest areas, while alkali soils often occur where the underlying rocks are chalk or limestone. Most plants prefer a soil that is neither too acid nor too alkali, but some are only happy in a particular soil. Heathers and rhododendrons, for example, prefer an acid soil.

Some plants are indicators themselves. Hydrangeas have pink blooms in alkaline soils and blue ones in acid soils.

Rainwater is not neutral. It is slightly acidic because carbon dioxide from the air is dissolved in it. This reacts with limestone, made of alkaline calcium carbonate. Minerals dissolved in the water gradually build up into the strange rock formations known as stalagmites (rising from the floor of caves) and stalactites (hanging from the ceiling).

HOW DO WASP AND BEE STINGS DIFFER?

ALTHOUGH both feel painful, wasp stings are alkali and bee stings are acid. That means that it is best to treat them with acid and alkali substances respectively.

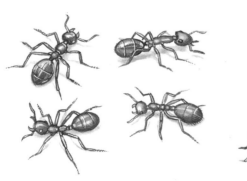

Both stinging ants and stinging nettles produce an acid called methanoic acid (formic acid). Ants use it to immobilize their prey, while nettles use it to protect themselves from being eaten.

fast facts

WHAT IS ACID-FREE PAPER?

Modern methods of making paper result in a product that is very slightly acid. Over a period of years, the acid in the paper starts to destroy it, which is why the paper in old books becomes yellow and brittle. Acid-free papers have been developed to ensure that important documents do not deteriorate.

WHAT IS NEUTRALIZATION?

When an acid and a base or alkali are mixed together in the right quantities, they result in a substance that is neither acid nor alkali. It is neutral, with a pH value of seven. Neutralization is the process of making a material neutral by adding its opposite.

WHY DO WE SOMETIMES HAVE ACID IN OUR STOMACHS?

We always have acid in our stomachs! It is quite a strong one, called hydrochloric acid, and it is produced by the body to help break down our food in the process known as digestion.

WHAT HAPPENS WHEN SULPHURIC ACID IS ADDED TO WATER?

When sulphuric acid is dissolved in water, an enormous amount of heat is produced. This is potentially very dangerous, so the acid must be added to the water rather than the water to the acid. By this means, the acid is diluted by the water, which is warmed by the reaction.

CAN DOCK LEAVES REALLY HELP NETTLE STINGS?

Nettle stings are acidic and dock leaves are slightly alkaline, so rubbing a sting with a dock leaf may help a little to dull the pain.

WHERE DOES ENERGY COME FROM?

Energy is what makes things happen. Nothing can live, move and grow, or give off light, heat or sound, without energy. There are many different kinds of energy, but nearly all the energy on our planet comes, directly or indirectly, from the Sun.

WHAT ARE THE DIFFERENT KINDS OF ENERGY?

CHEMICAL ENERGY is released when chemical reactions take place. It is stored in many different kinds of substances, such as foods and fuels. Kinetic energy is the energy of movement. An object that is being acted on by a force is said to have potential energy.

Chemical energy is stored in the food we eat. After we have eaten it, it is stored in our fat and muscles. When we move, some of the store of chemical energy in our bodies is converted into kinetic energy.

A rolling ball, a moving bicycle and a running person all have kinetic energy.

A ball being held in the air is being acted on by the force of gravity. If it is dropped, its potential energy will become kinetic energy.

Electrical energy can be converted into light energy, sound energy or heat energy.

HOW DOES A POWER STATION WORK?

COAL, OIL OR GAS may be used to fuel a power station. All of these are fossil fuels, formed millions of years ago when the bodies of plants and animals were crushed under enormous pressure.

When the fuel is burned, a chemical reaction takes place that converts its chemical energy into heat energy.

The heat energy is used to heat water until it becomes a gas: steam.

The steam is used to turn a turbine, converting the heat energy into kinetic energy.

A generator converts the kinetic energy into electrical energy.

The electrical energy is carried along wires to homes and factories, where it is converted into heat, light or sound energy by electrical appliances.

HOW DO HUMAN BEINGS GET THEIR ENERGY?

OUR ENERGY comes from the Sun – but not directly. Plants convert sunlight into chemical energy. We then eat the plants or other animals that have fed on them, so the chemical energy is stored in our bodies. For this energy to be released, chemical reactions need to take place in our bodies. These reactions require oxygen, which we take in from the air we breathe. That is why we get breathless when we are running and turning a lot of chemical energy into kinetic energy.

HOW CAN ENERGY BE STORED?

ENERGY from the Sun is stored in the leaves of plants, but it is also possible to store electrical energy in batteries. Inside a dry-cell battery there is a chemical paste called an electrolyte (which contains charged particles), a positive terminal (or electrode) and a negative terminal. When the battery is put into an electrical circuit, chemical reactions cause electrons to flow out through the negative terminal, through the circuit, and back through the positive terminal. When all the chemical reactions have taken place, the battery is "dead" and has to be replaced or, in the case of some batteries, recharged.

positive terminal

electrolyte

carbon rod

zinc casing forming
the negative terminal

This is a single cell. Larger batteries contain several single cells. Car batteries are not dry cells but contain dilute sulphuric acid and electrodes made of lead and lead oxide.

WHAT IS A JOULE?

A JOULE (J) is a small unit of energy. More commonly, we measure energy in kilojoules (kJ), which are units of a thousand joules each. A medium orange probably contains about 250kJ of chemical energy. The same weight of chocolates might contain 1700kJ of energy.

WHAT IS GEOTHERMAL ENERGY?

THE EARTH itself is a store of energy, as the rocks inside it are extremely hot. Water in underground streams and lakes can be heated by running over hot or molten rock. It may then come to the surface in hot springs or geysers. In some parts of the world the hot water or steam is used to turn turbines to produce electricity. This is called geothermal energy.

Steam may come out of the ground naturally in geysers, or water can be pumped underground and heated by hot rocks.

WHAT IS PERPETUAL MOTION?

Today we are concerned about conserving energy, ensuring that it is used efficiently so that we do not run out of non-renewable sources of energy too quickly. Once inventors dreamed of a perpetual motion machine, which would carry on working without more energy being supplied to it. In fact, this is impossible. No matter how efficient a machine is, some energy is lost as heat. Eventually, this uses up all the energy available to the machine unless more is supplied.

HOW CAN ROTTING PRODUCE ENERGY?

When plants or animals decay, they give off gases. One of these is a gas called methane, which can be used for heating water and homes.

CAN ENERGY BE DESTROYED?

One form of energy can change into another form but, like matter, it cannot be destroyed or created.

WHAT DOES A WATT MEASURE?

A watt (W) is a unit of power, which means the amount of energy used in a certain time. One watt is the same as one joule of energy used in one second. So a 100-watt light bulb is one that uses 100 joules in one second.

WHAT IS A CALORIE?

A calorie is a unit of energy that is sometimes used instead of the joule. One kilocalorie (Kcal) is equal to approximately 4.2 kilojoules (kJ).

WHAT IS A FORCE?

There are forces acting on us – and everything on our planet – all the time. The push and pull of forces is what keeps things where they are or starts them into motion. Forces enable something to stay the same size and shape or to change size and shape. They can slow down a moving object or speed it up, or change the direction of its motion. Whenever energy is being used, forces are at work.

ARE THERE DIFFERENT KINDS OF FORCE?

THERE ARE many different kinds of force. They are affecting everyday objects around us all the time. Here are just some of the many forces that we experience.

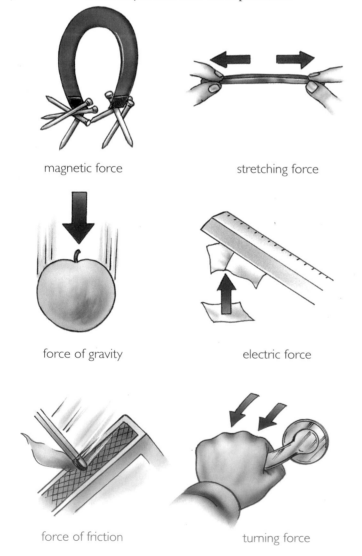

magnetic force

stretching force

force of gravity

electric force

force of friction

turning force

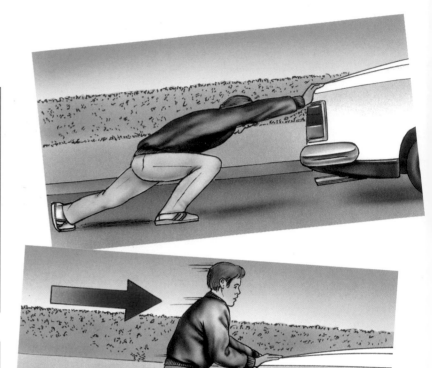

WHAT IS INERTIA?

WHEN A FORCE is applied to an object, it may change its position, movement or shape, but objects have a resistance to change that scientists call inertia. An object will always find it easier to carry on doing the same thing, unless a strong force acts on it. For example, if a car has broken down, a stronger force is needed to push it into motion than is required to keep it moving once it is on its way.

IS FRICTION A USEFUL FORCE?

FRICTION is a force that slows the motion of two surfaces when they move across each other. An engine has many moving parts. If they rub against each other, creating friction, the efficiency of the engine is affected. The friction creates heat and the engine needs more energy to work. The parts also wear down as they come into contact. To reduce the friction in an engine, a lubricant, such as oil, is put between the moving parts.

The grooves on a tyre help to push water on the surface of the road out of the way. This means that there is more friction between the tyre and the road, preventing the car from skidding.

There are also times when friction is useful. For example, if there were no friction between our feet and the ground, we would fall over. This can happen when a floor is polished or there is ice on the ground. There is less friction between our feet and these surfaces, so we easily slip.

HOW CAN THE DIRECTION OF FORCES BE CHANGED?

A DEVICE that can change the direction of a force is called a machine. It may be very simple, such as a lever. This can change a force pushing *down* on one end of the lever into a force pushing *up* on an object at the other end of the lever. A bicycle is able to move along because the crankshaft changes the force of your feet pushing *down* into the *turning* force of the wheels going round.

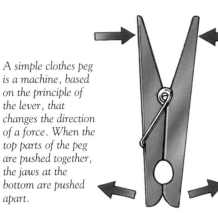

A simple clothes peg is a machine, based on the principle of the lever, that changes the direction of a force. When the top parts of the peg are pushed together, the jaws at the bottom are pushed apart.

WHAT HAPPENS WHEN MORE THAN ONE FORCE ACTS ON AN OBJECT?

MOST OBJECTS have more than one force acting on them at any one time. If an object is not moving, it is said to be in equilibrium, meaning that all the forces acting on it cancel each other out.

If both dogs are pulling with equal force, the shirt will not move. It will be in equilibrium. Of course, if the forces on it are too strong, the fabric itself will tear apart.

Often, the forces acting on an object are not balanced but combine together to have a certain effect, called the resultant. If the direction and size of all the forces acting on an object are known, the resultant can be calculated.

There are many forces operating on this balloon. The force of gravity is pulling it downwards towards the ground. The hot air is creating an upward force called lift. The pushing force of the wind is blowing the balloon along. The friction force of the air on the balloon is slowing it down. If the size and direction of all the forces are known, the direction and speed of the balloon can be worked out.

WHAT IS A CENTRIFUGAL FORCE?

FORCES act in a straight line unless something changes their direction. A carriage travelling around a fairground ride would go straight on if the track did not take it round in a circle, forcing it to change direction all the time. The forward-acting force keeps the carriage on the tracks, even when it is upside down. This is known as a centrifugal force.

IS GRAVITY A FORCE?

Gravity is a force of attraction between two bodies. It is present between any two objects, but it is only with very large items, such as planets and stars, that we notice it most of the time. The force of gravity of the Sun is so great that it keeps the planets of the Solar System in orbit around it.

WHAT IS A FORCE FIELD?

A force field is the area in which a force can be felt, such as the area around a planet within which the force of gravity operates.

HOW IS FORCE MEASURED?

Force is measured in newtons (N). One newton is the force needed to cause a mass of one kilogram to accelerate one metre per second per second ($1m/s^2$).

WHAT IS HOOKE'S LAW?

Hooke's Law, named after the Englishman Robert Hooke, says that the amount a body is stretched out of shape is in proportion to the force acting on it. That means that a spring can be used to measure forces, as the greater the force, the more the spring is stretched.

WHAT IS A CONTACT FORCE?

Some forces do not work unless one thing is touching another. These are known as contact forces. Other forces, such as gravity, work even if an object is not being touched.

WHAT IS A VECTOR QUANTITY?

A vector quantity is one that has both size (magnitude) and direction, as a force has. A quantity that has magnitude but not direction, such as temperature, is known as a scalar quantity.

WHAT IS A MAGNETIC FIELD?

A magnetic field is the area around a magnet in which its magnetic force operates. A magnetic object that is placed within the field will be attracted or repelled by the magnet. When iron filings (tiny slivers of iron) are placed near a magnet, they line up to show its magnetic field. In fact, each tiny piece of iron has become a small magnet. The mini-magnets show how strongly each part of the large magnet attracts them.

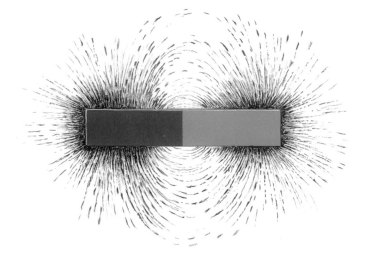

HOW IS AN ELECTROMAGNET MADE?

WHEN AN ELECTRIC CURRENT runs through a wire, it creates a magnetic field. If the wire is wound round and round an iron core, the coil and core become strongly magnetized whenever the current is turned on. The coil of wire is called a solenoid.

When the wires are connected to a power source so that current runs through them, the iron nail becomes a magnet and can attract iron and steel objects.

HOW DOES A COMPASS WORK?

THE EARTH has a core of molten iron and is itself a huge magnet. Its magnetic field acts as though there were a bar magnet running along the axis of the Earth. A compass contains a magnetized needle, which can turn freely. No matter which direction the compass is facing, the needle will turn to point towards the North Pole. The compass can then be rotated so that its north point lines up with the needle and the other directions can be read.

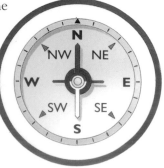

The abbreviations round a compass stand for North, North-East, East, South-East, South, South-West, West and North-East, reading clockwise from the top.

WHAT ARE THE POLES OF A MAGNET?

LIKE THE EARTH itself, each magnet has a north and a south pole. If it can turn freely, the north pole of a magnet will turn towards the North Pole of the Earth. The south pole of a magnet will be attracted towards the South Pole of the Earth. Confusingly, the Earth's North Pole actually has a south magnetic pole, which is why the north pole of a magnet is attracted to it. For the rule is that like poles repel each other (push each other away), while unlike poles attract.

The north and south poles of the two magnets attract each other.

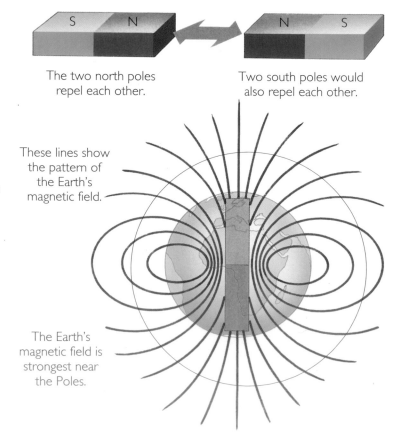

The two north poles repel each other.

Two south poles would also repel each other.

These lines show the pattern of the Earth's magnetic field.

The Earth's magnetic field is strongest near the Poles.

WHAT ADVANTAGES DO ELECTROMAGNETS HAVE OVER ORDINARY MAGNETS?

THE FACT that an electromagnet ceases to become a magnet when the current is turned off can be used to great effect in large and small machines. For example, a powerful magnet can lift very heavy weights of iron and steel in a factory, but that would be no good if the magnet could not be persuaded to release them. With an electromagnet, the current can be stopped and the load released.

An electromagnet can save people who live up several flights of stairs from having to walk down to the front door when the bell rings. They can simply find out who is calling by means of an intercom and then press a switch to let the caller in. The switch turns on a current that activates an electromagnet. The magnet attracts the door latch, pulling it back and allowing the visitor to enter. Then a spring allows the latch to slip back into place.

HOW DOES MAGNETISM CREATE A MAGNIFICENT LIGHT SHOW?

THE EARTH'S North and South Poles attract charged particles from the Sun. Within the atmosphere, these collide with molecules of gas to cause spectacular light shows, called the *aurora borealis* (northern dawn), which can be seen in the Arctic Circle.

When the weather conditions are right, the aurora borealis, also known as the northern lights, can sometimes be seen outside the Arctic Circle in the northern hemisphere.

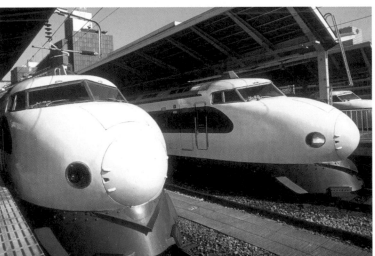

Maglev trains are very quiet for the passengers, as there is no sound of wheels rattling on tracks.

WHERE ARE TRAVELLERS MAGNETICALLY LEVITATED?

IN JAPAN, "maglev" trains run just above, not on, their tracks. Both the bottom of the train and the track itself are magnetic. The magnets repel each other, so the train hovers just above the track, enabling it to run with less friction and so reach higher speeds.

WHO DISCOVERED ELECTROMAGNETISM?

Electromagnetism was discovered by a Danish physicist called Hans Christian Oersted. In 1820, he noticed that an electric current could cause a compass needle to deflect. Previously, only magnets had been seen to do this.

HOW CAN MAGNETS HELP WITH RECYCLING?

Before cans used for food and drink are melted down to be recycled, they need to be separated into those made of steel and those made of aluminium. As steel is magnetic but aluminium is not, a huge magnet is held over the pile of cans and the steel ones are picked up by it, leaving the aluminium ones behind.

WHERE DOES THE WORD "MAGNET" COME FROM?

Magnets are so called because the ancient Greeks found magnetic rocks in an area called Magnesia, in what is now Turkey.

WHAT ARE FERROMAGNETIC METALS?

Ferromagnetic metals are those that can be magnetized: iron and steel.

WHAT WAS A LODESTONE?

A lodestone was an early compass, used by sailors to navigate their ships. It was a piece of magnetite, a a rock containing iron, that was naturally magnetic.

CAN MAGNETS WORK THROUGH NON-MAGNETIC MATERIALS?

Depending on its strength and the thickness of the material between it and a magnetic material, a magnet can still work. For example, it can be attracted to a refrigerator door through a piece of paper.

WHY IS ELECTRICITY SO USEFUL?

Electricity is a very flexible form of energy. It can easily be converted to heat, light or sound energy. It can be carried long distances through wires and cables. It is clean and safe if used in the right way. In fact, electricity is now so much a part of our lives that it is difficult to imagine being without it.

WHAT IS ELECTRICITY?

ELECTRICITY is the movement of electrically charged particles. Atoms contain positively charged protons and negatively charged electrons. Usually, these balance each other, so that the atom is electrically neutral, but electrons sometimes move from one atom to another, leaving the first positively charged and the second negatively charged. Just as unlike poles of magnets attract each other, so atoms with different charges attract each other. When electrons move through a substance, they create a flow of electricity called a current.

Once the brightest things to be seen at night were the Moon and stars. Electricity has enabled cities to be lit as brightly by night as by day.

WHAT IS STATIC ELECTRICITY?

STATIC ELECTRICITY is what sometimes makes a nylon jumper crackle and spark in dry weather. Or you may get a small electric shock from a metal surface after walking across a carpet made of artificial fibres. Rubbing something made of amber or plastic can cause it to pick up electrons from your clothes or hair, giving them a positive charge. If you then touch something with a slightly negative charge, a small spark may fly across just before you touch it, or, if it is light, the oppositely charged object may be attracted to you.

A balloon rubbed on your jumper picks up electrons from it. Your jumper is then slightly positively charged and the balloon is slightly negatively charged. As opposite charges attract, the balloon will cling to you.

HOW DOES A LIGHTNING CONDUCTOR WORK?

A LIGHTNING CONDUCTOR is a metal rod that is placed so that it points upwards above the highest point of a tall building. If lightning does strike the building, it is the lightning conductor, not the building itself, that the spark hits. The electrical charge then runs harmlessly down the lightning conductor to Earth.

We cannot see electricity, but we can see its effects. Lightning happens when the electrical charge of a cloud discharges itself to the Earth or to another cloud that has an opposite charge.

WHAT IS AN ELECTRIC CIRCUIT?

A CIRCUIT is a path along which an electric current can flow. Each part of the circuit must be connected to the next, and each must be able to conduct electricity. In a series circuit, there is only one path for the current to follow, and it passes through each component of the circuit in turn. If one component fails, the current will no longer be able to flow. Christmas tree lights are usually connected to each other in series. When one bulb blows, the circuit is broken and all the lights go out.

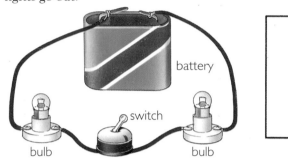

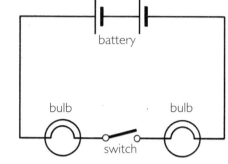

When the switch is turned on, the circuit is completed and the bulbs light. It does not matter what the order of the components is.

The same series circuit can be shown as an electrical diagram. Special symbols are used to represent the bulbs, the switch and the battery.

Instead of being connected in a series circuit, the same components could be connected in a parallel circuit. In this kind of circuit, there is more than one pathway for the electrical current to flow along.

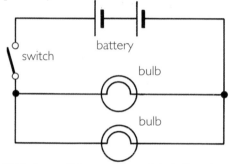

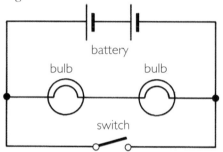

With this parallel arrangement of the bulbs, when the circuit is switched on, one bulb will still light if the other blows

The order of components in a parallel circuit is very important. This circuit will still work even when the switch is turned off, making the switch useless.

WHAT IS A CONDUCTOR?

MATERIALS that allow electric currents to pass through them are called conductors. One of the best conductors that is fairly cheap to obtain is copper, which is why many electric cables and wires are made of this metal.

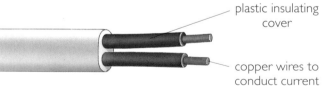

plastic insulating cover

copper wires to conduct current

Tools such as screwdrivers, which may be used on electrical appliances, have plastic handles to provide insulation for the electrician in case the current is accidentally turned on.

WHAT IS AN INSULATOR?

AN INSULATOR is the opposite of a conductor. It is a material that will not allow electrical current to run through it because its electrons are not free to move. Plastic is a very good insulator. That is why it is used to cover copper wire. The wire can then safely conduct electricity along its length without allowing it to come into contact with other conductors.

HOW CAN ELECTRICITY BE USED TO SEPARATE COMPOUNDS?

Some compounds can be separated into individual elements by passing an electric current through them when they are in a liquid state. This process is called electrolysis. For this to happen, the compound must be able to conduct electricity, and its elements must be held together by ionic bonds. Many industrial processes use electrolysis, especially those concerned with purifying metals or applying thin layers of metal to other objects.

WHAT IS AN ELECTROLYTE?

AN ELECTROLYTE is a liquid that can conduct an electric current. A metal may become an electrolyte if it is molten (melted) or dissolved in another liquid. Water can also conduct an electric current. That is why it is very dangerous to touch an electric socket with wet hands.

WHAT ARE CATHODES AND ANODES?

CATHODES AND ANODES are electrodes. These are carbon or metal rods that are connected to an electric current. When they are placed in an electrolyte, current can pass through the liquid from one electrode to the other, so completing the circuit. The cathode has a negative electrical charge and the anode has a positive electrical charge. Ions in the electrolyte are being held together because they have opposite electrical charges, which attract each other. These bonds are broken because the ions with positive charges are more strongly attracted to the negative charge of the cathode than they are to the negative charge of the ions with which they are bonded. In the same way, negatively charged ions are attracted to the anode.

WHAT IS ANODIZING?

WHEN A METAL reacts with oxygen, it forms a compound called an oxide. This happens on the surface of metals such as silver. As the oxide dulls the appearance of the metal, it is often rubbed off ornaments and jewellery, but in fact this simply presents a new surface of pure metal to the air to be oxidized. However, some metals, such as aluminium, are deliberately coated, by means of electrolysis, with a layer of their oxide. This process is known as anodization. It protects the metal underneath from oxidizing further.

Anodized aluminium foil can be coloured by dyeing the layer of oxide.

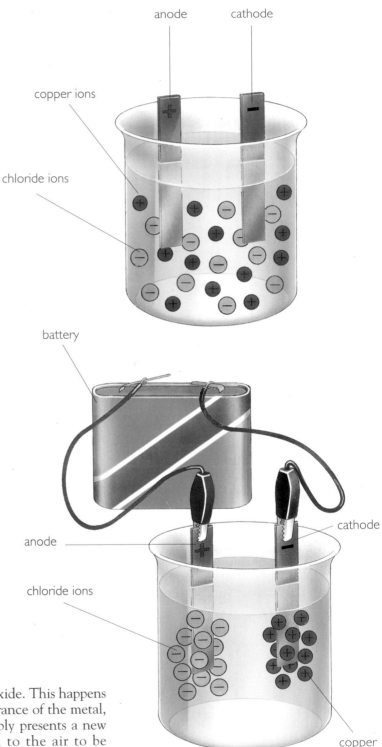

This diagram shows copper chloride being separated into copper and chlorine by means of electrolysis. The copper ions have a positive charge, so they are attracted to the negative charge of the cathode and form a coating on this electrode. Chloride ions have a negative charge, so they are attracted to the positive charge of the anode. Here they give up their extra electrons and so become chlorine gas.

WHAT IS ELECTROREFINING?

ELECTROREFINING, as the word suggests, is a way of purifying metals by using electrolysis. Copper can be purified by making the impure copper the anode in an electrolyte of copper sulphate. The cathode is made of pure copper. When an electric current is passed through the copper sulphate, positively charged copper ions from the anode are attracted to the cathode of pure metal. The impurities, which may be tiny amounts of other metals, such as mercury, gold and silver, fall to the bottom of the electrolyte.

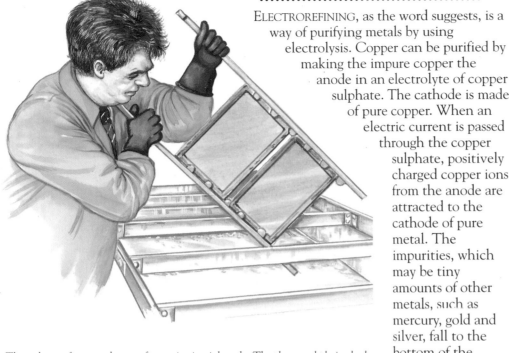

These sheets of copper plate are for use in circuit boards. The plates and plating bath have to be carefully arranged so that the copper is distributed evenly over the surface.

HOW DID HUMPHRY DAVY DISCOVER NEW ELEMENTS?

HUMPHRY DAVY (1778–1829) was an English chemist who conducted some early experiments using electrolysis. This process offered a way of isolating metals from the compounds in which they are naturally found. As a result, Davy discovered potassium, sodium and calcium because he was able to separate the metals into their pure form.

WHAT IS ELECTROPLATING?

ELECTROPLATING uses electrolysis to deposit a thin layer of metal on another substance. The item to be plated is used as one electrode. Copper, silver, tin and chromium are often applied to surfaces in this way.

fast facts

WHAT HAPPENS TO WATER WHEN A CURRENT IS PASSED THROUGH IT?

When water is used as an electrolyte, it separates into hydrogen and oxygen – the two elements that, as the compound H_2O, form water.

WHICH METALS ARE EXTRACTED FROM THEIR ORES BY ELECTROLYSIS?

Electrolysis is used for the extraction of very reactive metals. Aluminium, for example, is extracted in this way from bauxite that has been dissolved in molten cryolite, a substance containing aluminium and sodium.

CAN ELECTROLYSIS BE REVERSED?

When electrolysis is being used to plate an object with a layer of metal, it is sometimes possible to remove the plating by reversing the electrodes. In other words, the cathode becomes the anode and the anode the cathode.

WHICH KINDS OF OBJECT ARE ELECTROPLATED?

OBJECTS may be electroplated for protection or to enhance their appearance. Very often, the object itself is made from a much cheaper material than the plating.

Almost any solid object can be electroplated. Some parents have their baby's first shoes electroplated as a keepsake.

Plating may protect the material underneath. Tin plate on steel cans stops the steel from corroding. Chromium plating was once common on cars to prevent bumpers and headlights from rusting.

BWM 960

Items made from cheaper metals can be electroplated with silver to look like solid silver articles.

WHO DISCOVERED GRAVITY?

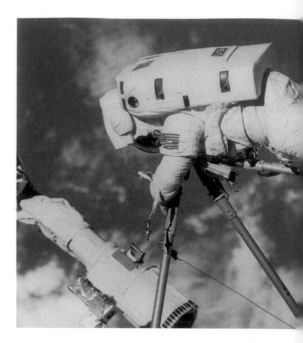

The fact that objects dropped from a height fall to the ground, that the Moon is near enough to be seen from Earth, and that we do not float into the air when we are standing still has, of course, been known for thousands of years. What was not known was the reason for these phenomena. It was a British scientist, Isaac Newton, who, in 1666, put forward the idea that the same force – gravity – might be responsible for all these events. Gravity is a force of attraction caused by the huge mass of the Earth.

HOW DOES GRAVITY AFFECT THE TIDES?

THE MOON, too, has gravity. Its gravitational pull is much less than the Earth's, as its mass is smaller, but it still has an effect on Earth. On the side of the Earth nearest the Moon, the oceans are pulled out by the Moon's gravity, causing a high tide. Exactly the same thing happens on the opposite side of the Earth, but this time because the Moon is exerting less pull on the waters of the oceans. As the Earth rotates on its axis, each part of the Earth is turned towards the Moon once in every twenty-four hours. That means that the seas have two high tides every twenty-four hours – once when they are facing the Moon and once when they are on the opposite side of the Earth from the Moon.

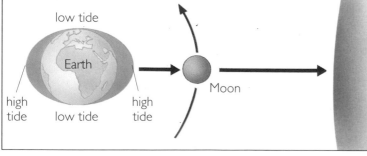

low tide

Earth

Moon

high tide   low tide   high tide

WHY DO ASTRONAUTS FLOAT IN SPACE?

OUTSIDE THE EARTH'S gravitational field, astronauts experience "weightlessness". Their mass has not changed, but with no gravity to act upon this mass, they have no weight. When working outside a spacecraft, astronauts are tethered to prevent them from floating away into space. Inside the spacecraft, liquids have to be sucked through straws. Liquid would not be held in an ordinary cup by gravity, as it is on Earth, but would spray all over the interior. One of the reasons that astronauts are spending longer and longer periods in space is so that scientists can study the effects of weightlessness on their bodies, so that future space flights can last for months or even years.

IS GRAVITY THE SAME ALL OVER THE UNIVERSE?

THE FORCE of gravity depends on the mass of the object exerting the gravitational pull. Generally, large planets have a greater gravitational force than smaller ones. As the Moon's mass is smaller than that of the Earth, it exerts a gravitational pull only a sixth as strong as the gravity on Earth. That is why astronauts appear to bounce along on the Moon's surface – the Moon is pulling them down much less strongly than on Earth. But the principle of gravity holds true throughout the universe.

This chart shows the force of gravity on each of the planets of our Solar System, compared to the gravity on Earth.

Mercury	Venus	Earth	Mars	Jupiter	Saturn	Uranus	Neptune	Pluto
0.38	0.9	1	0.38	2.64	0.925	0.79	1.12	0.05

WHAT IS A CENTRE OF GRAVITY?

THE CENTRE OF GRAVITY or centre of mass of an object is the point from which all its weight seems to act. The lower an object's centre of gravity, the more stable it is. That is why decanters for holding water or wine often have wide, heavy bases, giving them a low centre of gravity, to make them difficult to knock over. When an object is tilted, it is still stable while its centre of gravity is over its base. If the object is tilted further, so that its centre of gravity is no longer over its base, it becomes unstable and will fall over.

base   base

centre of gravity   centre of gravity is still over base

This toy has been designed so that when a young child knocks it over, it will almost always bounce back up. In other words, it is extremely stable. Similar principles are used to build boats that are very difficult to capsize and will right themselves if they do turn over.

IN WHICH SPORTS IS A LOW CENTRE OF GRAVITY IMPORTANT?

ANY SPORT that requires a participant or piece of equipment to be stable uses the principle of the centre of gravity.

Boxers aim not to be knocked down! They try to keep a wide-legged stance to give themselves a low centre of gravity and maximum stability.

A racing car has wide wheels and a low body, giving it a low centre of gravity. This makes it stable at high speeds and when cornering.

DOES GRAVITY PULL HEAVY OBJECTS MORE STRONGLY THAN LIGHT ONES?

AS OBJECTS are dropped and pulled towards Earth by its gravitational force, they accelerate, travelling faster and faster the further they fall. That is why a person falling one metre might sustain only bruises but a person falling one kilometre would be unlikely to survive. The body would be hitting the ground at a much higher speed. However, an Italian scientist called Galileo Galilei, working some years before Newton, showed that the weight of a body does not affect the speed with which it falls.

fast facts

HOW DO ROCKETS ESCAPE FROM THE EARTH'S GRAVITY?

The further away from the centre of the Earth that an object travels, the less the Earth's gravity pulls on it. In fact, you weigh very slightly less at the top of a mountain than at the bottom. At a certain distance, a rocket can escape the Earth's gravitational pull. A rocket uses up a great deal of fuel in the first part of its journey from Earth, as its booster rockets fire to push it beyond the planet's gravity.

WHY DO TIGHTROPE WALKERS OFTEN CARRY A POLE?

By carrying a pole, tightrope walkers are able to lower their centre of gravity and so increase their stability as they balance on the narrow rope.

HOW IS EARTH'S GRAVITY USEFUL IN COMMUNICATIONS?

It is not only the Moon that the Earth's gravity keeps in orbit around our planet. Satellites made by human beings are also circling the Earth. Radio signals can be bounced off them so that telephone calls, television programmes and other communications can be sent rapidly around the world.

DOES THE SUN HAVE GRAVITY?

The Sun is a massive body and so its gravity is very high. If you could jump to a height of one metre or one yard on Earth, you could not even jump three centimetres or one inch on the Sun. Of course, it would not be possible to stand on the surface of the Sun in any case!

A pingpong ball and a ball of lead of the same size and shape, dropped from the same height at the same moment, will reach the Earth together.

WHAT MAKES UP THE AIR WE BREATHE?

The air around us is a mixture of gases. Its content varies depending on where and when it is measured, but on average the air is made up of just over one-fifth oxygen and just under four-fifths nitrogen. There are also very small quantities of other gases, such as argon and carbon dioxide, some pollutants and water vapour, and tiny solid particles, such as soot and pollen.

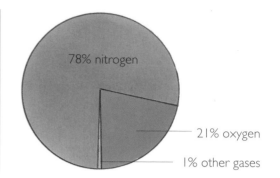

78% nitrogen

21% oxygen

1% other gases

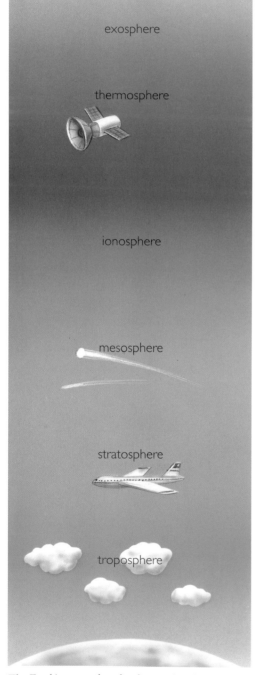

exosphere

thermosphere

ionosphere

mesosphere

stratosphere

troposphere

The Earth's atmosphere has layers of cooler and warmer air. On this diagram, warm air is shown in pale blue, becoming darker as it gets colder.

WHAT IS ATMOSPHERIC PRESSURE?

THE AIR around the Earth is pulled towards it by the planet's gravity. This causes it to press down on the Earth with a force known as atmospheric pressure. This is measured in units called millibars (mb). At sea level, the average atmospheric pressure is around 1000mb. It is changes in atmospheric pressure, caused by the air being heated by the Sun, that make the air flow from place to place, causing the winds and weather that we experience on Earth. Most weather events happen in the lowest layer of the Earth's atmosphere – the troposphere.

Cyclists aiming for high speeds crouch low over their machines to reduce the air resistance that would slow them down.

WHY IS THE SKY BLUE?

AS THE SUN'S LIGHT passes through the atmosphere, its rays are scattered by the tiny particles of pollen, soot and dust to be found there. As blue light is scattered most, the sky appears blue. At sunset and sunrise, sunlight has further to travel to reach us. Only red light can be seen because the blue light has been absorbed by the atmosphere.

WHAT IS AIR RESISTANCE?

ALTHOUGH we cannot see the air, it is still made of atoms and molecules, just like everything else. When an object passes through the air, these molecules push against it, causing a force of friction called air resistance.

HOW DOES A PARACHUTE WORK?

A PARACHUTE offers an enormous surface area on which air resistance can operate. The friction slows the descent of the parachutist, so that he or she can land safely. Without a parachute, a human body would accelerate towards the Earth, hitting it with fatal force.

WHAT IS A PNEUMATIC MACHINE?

A PNEUMATIC MACHINE is one that is driven by compressed air. If no other forces are acting on them, the molecules in gases, such as air, spread out to fill the space that is available to them. If the space is sealed and then reduced, the air is compressed – the molecules are pushed closer together. This means that the pressure that the compressed air exerts on the inside of its container is greater than the atmospheric pressure pushing down on the outside of the container. A pneumatic drill, also known as an air-hammer or jack-hammer, uses compressed air to push its bit forcefully against the ground being broken up. The compressed air is supplied to the drill through a hose by a machine called a compressor.

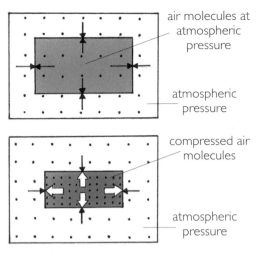

air molecules at atmospheric pressure

atmospheric pressure

compressed air molecules

atmospheric pressure

When air is compressed, the same number of molecules are squeezed into a smaller space. The pressure they exert is greater than the atmospheric pressure outside. This pressure can be used in pneumatic machines to drive a piston.

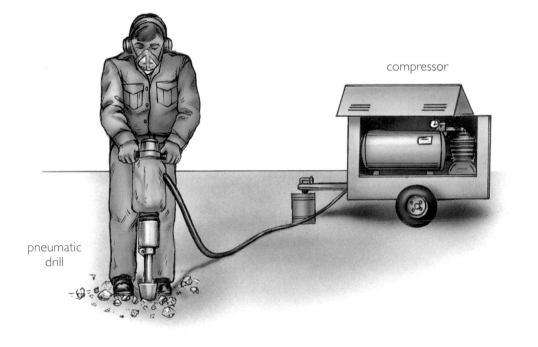

compressor

pneumatic drill

HOW DEEP IS THE EARTH'S ATMOSPHERE?

OUR PLANET'S ATMOSPHERE is not very deep compared with the diameter of the Earth. While you would have to travel 6370km (3956 miles) to reach the centre of the Earth, the edge of the Earth's atmosphere is only about 500km (310 miles) away.

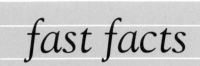

fast facts

WHAT IS A VACUUM?

A vacuum is a space with nothing in it – not even air.

WHAT IS AIR CONDITIONING?

Air conditioning is a way of cooling the air inside buildings, especially when the weather outside is very warm. The air is circulated through refrigerating pipes before being returned to the rooms inside the building.

WHY IS IT HARDER TO BREATHE AT THE TOP OF A MOUNTAIN?

Most of the gases in our planet's atmosphere are concentrated quite near to sea level. The higher you go, the less gas there is. That is why people talk about the air "becoming thinner" at high altitudes. There is less oxygen there to breathe. Mountaineers usually wear oxygen masks as they near the summits of the world's highest mountains.

WHAT HAPPENS WHEN RADIO WAVES HIT THE IONOSPHERE?

The ionosphere consists of electrically charged molecules of oxygen and nitrogen. These reflect radio waves that hit them, enabling them to be "bounced" back to a part of the Earth far away from the place from which they were sent.

WHO INVENTED THE HOVERCRAFT?

The hovercraft reduces friction between its base and the water by using a cushion of air. The air blows strongly down towards the water, lifting the hovercraft clear. A rubber skirt stops the air from escaping. The hovercraft was invented by Christopher Cockerell, a British scientist, in 1955.

WHY IS WATER VITAL TO LIFE ON EARTH?

All living things contain a large proportion of water. For example, around two-thirds of the human body is made up of water. Although most people could survive quite a long time without food, they would die within a few days if they had no water. More of the surface of the Earth is covered by water than by land – a fact that has an enormous effect on the climate of all parts of the Earth. Although it is a simple compound of oxygen and hydrogen, water plays a very complex role on our planet.

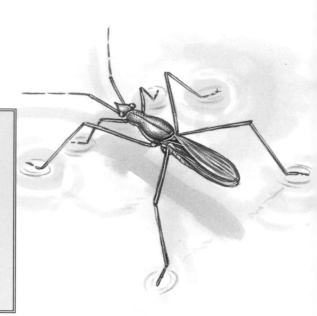

WHAT IS A SOLUTION?

IN CHEMICAL TERMS, a solution is not the answer to a problem but a mixture of a solid substance dissolved in a liquid. The solid is called a solute and the liquid is called a solvent. Some solids dissolve very easily and are said to be soluble. Something that will not dissolve in liquid is insoluble.

WHAT IS SURFACE TENSION?

WATER MOLECULES are attracted to each other strongly, which is why they stay as a liquid until heated to a temperature where the bonds between them are broken and they rise into the air as vapour. At the surface of still water, there are no water molecules above pushing or pulling against the surface molecules, so the surface molecules are even more strongly drawn together than usual. This causes them to act as though they form a skin over the surface. It is this effect that is called surface tension.

Insects that are as light as this pond skater can literally walk on water. Their feet make little indentations where they press down on the "skin".

Some drinks are supplied in concentrated form, as syrups of sugar and flavouring. When water is added, the syrup is diluted. A solution has been made.

Milk contains a large proportion of water, but it is not a solution. It is a suspension: a mixture of tiny particles of fat and other substances floating in water.

The surface tension of water makes it possible for a container to be more than full! With care, an object such as a needle, which would normally sink in water, can be made to float on the surface "skin".

CAN GASES BE DISSOLVED IN WATER?

GASES, as well as solids, can be soluble. For example, fizzy drinks have carbon dioxide gas dissolved in them. Inside the can or bottle, the carbon dioxide is at higher pressure than the outside atmosphere. When the bottle is opened, there is often a loud pop or fizz as the pressure is equalized and the carbon dioxide starts to escape into the air. If left for a few hours, the drink will lose most of its dissolved gas and taste "flat".

Fish breathe oxygen from the water with their gills. If pollution decreases the amount of oxygen dissolved in the water, fish cannot survive.

WHAT IS DISTILLED WATER?

BECAUSE WATER is an excellent solvent, we very rarely find it in a pure form. Even water from the tap has tiny amounts of a number of chemicals dissolved in it. If pure water is needed, it can be obtained by distillation.

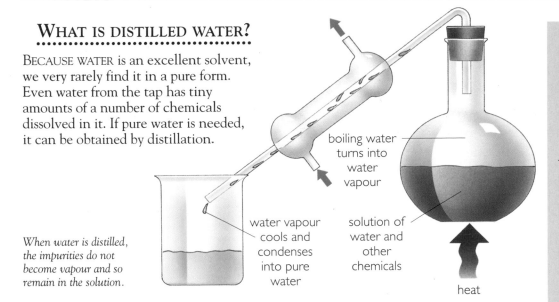

boiling water turns into water vapour

water vapour cools and condenses into pure water

solution of water and other chemicals

heat

When water is distilled, the impurities do not become vapour and so remain in the solution.

WHY IS EVAPORATION USEFUL?

EVAPORATION is another way of separating water from chemicals dissolved in it. It works in the same way as distillation, except that evaporation is usually used when it is the substances in the water that are needed, not the water itself. The water is usually allowed to drift away as steam. In other words, distillation is used to obtain the solvent, while evaporation is used to obtain the solute.

HOW CAN DRYING GOODS PRESERVE THEM?

LIKE all other living things, bacteria need water to survive and reproduce. If foods, such as pulses and cereals, are dried, most bacteria cannot attack them, so they are very slow to decay.

Pasta is made of a mixture of flour and eggs. It is shaped when damp and then dried. In this form, it will keep for months. When it is boiled in water, pasta takes in water molecules and becomes soft. Pulses are dried peas and beans. Before they can be eaten, they are soaked in water to replace the liquid they lost in drying.

The sea is salty because there are many minerals dissolved in it. Some people prefer to use sea salt to flavour their food. This is obtained simply by boiling sea water, so that it evaporates. The water escapes as steam, while the salt is left behind as crystals.

WHAT IS HARD WATER?

WATER is said to be "hard" when it has certain minerals dissolved in it. The most noticeable effect of hard water is that soap does not lather well in it, instead forming a kind of scum. There are two kinds of water hardness, depending on which chemicals are dissolved in it. Temporary hardness can be removed by boiling the water. The chemicals become a solid, which is the scale that sometimes furs up kettles and shower heads. Permanent hardness can be removed by using a water softener, which exchanges the calcium and magnesium ions that cause the hardness with sodium ions.

Oils and fats do not mix with water, so washing greasy clothes or hair in water alone will not clean them. Soap contains ions that are attracted to water at one end and to grease at the other. This end of each ion attaches itself to the grease, while the other end, attracted to the water, pulls the grease away from the fabric or hair. Hard water is a problem because the ions react with the chemicals in the water to form scum.

fast facts

WHY DO WATER PIPES SOMETIMES BURST IN COLD WEATHER?

Water expands when it freezes. If it is trapped in a pipe with no room for expansion, water may burst even a strong pipe as it freezes. Good insulation around pipes can keep the water inside above freezing point and prevent problems in all but the very coldest weather.

HOW DOES ANTIFREEZE WORK?

As liquids are cooled, they become solid, but this happens at a different temperature for each liquid. Water freezes at 0°C (32°F). By mixing water with a liquid, called antifreeze, that freezes at a much lower temperature, motorists can ensure that the water in their cars does not freeze in winter weather.

WHAT IS SATURATION?

Solutes can be added to a solvent only until its saturation point is reached. This is the point at which the liquid cannot dissolve any more of the solid.

WHAT IS DESALINATION?

In some parts of the world, there is little rain or fresh water. One answer is to remove the salt from sea water to make drinking water. This process is called desalination.

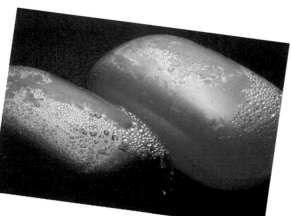

WHAT TRAVELS FASTEST IN THE UNIVERSE?

Nothing that has a physical existence travels faster than light. In a vacuum it travels at 300,000km (186,000 miles) per second. We tend to think that we are seeing things as they are, but that is not quite true. We are seeing them as they were at the moment that the light left them to travel to us. Of course, for most purposes, as light travels so quickly, this makes no difference at all. It is only when we are looking at the stars, which are unimaginably huge distances away, that we really are seeing the distant past. Light from our Sun takes about eight minutes to reach the Earth, but it takes less than a tenth of a second to travel across the Atlantic.

DOES LIGHT ALWAYS TRAVEL IN A STRAIGHT LINE?

BEAMS OF LIGHT do travel in straight lines, but those lines can be deflected. Light travels at different speeds in different substances. When the light passes from one substance to another, its beam bends. This is called refraction.

WHAT IS ELECTROMAGNETIC ENERGY?

LIGHT is not the only kind of energy to travel at the speed of light! In fact, every kind of energy in what is called the electromagnetic spectrum travels at that speed. Electromagnetic energy travels in waves. Only a small part of the electromagnetic spectrum is visible to us – the part that makes up the colours of the rainbow – but all of it has proved to be useful to us.

HOW ARE ELECTROMAGNETIC WAVES MEASURED?

THE DISTANCE from the peak of one wave to the peak of the next is called its wavelength. The height of a wave, from its rest position to a peak or trough, is its amplitude. The number of waves per second is known as the frequency and measured in hertz (Hz).

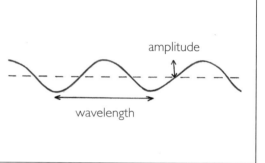

radio waves   microwaves   infra-red radiation   visible light   ultraviolet rays   x-rays   gamma rays

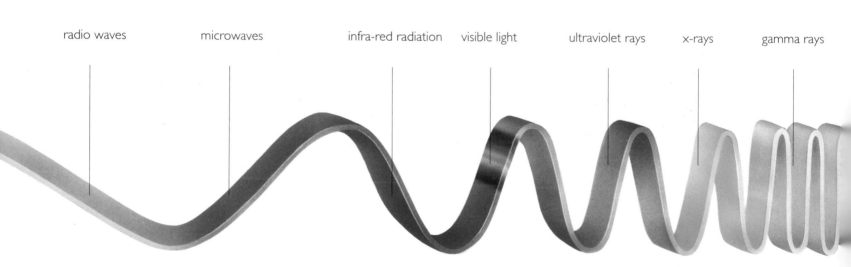

The longest wavelengths of electromagnetic energy are radio waves. They are used for communications and entertainment – radio and television.

Microwaves are best known for their use in microwave ovens.

Infra-red rays cannot be seen, but they can be felt as warmth. Infra-red cameras allow photographs to be taken in the dark. They create images showing areas of heat and cold.

Visible light appears colourless to us, but it is made up of different colours, each one of which has its own wavelength.

Ultraviolet (UV) rays are what cause some people's skin to tan. We now realize that large amounts of these can be harmful, but small amounts help our bodies to produce vitamin D.

X-rays can pass through the soft parts of the bodies of animals but are absorbed by their skeletons, which can be shown on x-ray film. X-rays are harmful in large quantities but useful in small ones.

Gamma rays are given off by radioactive materials. They can harm living cells.

HOW CAN SHADOWS MEASURE TIME?

AS THE EARTH turns each day, shadows cast by the Sun move and change length. This fact has been used for thousands of years to measure the time of day. A sundial has a time scale and a central pole called a gnomon. The shadow cast by the gnomon falls on the scale and the time can be read.

WHICH MATERIALS REFLECT LIGHT?

MOST THINGS do not create their own light. We can see them because they reflect light coming from another source, such as the Sun or a light bulb. A very smooth surface reflects more light than a rough one. Surfaces that are extremely smooth, such as mirrors, are the best reflectors.

A car wing mirror is slightly curved so that the image is smaller and more of the view along the side of the car can be seen.

Enormous buildings with glass sides seem almost to disappear as they reflect the images of everything around them.

Builders and designers can use reflections to great effect. Here the water acts as a mirror, making the arches of the bridge appear circular, not semi-circular.

HOW DOES THE HUMAN EYE WORK?

THE HUMAN EYE is a ball containing a kind of jelly that keeps it round, just as the air in a balloon keeps that round. At the front is a lens, through which light can enter the eye. The lens can change shape to focus light from different distances. Like a slide projector, the lens throws an image onto the back of the eye, which is called the retina. In fact, the image is upside down, but your brain, which makes sense of everything you see, sorts out the image so that you "see" it the right way up.

HOW DO SPECTACLES IMPROVE VISION?

Sometimes the lens in the human eye causes the image to fall behind or in front of the retina. This results in a blurred image. Vision can be corrected by placing another lens in front of the eye. This adjusts the image so that it falls directly on the retina and can be seen clearly. The corrective lens may be worn in spectacles or on the surface of the eye itself, as a contact lens.

WHAT ARE LASERS?

The word *laser* stands for Light Amplification by the Stimulated Emission of Radiation. Laser light has very focused beams that give it power and precision. Lasers are used for delicate medical and industrial cutting operations, to read barcodes and to make holograms.

WHAT IS GEOTROPISM?

Many seeds germinate in the dark, underground. Yet when shoots first appear, they at once start to grow towards the light. This behaviour is known as geotropism.

WHAT IS FLUORESCENCE?

Some substances absorb non-visible electromagnetic energy, such as UV rays, and then release it as bright, visible light. They are said to be fluorescent. Modern washing powders contain fluorescents to make washed clothes look whiter and brighter.

WHAT IS THE BLIND SPOT?

THE BACK of the eye is very sensitive, but at one point the optic nerve leads to the brain. If the image falls on this point, called the blind spot, it cannot be seen. The blind spot is particularly important for drivers, as there is a point behind them on either side where their vision can be misleading as they check for vehicles behind before overtaking.

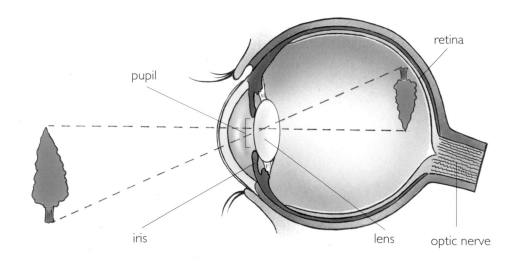

retina
pupil
iris
lens
optic nerve

WHAT ARE THE COLOURS OF THE SPECTRUM?

Although light appears to be white or colourless, in fact it is made up of all the colours of the spectrum. Each colour has a different wavelength. The colours can be seen if a beam of light is split by a prism. The prism refracts each of the wavelengths differently and so splits them into a visible band of colours. Although the colours merge together so that it is hard to see them separately, there are seven of them: red, orange, yellow, green, blue, indigo and violet.

In nature, the colours of the spectrum can sometimes be seen as a rainbow. Drops of rain in the air have acted as prisms to split the light into its seven colours. One way to remember the order of the colours is to memorize the sentence, "Richard Of York Gave Battle In Vain."

WHAT HAPPENS WHEN COLOURED LIGHTS ARE MIXED?

WE ARE USED to thinking of red, yellow and blue as the three primary colours. Paints of these colours can be mixed to create the other colours of the spectrum. But coloured lights work in a different way. The primary colours of light are red, green and blue. When lights are mixed in pairs, they create the secondary colours of magenta, cyan and yellow. When all three colours are mixed together in equal amounts, white light is the result.

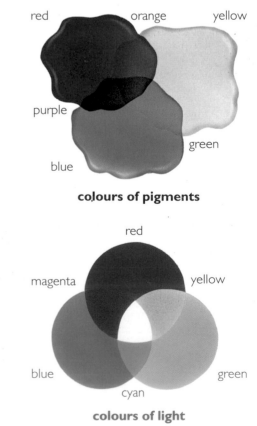

colours of pigments

colours of light

HOW CAN COLOURS FOOL THE EYE?

OPTICAL ILLUSIONS are often said to fool the eye, but it is the brain, which interprets the information that our eyes take in, that is really fooled. Our brains are working hard all the time to make sense of the world we see. They have so much information to process, coming in from all our senses, that they take short cuts, working on patterns they have met before. Sometimes those patterns do not make sense of a new situation.

Even in black and white, our brains can be confused. This picture can be seen as two faces or as a vase but not as both at once. The information being given to the brain is the same in either case.

The red squares in the middle of the coloured squares are the same size each time, but some colours appear more prominently to our brains, so some squares seem to be bigger than others.

WHY WERE THE COLOURS OF THE OLYMPIC RINGS CHOSEN?

THERE ARE five Olympic rings, to represent the five continents of the world. The colours – blue, black, red, yellow, green – were chosen because every national flag in the world includes at least one of these colours.

HOW DO COLOURS WORK AS CODES?

AS WE TAKE IN the huge amounts of information around us, different colours take on various meanings. They work as a kind of code. For example, everyone knows without thinking about it that red means "stop" and green means "go" at a traffic light. Seeing the colour is much quicker than reading or hearing the word. Similarly, certain colours become associated with certain products. When you go out to buy a can of drink, you probably do not have to *read* the label. You simply look for a certain combination of colours on the can.

HOW CAN MIXED COLOURS BE SEPARATED?

WHEN COLOURS are mixed together to form a coloured ink, it seems impossible to separate them, but chromatography is a method that may work. If a drop of ink is placed in the middle of a piece of filter paper and then some water is dropped on top of it, some of the dyes in the ink will travel across the paper more easily than others, resulting in rings of different colours spreading out from the centre. This method is also used by scientists to test whether chemicals are pure.

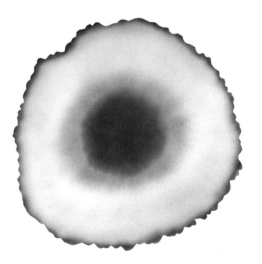

WHAT IS A COLOUR WHEEL?

GARDEN AND INTERIOR DESIGNERS sometimes make use of a colour wheel. This helps them to choose colours that are in harmony with each other when that is appropriate. When a more striking effect is required, colours that contrast can be chosen. One half of the wheel has colours that give a warm feeling, while the other half has cooler hues.

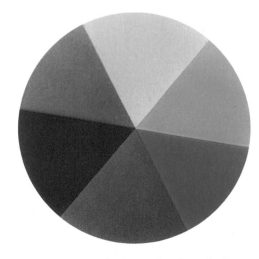

Colours opposite each other on the colour wheel generally contrast, while colours next to each other harmonize.

fast facts

WHAT IS COLOUR BLINDNESS?

Some people cannot distinguish easily between red and green. This type of "colour blindness" is more common in boys than in girls. About one out of every fifteen boys is affected but only one out of a thousand girls.

WHAT IS POINTILLISM?

Pointillism is a painting technique, used most famously by the Impressionist painter Georges Seurat, which uses tiny dots of pure colour to build up images. Viewed from a distance, these seem to blend together to produce a wide range of colours and tones.

WHAT IS SEPIA?

Sepia is a reddish-brown pigment (colour) made from the black, inky fluid secreted by cuttlefish. It was used for drawings and watercolour painting before artificial pigments were created. Giving a photograph a sepia tint is still a way of making it look instantly older.

HOW CAN PIGMENTS REVEAL FORGERIES?

Pigments for painting once came only from natural sources, such as the earth, plants and rocks. Many modern pigments are made by chemical processes. By analyzing the paint on a canvas, scientists can tell whether it could have been painted at the date claimed for it. Forgers rarely take the trouble to use original pigments.

HOW DO WE SEE COLOURS?

On the retina of the human eye are about seven milllion cells, shaped like cones, that help us to see colour. There are three different kinds of cone. Each can respond to one of the primary colours: red, green and blue.

CAN SOUNDS BE HEARD IN SPACE?

Like light, sound travels in waves, but while light can travel through a vacuum, sound cannot. Sound energy moves through vibration. Part of the instrument making the noise vibrates (moves backwards and forwards very quickly). This in turn pushes against the air, causing the air molecules to collide, transferring the sound energy from molecule to molecule away from its source, until it reaches our ears. Sound does not only travel through air molecules. It can also cause the molecules of other gases, liquids and even solids to vibrate. But space is silent. There are no molecules for the sound waves to vibrate.

WHAT IS SONAR?

SONAR uses ultrasonic sounds to find out where and how far away something is. This is called echo-location. The sounds are transmitted and bounced back by the object. The time that passes between the transmission and the reception of the reflected sound tells how far away the object is. Sonar is used particularly at sea to establish the depth of water beneath a boat.

Dolphins use ultrasound for echo-location to find food and avoid predators. They also communicate with each other using ultrasonic frequencies.

HOW IS SOUND MEASURED?

SOUNDS travel as waves. It is the shape of the wave that determines the kind of sound that is produced. The pitch of a sound (whether it is high or low) depends on the frequency of the sound waves. The frequency is how many waves, or vibrations, the sound makes in one second. This is measured in hertz (Hz). One vibration per second is one hertz. How loud the sound is depends on the magnitude (or height) of its waves. The more energy the waves carry, the louder the sound. Loudness is measured in decibels (dB).

As sounds push air molecules together, air pressure rises. Between vibrations, air pressure falls. It is this change in air pressure that can be shown as waves on a screen when sounds are made near a microphone.

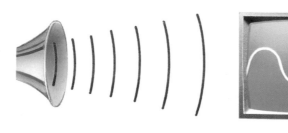

WHAT IS MUSICAL NOTATION?

MUSICAL NOTATION is a way of writing down musical sounds so that a singer or instrumentalist can reproduce them as the composer intends. As well as showing the pitch and length of the sounds, the notation gives information about how the notes should be played.

This is a treble clef. It shows the pitch of the notes on this stave (five lines).

This is a key signature. It shows whether certain notes should be flattened or sharpened throughout the music.

A quaver is half a beat long.

The bar line divides the music into bars.

This is a time signature. It shows that there are three beats of music in each bar (small section).

A crotchet is one beat long.

pp
This is short for the Italian word *pianissimo*. It shows that the music should be played very quietly.

A minim is two beats long.

The higher on the stave a note is, the higher its pitch. The first two notes are an octave apart. The upper note has twice the frequency of the lower note.

WHAT IS A SONIC BOOM?

SOME AIRCRAFT can travel faster than the speed of sound. They travel ahead of the sounds they make. This produces a build-up of sound energy behind them that becomes a shock wave, heard as a sonic boom.

Aircraft travelling faster than the speed of sound are said to be moving at supersonic speeds. The speed of sound is described as Mach 1. Concorde, which can travel at twice the speed of sound, reaches Mach 2.

WHAT ARE HARMONICS?

MOST SOUNDS are not pure sounds of a single wavelength and frequency. Other frequencies are mixed in with the sound, creating the particular texture and tone of an individual voice or instrument. These frequencies are called harmonics.

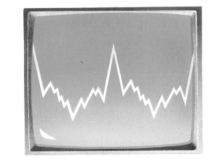

Complex sounds produce distinctive sound waves when viewed on a screen. These are so individual that a person's voice can be recognized from the wave patterns it makes. Voice-recognition systems use this fact to ensure that only certain people have access to buildings or computer files.

WHAT ARE THE INSTRUMENTS OF AN ORCHESTRA?

AN ORCHESTRA has instruments that produce sounds in different ways, but all cause air to vibrate to carry the sound to listening ears. String instruments have vibrating strings that are bowed or plucked. Wind instruments cause a column of air to vibrate when the player blows into them. Instruments that create sounds by being struck or shaken are percussion instruments. Brass instruments resonate when air is blown into them.

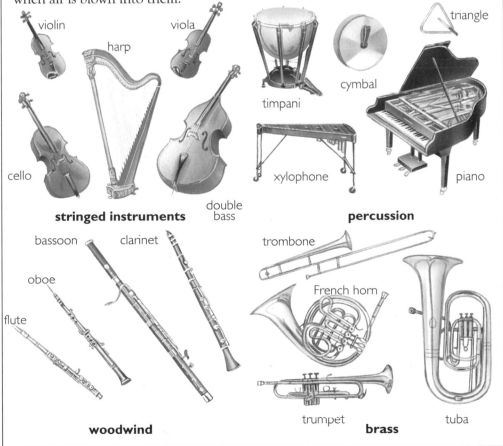

violin

viola

harp

triangle

timpani

cymbal

xylophone

piano

cello

double bass

stringed instruments

percussion

bassoon

clarinet

trombone

oboe

French horn

flute

trumpet

tuba

woodwind

brass

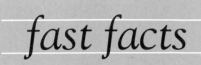

HOW FAST DOES SOUND TRAVEL?

All sounds travel at a speed of 343m (1125ft) per second at room temperature.

CAN SOUNDS BE DANGEROUS?

Sounds over 120dB can be painful to human ears and even cause deafness. There are laws about the level of sound that workers are exposed to in factories or when operating machinery.

WHAT IS ULTRASOUND?

Sound with a frequency of more than 20,000Hz is called ultrasound or described as ultrasonic. Ultrasound can be used to build up a picture of what is happening inside our bodies. Like x-rays, ultrasonic sound waves travel into the body and are bounced back by the organs inside. A screen can display the reflected sounds as a picture.

CAN A SINGER REALLY SHATTER GLASS?

Almost all materials can vibrate, but they do so at different frequencies. If a sound of the same frequency as an object's natural frequency is played near it, the object vibrates in sympathy. This is called resonating. If a singer sings a pure note of the same frequency as a glass's natural frequency, the glass may resonate so powerfully that it shatters.

WHAT SOUNDS CAN ANIMALS HEAR THAT WE CANNOT?

Human beings can normally hear sounds in the range of 20-20,000Hz but that does not mean that sounds do not exist outside those frequencies. Dogs can hear sounds up to 50,000Hz, and bats navigate by using ultrasound at frequencies of up to 120,000Hz.

CAN SOMETHING BE HOT AND COLD AT THE SAME TIME?

When we describe an object as hot, we are really comparing it with something else. The word does not mean anything by itself. We can say that we feel hot after exercise, that a cup of coffee is hot, and that the surface of the Sun is hot, but we mean something quite different each time.

An object can be hot compared with an ice cube but cold compared with boiling water. In fact, both the ice cube and the boiling water contain heat energy, but their temperatures are quite different. Temperature is a measure of how hot something is compared with an agreed scale.

A small object with a temperature of 100°C may not have as much heat energy as a very large object with a temperature of 0°C.

WHAT IS CONVECTION?

HEAT ENERGY is always on the move. It flows from a hotter object towards a cooler one until both are the same temperature. In liquids and gases, heat energy usually moves by convection. This means that the molecules nearest to the heat source begin to move more rapidly and spread apart, so that this area of the fluid is less dense. As the less dense part of the liquid or gas rises, denser parts sink to take its place.

The upwardly moving currents of warmed liquid or gas are known as convection currents. In the air, convection currents are called thermals. Birds (and even gliders containing passengers) are able to rise with them.

HOW DOES CONDUCTION WORK?

IN SOLIDS, heated particles also begin to vibrate in their positions, but while the substance remains solid, they cannot move upwards. Instead, one moving particle bumps into the next and so transfers some energy. This continues until the heat energy is transferred throughout the solid. If enough heat energy is transferred to the solid, the particles move so rapidly that they break free from each other and the substance melts to become a liquid.

Solids through which heat passes easily are said to be good conductors. Metals, such as copper, conduct heat quickly and evenly, which is one reason why cooking pans are often made from them.

WHAT KIND OF HEAT ENERGY IS RADIATION?

RADIATION is a means of transferring heat that does not cause particles to vibrate. Instead, it travels in waves, called infra-red rays. Infra-red radiation has a longer wavelength than light but travels at the same speed. Unlike other methods of heat transfer, radiation can work in a vacuum.

The Sun's heat travels through space by radiation. Ice reflects radiation, which is one reason why the temperature at the Poles is always low.

HOW DOES A THERMOSTAT WORK?

THERMOSTATS are devices that switch an appliance on and off when certain temperatures are reached. They work on the principle that some materials conduct heat better than others. A strip made of two metals, such as copper and iron, is connected to an electrical circuit. As the strip is warmed, the molecules in the upper metal vibrate more strongly than those in the lower one. The upper metal expands and bends, pulling the lower metal up and breaking the circuit. No more heat is transferred until the metal cools and drops back into position, completing the circuit again.

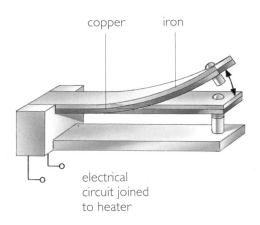

copper   iron

electrical
circuit joined
to heater

A scale on the glass tube shows the temperature in degrees Centigrade or Fahrenheit.

A narrow part near the base of the column of liquid stops the liquid from flowing back into the bulb before the temperature can be read. That is why thermometers are shaken before use to return all the liquid to its lowest point.

As it warms, the liquid inside the glass tube rises

HOW IS HEAT ENERGY MEASURED?

HEAT ENERGY, like other forms of energy, is measured in joules (J). Temperature is measured in degrees Fahrenheit (°F), Celsius (°C) or Kelvin (K). In Fahrenheit, water freezes at 32° and boils at 212°. The Celsius scale is based on the boiling and freezing points of water, so these are 100°C and 0°C respectively. Kelvin units are the same as Celsius degrees but they start from the lowest temperature possible. On this scale, water freezes at 273K.

HOW DOES A THERMOMETER WORK?

AS SUBSTANCES get hotter, their molecules move around more rapidly and they may take up more space. A thermometer contains a liquid that expands as it gains heat energy. This causes the level of the liquid to rise in a narrow tube. A scale beside the tube allows the temperature to be read.

HOW DO FIREFIGHTERS PROTECT THEMSELVES FROM HEAT?

FIREFIGHTERS need to wear clothing that is both fire retardant (slow to catch on fire) and offers good insulation (does not conduct heat easily). Fireproof clothing often has a shiny surface, because this helps to reflect the radiated heat away from the body.

ARE HUMAN BEINGS THE ONLY ANIMALS TO USE TOOLS?

The simplest tools often act as extensions of parts of the body. For example, if your arms are too short to reach a ball that has fallen into a pond, you may use a stick to lengthen your reach. The stick is a tool. Many non-human animals use simple tools: chimpanzees use sticks to scoop ants from their mounds; thrushes drop snails' shells onto a flat stone or "anvil" to crush them; some vultures drop stones onto other birds' eggs to break the shells. Tools, used by humans or other animals, help to make work easier to do.

Lifting your body to the top of the slide would be difficult if you had to go straight upwards. The steps are a kind of slope, making it easier to reach the top.

It would be hard work for one child to lift another into the air over and over again. A see-saw makes it easy because it is a kind of lever.

This cart and bricks would be much too heavy for a small child to lift and carry. Wheels make it possible for a small force to move them long distances.

A bicycle has gears that change the amount of force needed to turn the pedals.

IN SCIENTIFIC TERMS, WHAT IS WORK?

TO A SCIENTIST, work is done when a force causes something to move. The unit of measurement used for work is the joule. A joule of work is done when a force of one newton moves something one metre (3.3 feet). The force needed to lift a small apple is about one newton.

WHAT ARE SIMPLE MACHINES?

LEVERS, wedges, slopes, screws, wheels, gears and pulleys are all known as simple machines. They make work easier by enabling a small force to move a large load. Machines may magnify (increase) a force or a movement.

HOW CAN A SLOPE MAKE WORK EASIER?

A SLOPE, or inclined plane, makes work easier because the force needed to move a load is spread out over a longer distance. The amount of work needed to move an object from one point to another does not change, but as the distance is lengthened, less force is needed.

Steps are a form of inclined plane. The shallower the steps, the further you have to travel, and the easier the climb is.

HOW CAN THE PRINCIPLE OF THE SCREW BE USED?

A SCREW is really an inclined plane wrapped around a cone or cylinder. It works on the opposite principle to a staircase. This time, by lengthening the distance travelled in the circular motion of the screw, the forward force (as the screw moves into the wood or metal) is magnified.

HOW DO LEVERS WORK?

THERE are three different kinds of lever, depending on where the force applied and the load are in relation to each other. A lever is a rod that can turn on a pivot, or fulcrum.

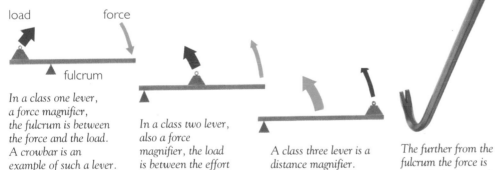

In a class one lever, a force magnifier, the fulcrum is between the force and the load. A crowbar is an example of such a lever.

In a class two lever, also a force magnifier, the load is between the effort and the fulcrum. Nutcrackers are class two levers.

A class three lever is a distance magnifier. It has the force between the fulcrum and the load. Tweezers are class three levers.

The further from the fulcrum the force is applied, the larger the load that can be moved, which is why a crowbar has a long handle.

WHY IS THE WHEEL SO USEFUL?

STRICTLY SPEAKING, a wheel on its own is not very useful, but a wheel on an axle is the basis of a huge number of machines. A wheel can be used to magnify a force. A steering wheel, for example, has a force applied to the outer edge, which moves a much longer distance than the centre (axle). The axle moves a much shorter distance and therefore exerts a greater force. When a force is applied to the axle, a wheel can be used to magnify distance, which is what happens in wheeled vehicles. A force applied to the axle moves a much greater distance at the outer edge of the wheels. Finally, a wheel can be used to change the direction of a force. Wheels convert the circular motion of the axle into the forward motion of the vehicle.

fast facts

WHEN WAS THE WHEEL INVENTED?

The wheel was probably invented around 3300BC by the Mesopotamians. However, free-rolling logs, the forerunners of wheels, were probably used in many parts of the world long before that.

HOW IS WORK CALCULATED?

Work done (J) = force (N) x distance moved in the direction of the force (m).

WHAT IS ARCHIMEDES' SCREW?

Archimedes' screw is a device that uses the principle of the screw to lift water from a lower level to a higher one. The screw is inside a tube. With each turn, water trapped between the thread of the screw and the side of the tube is raised up the tube.

WHAT IS A GEAR?

A gear is a toothed wheel. Its teeth can fit into the teeth of another gear, so that when one turns, the other turns also. By using combinations of gears, engineers can change the magnitude or direction of a force. This technique is often used to slow or speed up machines. For example, a large gear, turning slowly, will make a smaller gear turn more quickly.

HOW CAN WHEELS HELP LIFT HEAVY LOADS?

PULLEYS are wheels with grooves through which a rope can run. It is much easier to pull something down than to lift it up, as you can use your body weight to help. A pulley enables a downward force to be converted into an upward force. Lifts often use this principle by employing a counterweight. The dropping *down* of the lift causes the counterweight to *rise*. Then the dropping of the counterweight helps the lift to go up again.

WHAT IS AN ELECTRONIC CIRCUIT?

An electronic circuit is made up of a number of components linked together to form a circuit through which electricity flows. Components are devices that have different jobs within the circuit. They may be fixed in position on a circuit board. Electronic components can be made so tiny that thousands of them will fit into a chip a fraction of the size of a postage stamp.

On a circuit board, individual components are held in position by soldering. The wiring that connects them runs along the underside of the board.

WHAT ARE THE MOST COMMONLY USED ELECTRONIC COMPONENTS?

ELECTRONIC COMPONENTS affect the way that current flows around a circuit. Four of the most commonly used are capacitors, diodes, resistors and transistors.

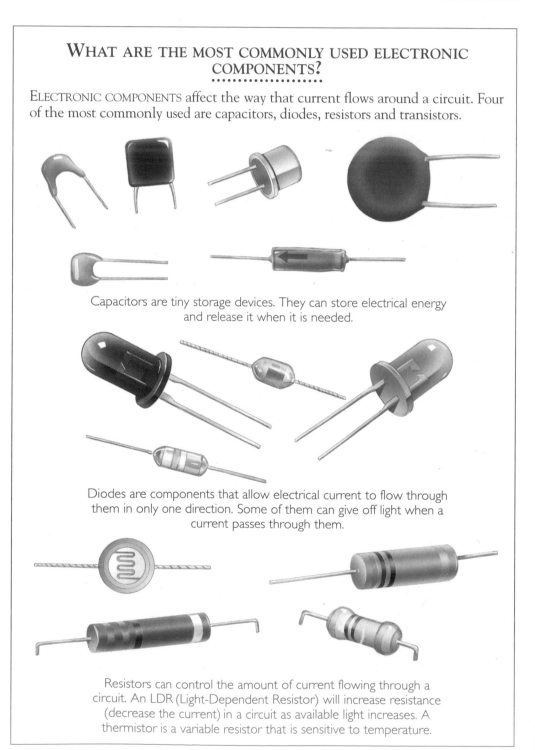

Capacitors are tiny storage devices. They can store electrical energy and release it when it is needed.

Diodes are components that allow electrical current to flow through them in only one direction. Some of them can give off light when a current passes through them.

Resistors can control the amount of current flowing through a circuit. An LDR (Light-Dependent Resistor) will increase resistance (decrease the current) in a circuit as available light increases. A thermistor is a variable resistor that is sensitive to temperature.

WHAT IS A SILICON CHIP?

A SILICON CHIP is also known as an integrated circuit. It is a complete circuit, perhaps containing thousands of electronic components, that is printed on a thin wafer of an element called silicon. The chip is protected by a covering called a capsule, which is the part we normally see. Little metal feet allow the chip to be connected to other chips and components.

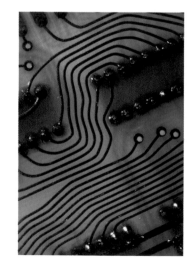

HOW ARE INTEGRATED CIRCUITS CONNECTED?

SILICON CHIPS are too small to be connected by ordinary wire, however fine it is. Instead, minute "tracks" of a conducting material such as copper are printed on the circuit board to link the silicon chips.

WHY DO ELECTRONIC CIRCUITS USE BINARY CODE?

ALTHOUGH APPLIANCES containing electronic circuits can perform very complicated tasks and even appear to think for themselves, they are operated entirely by electrical current. This cannot "think" but it can be turned on or off, increased or decreased, or caused to change direction by electronic components. The activity in any one part of a circuit depends on whether electrical current is detected or not. This can be represented by a 1 if a current is detected or a 0 if it is not. Binary code uses only the digits 0 and 1, so it enables an electronic device to perform calculations.

HOW DOES AN ELECTRONIC CALCULATOR WORK?

AN ELECTRONIC CALCULATOR has many integrated circuits inside, capable of making complicated calculations. The key pad sends signals through the circuits. The display shows the digits as they are keyed in and gives the answer when the calculation is finished. Keys marked with an M cause circuits to memorize certain numbers so that they can be reintroduced later in the calculation. As there is a key for entering the decimal point, the calculator can deal with both very small and very large numbers.

WHAT IS A LOGIC GATE?

LOGIC GATES are combinations of resistors that make it possible for an electronic circuit to carry out calculations. Different kinds of gates affect the output of electrical current, depending on the input. Most logic gates have two input points and one output point.

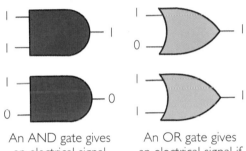

An AND gate gives an electrical signal only if it receives a signal at both input points.

An OR gate gives an electrical signal if either or both input points receive a signal.

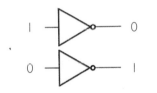

A NOT gate gives an electrical signal if the input point does NOT receive a signal. If the inpoint point does receive a signal, there is no output. The effect of this is always to reverse the signal.

WHAT IS A LIQUID CRYSTAL DISPLAY?

MANY ELECTRONIC DEVICES nowadays have liquid crystal displays. Watches, music centres, calculators and even cars give information by means of liquid crystals. These are crystals, held inside cells, that become opaque or change colour when they are heated. The circuits behind the display pass a voltage across the crystals, so that some of them change while the others remain the same. In this way, numbers, letters and symbols can be displayed.

The cells are often straight lines arranged as a figure eight. Individual cells can be coloured to form a variety of numbers, letters and symbols.

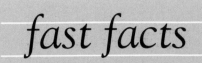

WHERE IS SILICON VALLEY?

Silicon Valley is an area south of San Francisco, California, in the United States, where there are many companies concerned with electronics and computers.

WHAT IS THE BIGGEST ADVANTAGE OF THE SILICON CHIP?

By far the biggest advantage of the silicon chip is its size. Even very small devices can now be "smart", containing thousands of electronic circuits to enable them to perform complicated tasks or do several jobs at once. However, scientists are working on even smaller chips, which would enable almost all everyday objects, such as your clothing, to contain electronic components.

WHAT IS AN LED?

An LED is a Light-Emitting Diode. It does not use a bulb, so rarely fails and may be used, for example, in the light that shows whether an electrical device is switched on.

WHAT IS THE DIFFERENCE BETWEEN DIGITAL AND ANALOGUE SIGNALS?

Analogue signals, like sound waves, flow in a continuous wave. Digital signals contain the same information but are broken up into pulses, which can be expressed in binary code and are therefore in a form that electronic circuits can use.

WHAT IS A SEMICONDUCTOR?

Semiconductors are materials that conduct electricity more or less well, depending on certain outside conditions. In silicon chips, they are made by adding other chemicals to very thin layers of silicon.

HOW CAN TIME BE MEASURED?

Our experience of time is that it flows forwards. It cannot be stopped or reversed but goes on in a continuous stream. We can only measure time in relation to other things that have a regular pattern: the rising of the Sun, the swinging of a pendulum or the vibration of a crystal.

WHAT IS A DAY?

A DAY is the time that it takes for the Earth to turn once around its axis, or one day and one night. It is probably the earliest measurement of time used, although early people had no idea that the Earth was turning. They assumed that the Sun was moving, because it appeared to rise above the horizon each morning and disappear behind the opposite horizon at night.

The Earth orbits the Sun once every 365.24 days. This is one year.

The Moon circles the Earth once every 27.3 days.

The Earth takes 24 hours to turn on its axis. This is one day.

WHAT IS THE DIFFERENCE BETWEEN A LUNAR AND A CALENDAR MONTH?

AFTER THE DAY, the next measurement of time that early people used was probably the month. They noticed that the Moon changed shape on a regular cycle, with 28 days passing from one full Moon to the next. In fact, the true figure is about 29.5 days. This is a lunar month. The phases of the Moon do not divide exactly into the 365 or 366 days in a year, so over time the months that we use today, known as calendar months, came to have slightly different lengths. April, June, September and November have 30 days each. All the other months have 31 days, except February, which has 28 days, or 29 in a leap year.

WHY DO WE HAVE LEAP YEARS?

THE YEAR is not an exact number of days but about 365 and one quarter days. By adding an extra day into the calendar every four years, we ensure that the year does not gradually become out of step with the seasons.

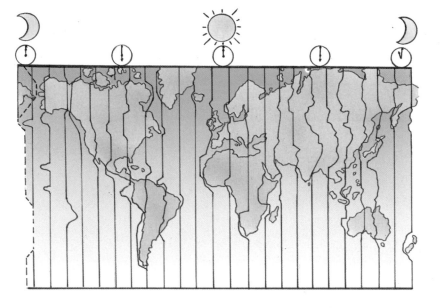

WHAT ARE TIME ZONES?

AS THE EARTH SPINS, different parts of it face the Sun. Therefore, it cannot be the same time all over the world at the same moment. When it is the middle of the night in one country, it is dawn in another part of the world. To keep expressions of time consistent in every part of the world, the Earth is divided into 24 time zones, each one exactly an hour apart.

WHAT IS GREENWICH MEAN TIME?

GREENWICH MEAN TIME is the local time at the Greenwich Observatory in London, England. The line of 0° longitude, along which the Sun passes overhead exactly at noon, runs through the Observatory. Greenwich Mean Time (GMT, also known as Universal Time, or UT) is used as a standard time all over the world.

WHAT WERE THE FIRST CLOCKS LIKE?

IT WAS probably the Babylonians who first divided the day into 24 hours, with 60 minutes in each hour. These are numbers that can easily be divided by 2, 3 and 4. The very first clocks, like the first calendars, were based on the Sun, using the movements of its shadow to read the time from a marked area of Earth or stone. Later methods of time measurement were based on actions that happened at a fixed rate, such as the pull of gravity on grains of sand.

Prehistoric standing stones may have been used as clocks or calendars.	Water clocks measured either the water that had dripped from a container, or the water left inside, to tell the time.	Hourglasses were used from the early middle ages. Sand drained from one bulb to the other in a few minutes or as much as two hours.	Candle clocks were used in the ninth century but were not very accurate as a draught could cause the candle to burn more quickly.

DOES THE WHOLE WORLD USE THE GREGORIAN CALENDAR?

FOR INTERNATIONAL COMMUNICATIONS, the whole world does use the Gregorian calendar, but other religious and traditional calendars are still in use around the world. The Jewish calendar has a year that varies between 353 and 385 days. The Muslim calendar has 354 or 355 days in a year.

fast facts

WHAT DID CHRISTIAAN HUYGENS INVENT?

Christiaan Huygens, a Dutch physicist, invented the first pendulum clock in the middle of the seventeenth century.

WHY WAS 46BC KNOWN AS "THE YEAR OF CONFUSION"?

Julius Caesar was the first person to try to take account of the fact that the year is slightly longer than 365 days. He instituted the Julian calendar in 46BC, but because the lack of leap years in previous years had made the year and seasons out of step, he decreed that the first year of the new calendar should have 445 days. The difficulties this caused resulted in the nickname "the year of confusion".

WHAT HAPPENED ON 5 OCTOBER 1582?

On 4 October 1582, Pope Gregory XIII introduced the Gregorian calendar, which was the most accurate yet and is still in use today. Like Julius Caesar before him, he needed to make an adjustment, so he declared that 4 October would be followed by 15 October. Therefore, strictly speaking, nothing at all happened on 5 October 1582.

WHY ARE THE 1900s KNOWN AS THE TWENTIETH CENTURY?

Our calendar is measured from an early estimate of the date of the birth of Christ. The next hundred years after this are called the first century. That means that the next century, with years beginning with the digit 1, is the second century, and so on.

WHAT ARE DECIMAL NUMBERS?

Decimal numbers use 10 digits, which are combined to make numbers of any size. The position of the digit determines what it means in any number. For example, the 2 in the number 200 is ten times the size of the 2 in the number 20. Each position of a number gives a value ten times higher than the position to its right. So 9867 means 7 units, plus 6 x 10, plus 8 x 10 x 10, plus 9 x 10 x 10 x 10. As decimal numbers are based on the number 10, we say that this is a base-10 number system.

HOW ARE ROMAN NUMERALS USED?

THE ROMANS had a number system with a base of 10, as we do, but they used different numerals to write it down. For the numbers one to nine, instead of using nine different numerals, they used only three different letters, combining them to make the numbers. This made it very difficult for them to do even simple calculations, so their advances in mathematics and related fields were not as great as might have been expected from such a far-reaching civilization.

I	1	XX	20
II	2	L	50
III	3	C	100
IV	4	M	1000
V	5		
VI	6		
VII	7		
VIII	8		
IX	9		
X	10		

Roman numerals are still used for certain purposes. They appear on watch and clock faces (usually with IIII instead of IV for 4) and when numbers have a certain importance, such as in the title of a monarch.

WHAT IS THE BINARY SYSTEM?

THE BINARY SYSTEM is another way of counting. Instead of being a base-10 system, it is a base-2 system, using only two digits: 0 and 1. Again, the position of a digit gives it a particular value. 1010101 means 1 unit, plus 0 x 2, plus 1 x 2 x 2, plus 0 x 2 x 2 x 2, plus 1 x 2 x 2 x 2 x 2, plus 0 x 2 x 2 x 2 x 2 x 2, plus 1 x 2 x 2 x 2 x 2 x 2 x 2. 1010101 is the same as 85 in decimal numbers.

WHAT IS AN ABACUS?

AN ABACUS is a frame of beads used in China and neighbouring countries for making calculations. A skilled abacus user can produce answers to some calculations almost as quickly as someone using an electronic calculator.

64	32	16	8	4	2	1	
						1	= 1
					1	0	= 2
				1	0	1	= 5
			1	0	1	0	= 10
		1	0	0	0	1	= 17
1	0	1	0	1	0	1	= 85

An abacus usually has wires or bamboo rods with five beads at the bottom and two beads at the top.

WHAT IS GEOMETRY?

GEOMETRY is the branch of mathematics that is concerned with points, lines, surfaces and solids, and their relation to each other. Shapes, both flat and three-dimensional, are an important part of geometry. When we describe something as geometric, we mean that it has a regular, often angular pattern of lines or shapes.

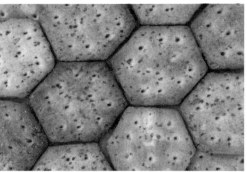

One branch of geometry is concerned with tesselation, which means covering a surface by repeated use of a single shape. This has many applications in construction and industry. These hexagonal biscuits, for example, can be cut from dough with no wastage at all.

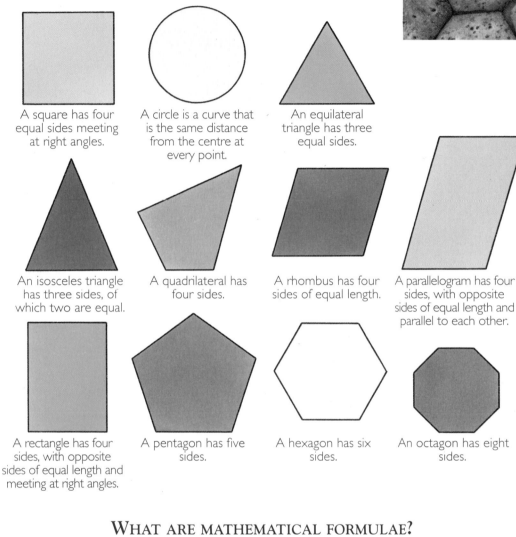

A square has four equal sides meeting at right angles.

A circle is a curve that is the same distance from the centre at every point.

An equilateral triangle has three equal sides.

An isosceles triangle has three sides, of which two are equal.

A quadrilateral has four sides.

A rhombus has four sides of equal length.

A parallelogram has four sides, with opposite sides of equal length and parallel to each other.

A rectangle has four sides, with opposite sides of equal length and meeting at right angles.

A pentagon has five sides.

A hexagon has six sides.

An octagon has eight sides.

WHAT ARE MATHEMATICAL FORMULAE?

MATHEMATICAL FORMULAE are useful rules expressed using symbols or letters. The formulae below show the volume of various three-dimensional shapes. $\pi = 3.142$

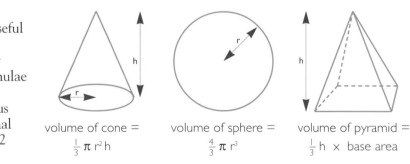

volume of cone = $\frac{1}{3}\pi r^2 h$

volume of sphere = $\frac{4}{3}\pi r^3$

volume of pyramid = $\frac{1}{3}h \times$ base area

$a^2 + b^2 = c^2$ or
$(a \times a) + (b \times b) = (c \times c)$

WHO WAS PYTHAGORAS?

PYTHAGORAS was a Greek living in the sixth century BC. He was a mathematician and scientist who is now best remembered for Pythagoras' Theorem, a formula for calculating the length of one side of a right-angled triangle if the other sides are known. However, this theorem was, in fact, already known hundreds of years earlier by Egyptian and Babylonian mathematicians.

fast facts

WHAT IS ALGEBRA?

Algebra is a branch of mathematics in which letters or symbols are used in place of numbers. At its simplest level, this means that if we know that there are 40 boys in a group of 100 children, we can say that g stands for the girls in the group and

$$40 + g = 100 \quad \text{or}$$
$$g = 100 - 40 \quad \text{so}$$
$$g = 60$$

WHAT IS THE LARGEST POSSIBLE NUMBER?

There is no such thing as the largest possible number. No matter how big a number you think of, someone else can simply add one to it to make a bigger number.

WHAT IS A PLANE FIGURE?

A plane figure is a flat shape, with only two dimensions, like the geometric shapes above.

WHAT IS A PRIME NUMBER?

Prime numbers are those that can only be divided by themselves and 1. For example, 23 is a prime number, as it can only be divided by 23 and 1. However, 24 can be divided by 1, 2, 3, 4, 6, 8, 12 and 24.

WHAT IS A POLYHEDRON?

A polyhedron is a three-dimensional figure with flat (plane) faces, such as a pyramid.

WHAT IS ALCOHOL?

Alcohol is an organic compound. That means that it is one of the substances studied in a whole branch of chemistry called organic chemistry. Organic chemistry concerns carbon compounds, many of which are made by living (organic) things. Alcohol is a compound of carbon, oxygen and hydrogen. There are many kinds of alcohol, with different properties and uses in industry. Ethanol and glycerol are both useful forms of alcohol.

HOW DOES FERMENTATION PRODUCE ALCOHOL?

FERMENTATION is a natural process that uses a kind of fungus called yeast. When given the right conditions of warmth and moisture, yeast will digest sugars in fruit or other plant materials and give off carbon dioxide gas and alcohol. Fermentation is used on a huge scale to make alcoholic drinks and ethanol for use in industry.

HOW WAS ALCOHOL DISCOVERED?

IT IS LIKELY that the effects of alcohol were discovered before the chemical! Grapes may have a natural yeast on their skins that will cause the fruits or juice squeezed from them to ferment in warm conditions without the addition of further yeast. Early peoples may have discovered that fermented grape juice had an unusual flavour and effect on the body.

WHAT IS THE CARBON CYCLE?

CARBON is an essential element in all living things. It is constantly being recycled on Earth in the carbon cycle shown below.

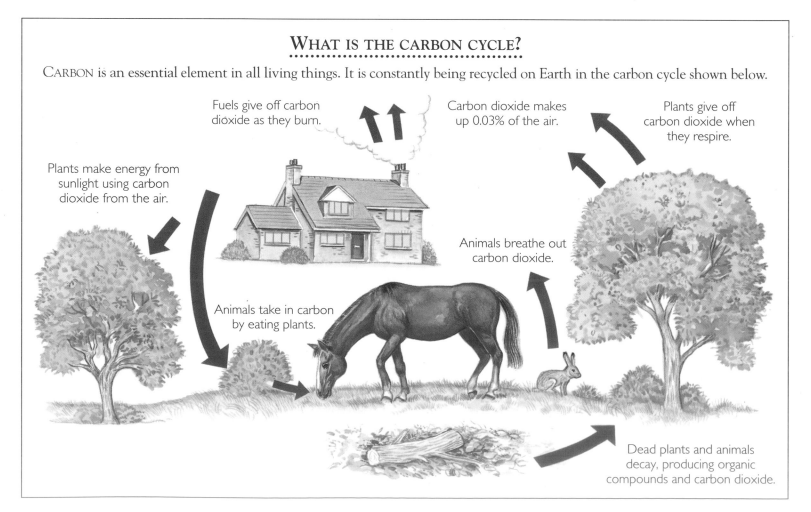

Fuels give off carbon dioxide as they burn.

Carbon dioxide makes up 0.03% of the air.

Plants give off carbon dioxide when they respire.

Plants make energy from sunlight using carbon dioxide from the air.

Animals breathe out carbon dioxide.

Animals take in carbon by eating plants.

Dead plants and animals decay, producing organic compounds and carbon dioxide.

WHAT ARE CARBOXYLIC ACIDS?

CARBOXYLIC ACIDS contain carbon, oxygen and hydrogen. Many naturally occurring acids are carboxylic acids, such as the acid that causes nettles to "sting" and the acid in vinegar. This is called ethanoic acid. It is created when alcohol reacts with oxygen (oxidizes).

Some carboxylic acids are found in fats and oils from animals and plants. They are called fatty acids. When they react with alcohol, they create compounds called esters, which give flowers their scent. Some expensive perfumes are still made by distilling the scent from flowers and preserving it in alcohol.

WHAT IS A HOMOLOGOUS SERIES?

A HOMOLOGOUS SERIES is a group of compounds that are made of the same elements and share some of the same properties and features but have different numbers of atoms in their molecules. Alkanes, alkenes and alcohols all form homologous series.

Cosmetics contain many organic compounds. Solvents dissolve other ingredients to produce a liquid consistency. Pigments give the cosmetics a wide range of colours. Oils give a smooth texture that is resistant to moisture.

Aniline is one of the many organic compounds that can be extracted from coal tar. It forms an important part of aniline dyes, which give very bright colours for textiles.

Plastics, made from organic compounds such as ethene, can be incredibly strong. The bodies of racing cars are made from plastic reinforced by fibres.

WHAT IS AN ALKANE?

An alkane is a compound of carbon and hydrogen (a hydrocarbon) in which the atoms are held together by single covalent bonds. Methane, propane and butane, gases used as fuels are examples of alkanes.

WHAT IS AN ALKENE?

An alkene is also a hydrocarbon but its atoms are held together by double covalent bonds. Alkenes are very reactive and can be used in industry to make many products, such as plastics, dyes and paints.

WHAT CAN WE TELL FROM THE NAMES OF ORGANIC CHEMICALS?

The names of some organic compounds tell us how many carbon atoms there are in their molecules. Compounds whose names begin with "meth" have one carbon atom. Molecules with two carbon atoms have names beginning with "eth", while three carbon atoms in a molecule are indicated by a name beginning with "prop".

WHY IS CARBON ABLE TO FORM SO MANY COMPOUNDS?

Carbon is extraordinary in that it can form over two million different organic compounds. This is because carbon atoms are able to bond with each other and with other atoms in single, double and triple covalent bonds, forming molecules in the shape of strings or rings.

WHAT IS A CHLOROFLUOROCARBON?

A chlorofluorocarbon, as its name suggests, is a compound of chlorine, fluorine and carbon. Chlorofluorocarbons were widely used in aerosols, but it was feared that they helped to destroy the ozone layer, so they are now avoided where possible.

WHY DO WE NEED ACCURATE MEASUREMENT?

For many purposes, an approximate idea of a length or weight or distance is fine. We may say that something is five-minutes' walk away, for example. That does not tell us how far it is – that would depend on how quickly a person walked – but it does give a rough idea that it is neither hundreds of kilometres nor just a few centimetres distant. However, if you need to know whether a new car would fit in your garage, you need a more accurate measurement, at least within a few centimetres. An Olympic highjumper, in fierce competition, will certainly need to measure to the nearest centimetre. And so it goes on, until scientists measuring the size of atoms need units of measurement much too small to be seen with the naked eye. The important thing is that units of measurement must be standard (agreed by everyone who uses them).

A Roman mile was 1000 paces long.

A foot was as long as ... a foot!

At one time, the timing of international athletics races was measured by an official with a stopwatch. Now winning margins of as little as one hundredth of a second are recorded by electronic timers.

WHAT WAS THE EARLIEST SYSTEM OF MEASUREMENT?

IT IS LIKELY that the first systems of measurement were based on the human body. As every person had a body, they could use themselves as reference! Of course, since people vary greatly in size, this was not a very accurate system.

From elbow to fingertips was one cubit.

The width of the hand was four fingers.

WHAT ARE SI UNITS?

SI UNITS are internationally agreed units for scientific measurements. SI stands for a French phrase: Système Internationale d'Unités (International System of Units). The base units are those used for the basic measurements that can be made, while derived units are those that need to be worked out using one or more base units. For example, a newton is the force needed to accelerate a mass of one kilogram by one metre per second.

BASE UNITS

Quantity	Unit	Abbreviation
distance	metre	m
mass	kilogram	k
time	second	s
electrical current	ampere	A
temperature	kelvin	K
amount of substance	mole	mol
luminous intensity	candela	cd

DERIVED UNITS

Quantity	Unit	Abbreviation
frequency	hertz	Hz
energy	joule	J
force	newton	N
power	watt	W
pressure	pascal	Pa
electrical charge	coulomb	C
electromotive force	volt	V
electrical resistance	ohm	Ω
electrical conductance	siemens	S
electrical capacitance	farad	F
magnetic flux	weber	Wb
inductance	henry	H
luminous flux	lumen	lm
illumination	lux	lx

HOW ARE LATITUDE AND LONGITUDE MEASURED?

IN ORDER to be able to pinpoint where we are on the Earth, we cover it with a grid of imaginary lines. Those running from North to South are called lines of longitude, while those running from East to West are called lines of latitude. These lines are measured in degrees. The line of longitude running through Greenwich, England is taken as 0° and lines on either side of it are so many degrees East or West. The line of latitude that is counted as 0° runs around the equator. Lines either side of it are said to be so many degrees North or South. Each degree is divided into sixty minutes (60').

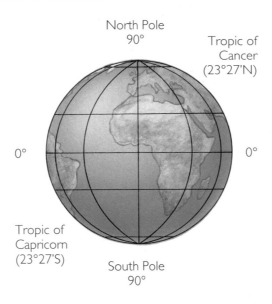

North Pole
90°

Tropic of Cancer
(23°27'N)

0°   0°

Tropic of Capricorn
(23°27'S)

South Pole
90°

HOW CAN STANDARD UNITS BE USED FOR VERY SMALL AND VERY LARGE MEASUREMENTS?

METRIC UNITS can be multiplied or divided by 10 as often as is needed to create units of a useful size for measuring the object under consideration. For example, a unit of 1000 metres, which is the same as 10 x 10 metres, and can be written as 10^2 metres, is called a kilometre. The prefix "kilo", meaning one thousand, can be applied to other units. A kilogram (kg) is equal to one thousand grams. Similarly, there is a prefix meaning one thousandth (10^{-3}): milli-. So one milligram is the same as a thousandth of a gram. On the right is a list of other prefixes and their meanings.

Prefix	Symbol or abbreviation	Factor
deca-	da	10
hecto-	h	10^2
kilo-	k	10^3
mega-	M	10^6
giga-	G	10^9
tera-	T	10^{12}
peta-	P	10^{15}
exa-	E	10^{18}
deci-	d	10^{-1}
centi-	c	10^{-2}
milli-	m	10^{-3}
micro-	μ	10^{-6}
nano-	n	10^{-9}
pico-	p	10^{-12}
femto-	f	10^{-15}
atto-	a	10^{-18}

HOW ARE ANGLES MEASURED?

ANGLES are measured in degrees, using a protractor. There are 360° in a circle, and 90° in a right angle. A triangle has a total of 180° in its three inner angles, so that if the size of two angles is known, it is always possible to work out the third. Since pairs of inner and outer angles must add up to 360°, it is also possible to work out the inner angles if two of the outer angles are known.

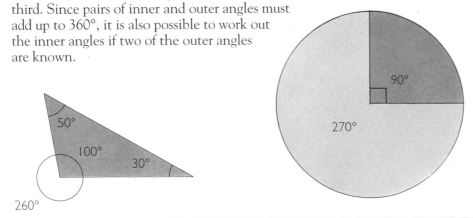

50°
100°
30°
260°

90°
270°

HOW LONG IS A METRE?

When the metre was first defined in 1791 by the French Academy of Sciences, it was expressed as the distance from the North Pole to the equator along a line passing through Paris, France, divided by 10,000,000,000.

HOW CAN CELSIUS BE CONVERTED INTO FAHRENHEIT TEMPERATURES?

To convert Celsius into Fahrenheit, multiply the degrees Celsius by 9, divide the answer by 5, and add 32. To convert Fahrenheit into Celsius, subtract 32 from the degrees Fahrenheit, multiply by 5, and divide by 9.

HOW ARE THE VAST DISTANCES OF SPACE MEASURED?

The distances in space are so huge that dealing with them in metres would result in numbers stretching right across this page. Instead, astronomers usually talk about a star being a certain number of light years away. Since light is the fastest thing in the universe, the distance it can travel in a year is enormous. In fact one light year is almost 100,000,000,000,000 kilometres.

WHAT IS THE PRIME MERIDIAN?

This is another way of referring to the line of longitude running through Greenwich, England.

WHAT IS TRIGONOMETRY?

Trigonometry is the measurement and calculation of angles, and their relationship to the lines that join them, especially in triangles.

WHAT IS A ROBOT?

A robot is a machine that can carry out a complicated series of actions automatically. Electronic circuits make it able to move, which may be controlled by radio signals from a distance. When we think of robots, we may think of machines shaped approximately like human beings, but robots can be any shape or size.

HOW ARE ROBOTS USED FOR DANGEROUS JOBS?

THERE ARE MANY SITUATIONS in which human beings can operate safely only by wearing bulky protective clothing and working for short periods at a time. Sometimes even that is not enough to protect them. If it is suspected that a booby-trapped bomb has been left in an abandoned vehicle, for example, a controlled explosion may be the only way of deactivating it. No matter how much protection a bomb disposal expert has, the explosion could be fatal if he or she is nearby. The answer is to use a robot carrying an explosive charge. The robot can be sent into the danger zone while experts remain at a safe distance. Although no one wants to destroy an expensive machine, the alternative is much worse.

In recent years, minefields have often caused dreadful injuries to civilians long after a war has ended. Clearing them is extremely dangerous. This is another area in which robotics can save lives.

This is the interior of a nuclear reactor containment dome. Within radioactive environments, robots can perform tasks that would be dangerous for human beings.

HOW ARE ROBOTS USED IN INDUSTRY?

AS WELL AS BEING USEFUL in dealing with chemicals that would be dangerous to humans, robots have their uses in manufacturing industry. On production lines, the same action is done over and over again as part-made products pass along a conveyor belt. This is very tedious for human workers. Specialist robots, which can perform only one action, are ideal for this work, but humans are still needed to control them and to act if something goes wrong, as most robots are not designed to respond to unusual situations.

These robots are welding cars on a production line. They can work quickly and accurately twenty-four hours a day if necessary.

WILL ROBOTS EVER BE ABLE TO THINK FOR THEMSELVES?

IN MANY WAYS, robots already do think for themselves, in the sense that they may have the ability to assess all the information available in a particular situation and make a decision based on what they "know". Some robots can also "learn", so that if an action is unsuccessful, they do not repeat it. But any robot is only as good as the electronic circuits that cause it to move and the engineering that has enabled it to respond physically to electronic signals. As computer technology becomes more sophisticated, so will robots. It is likely that they will play an important role in all our lives in the twenty-first century.

fast facts

HOW CAN COMPUTERS BEAT CHESS EXPERTS?

Computers are able to perform calculations at lightning speed. Before making a chess move, they can review all available moves and choose the best one. But chess experts can sometimes beat a computer by understanding the basis on which it makes decisions.

WHERE DOES THE WORD "ROBOT" COME FROM?

The word "robot" was first used in a Czech play in 1920. It comes from the Czech word for work or labour.

WHAT IS AN ANDROID?

An android is a robot shaped like a human being.

ARE HUMAN-SHAPED ROBOTS USEFUL?

In most cases, a robot does not need to be shaped like a human, but sometimes this can be useful. People who have lost limbs can now be fitted with a robotic arm, leg, hand or foot that is made to look as much like a living body part as possible.

CAN ROBOTS FEEL?

Robots cannot feel emotions but they can be built to have senses. Television cameras and light sensitive cells can "see" for the robot, while touch-sensitive pads enable it to grip a very delicate object without crushing it.

WHAT IS ANIMATRONICS?

A METHOD of animating models by using specially developed robotic techniques is called animatronics. It is specially useful for museum displays and cinema work, where animatronic models of such creatures as dinosaurs, monsters or aliens can "act" alongside human actors.

Animatronic dinosaurs have realistic "skin" covering the engineering and electronics inside.

HOW HAVE ROBOTS BEEN USED IN SPACE TRAVEL?

ROBOTS have already been sent to distant planets, such as Mars. They are able to land on surfaces that might be hostile to human beings, to take soil and atmospheric samples, analyze them and send the results back to Earth. Missions "manned" by robots are much cheaper than those including humans, and robots do not necessarily have to be brought home again!

A robotic arm on the space shuttle enables astronauts to carry out repairs on satellites and space stations.

WHAT IS VIRTUAL REALITY?

VIRTUAL REALITY is a series of effects produced by a computer that enables someone wearing special equipment to feel as if they are really within an artificially created world. The person experiencing the effect wears a helmet through which sounds and pictures are relayed, but this is not like watching a movie. The computer technology makes it possible to turn round and "see" what is behind you. You can also move through the created world, exploring and having adventures. Wearing electronically controlled gloves and other clothing even makes it possible for you to "feel" objects in the virtual world.

In virtual reality, you can experience worlds as strange as the imagination of the programmer can create. But virtual reality is not just amazing entertainment. It can be used for training, especially where real experience could be dangerous or very expensive. Pilots, firefighters, divers and astronauts are just some of the people who can benefit from virtual reality training.

WHAT IS THE DIFFERENCE BETWEEN SPEED AND VELOCITY?

Speed is a measure of how quickly something is moving. Usually when we are talking about speed, we mean average speed. This is the time that it takes to travel from one point to another divided by the distance travelled. So speed is expressed in units such as kilometres per hour (km/h) or metres per second (m/s). Velocity, however, is a vector quantity. It measures the direction of movement as well as the speed.

The velocity of a flying bird can change even if its speed remains constant, as it can change direction.

WHAT IS RELATIVE VELOCITY?

RELATIVE VELOCITY is the velocity that one object has when viewed from another moving object. It is something that we are frequently aware of throughout the day, although we are not thinking in scientific terms. For example, if you are sitting still and a dog walks past, it seems to be moving quite quickly. If you later go for a run and pass the dog, still moving at the same velocity, it will seem to be travelling much more slowly.

The aeroplanes are moving in formation, at the same speed and in the same direction. Viewed from the ground, they are clearly moving very quickly, but their velocity in relation to each other (relative velocity) is zero.

WHAT IS ACCELERATION?

ACCELERATION is a change in the velocity of an object. We often think of it as "speeding up", but there is also negative acceleration, known as deceleration. Acceleration is measured in metres per second per second (m/s^2). A change of direction is also an acceleration, as the velocity is changed.

A sprinter accelerates from zero velocity by pushing against the blocks. This propels her forward, but she will still be accelerating for several metres before she reaches her fastest velocity. Her momentum carries her forward even after she has passed the finish line, but as she stops using energy to push her feet against the ground, she gradually slows and stops.

fast facts

HOW FAST CAN THE FASTEST HUMAN RUN?

The fastest male sprinter in the world reaches speeds of over 43km/h (almost 27mph) over very short distances.

WILL WOMEN EVER BE ABLE TO RUN AS FAST AS MEN?

Since records have been kept, the difference between male and female speed in athletics has been narrowing. Because men are usually taller and more muscular, it is likely that some men will always be faster than the fastest women at shorter distances. But at longer distances – longer even than the marathon – the difference between the genders is much less marked and may one day be negligible.

HOW ARE FAST-MOVING VEHICLES SLOWED DOWN?

Most vehicles are slowed by braking, which means applying a force to the wheels to slow their turning motion. However, some aeroplanes and cars that move at very high speeds use parachutes to slow their forward motion. Air resistance acting on the parachute counters the forward motion of the vehicle, causing it to slow.

CAN ANYTHING KEEP MOVING FOR EVER?

Nothing can keep moving for ever, as friction or lack of energy input will gradually slow it down. The turning of the planets and other astronomical movements will continue for millions and millions of years, but even those will be affected when the star around which they orbit ages and dies.

WHAT IS TERMINAL VELOCITY?

WHEN SOMETHING IS DROPPED and is pulled by gravity towards the Earth, it accelerates as it falls until it reaches a velocity from which it can accelerate no further. This is called its terminal velocity. Terminal velocity happens when the force of the air resistance against the falling object increases to the point where it equals the force of gravity pulling the object. The terminal velocity of an object depends on how much air resistance it experiences. This is not affected by its weight but by its surface area and the streamlining of its shape.

A body experiences more friction passing through water than through air. That is why swimmers in a race try to dive as far as possible through the air before they enter the water. To reduce air resistance and increase their speed through the air as much as possible, they maintain a streamlined shape, with legs and arms held tightly in line with the body.

HOW FAST ARE YOUR REACTIONS?

INVOLUNTARY REACTIONS, which happen without conscious thought, such as blinking an eye when an object approaches it, happen in fractions of a second. You can make a comparison of the speed of your *conscious* reactions and those of a friend by asking him or her to hold a ruler upright from the bottom. Put your fingers around the ruler without touching it. As your friend shouts "Go!" and drops the ruler, close your fingers as quickly as you can. Use the ruler's scale to compare measurements with friends.

WHAT ARE NEWTON'S LAWS OF MOTION?

IN THE SEVENTEENTH CENTURY, Sir Isaac Newton developed three laws of motion that can be illustrated by a boy standing in a boat.

Newton's First Law of Motion states that an object will stay still or continue to move at the same velocity unless it is acted on by a force. Several forces are, in fact, acting on the boy and the boat, but they are balanced, so neither moves.

Newton's Second Law says that when a force acts upon an object, it will cause it to move, change direction, speed up or slow down. A gust of wind blowing against the boy and boat pushes them towards the bank.

Newton's Third Law states that every action produces an equal and opposite reaction. As the boy pushes himself forward, the boat pushes itself backward! The same thing happens when a gun is fired. When the bullet moves forward, the gun recoils.

WHAT IS MOMENTUM?

ALL MOVING OBJECTS have momentum. It is their tendency to keep moving unless a force acts upon them. Momentum is calculated by multiplying the mass of an object by its velocity. The greater its mass, the greater its momentum. That means that a train travelling at 25km/h (15mph) along a straight track has a greater momentum than a bird flying at the same speed above it. A much greater force will be needed to stop the train than to stop the bird.

What is the ideal temperature for life?

Living things have evolved and adapted over millions of years to live successfully in very different temperatures. Penguins at the South Pole may live quite happily in temperatures of –50°C (–58°F), while some bacteria live near deep-sea vents that are gushing out water at close to boiling point.

How does a refrigerator work?

A REFRIGERATOR is basically a box that is very cold inside. The heat inside the box is made to move outside, where it flows out into the air. This is achieved by means of a pipe that contains a fluid called a refrigerant. The refrigerant flows around the pipe, becoming a vapour and then condensing back into a liquid. As it becomes a vapour, the refrigerant takes heat from inside the refrigerator. When it becomes a liquid again, it gives off the heat outside at the back of the refrigerator. This cycle of evaporation and condensation is caused by changes in pressure as the fluid is pumped from a high pressure part of the pipe (the condenser) into a lower pressure area (the evaporator).

Can the sea freeze?

THE MINERALS dissolved in sea water, which make it taste salty, lower the temperature at which the water will freeze. But at the temperatures found at the far north and south of the globe, the sea is frozen all the time. Further from the Poles, it may also freeze in winter. In fact, the North Pole is permanently frozen sea – there is no land beneath the ice.

The condenser is where the refrigerant turns back into a liquid.

Strongly built ships called icebreakers are needed to keep some shipping lanes open during the winter when the sea freezes over. Ships with less strong hulls can be crushed by the ice.

Where do icebergs come from?

ICEBERGS are huge chunks of ice that break off from the frozen seas at the North and South Poles as the weather becomes warmer. They can be enormous and are all the more dangerous for shipping because nine-tenths of the iceberg is invisible under water. The famous *RMS Titanic* was sunk by an iceberg in 1912.

A pump compresses the vapour, so that it is at higher pressure in the condenser than in the evaporator.

HOW WAS ICE-CREAM MADE IN THE DAYS BEFORE ELECTRICITY?

TWO THINGS have to happen to the mixture of dairy products and flavourings that make up ice-cream: they must be frozen and they must be stirred, to prevent large ice crystals from forming. Before electrical freezing machines were available, the ice-cream mixture was put into a churn, around which a mixture of salt and ice was packed. Heat from the ice-cream mixture gradually passed into the colder ice, until the cream itself was frozen. Meanwhile, the mixture was stirred by means of a paddle connected to a handle outside the tub. This became harder work as the icecream froze!

Iced desserts were probably first made by the Chinese as long ago as 3000BC.

WHY DO SOME FOODS FREEZE SUCCESSFULLY WHILE OTHERS DO NOT?

PLANTS AND ANIMALS are made up of cells, each of which is surrounded by a cell wall. Some foods contain a great deal of water. As the water freezes, it expands, breaking the cell walls. When the food is defrosted, its texture has been changed and what remains may well be just a mushy mass. It is not dangerous to eat this food, but it may not look or taste very pleasant.

Melons, which have a very high water content, do not freeze successfully. Other fruits may still be edible after freezing but have a different texture.

WHY IS THERE FROST MORE OFTEN ON A CLEAR NIGHT THAN ON A CLOUDY ONE?

FROST IS FORMED overnight when the air temperature drops below 0°C (32°F) and the dew freezes. Clouds in the sky act as insulation, preventing the heat from the Sun that has built up in the land, sea and air during the day from escaping. This means that the temperature is less likely to drop below freezing. When the sky is clear, the day's heat is able to escape easily, and a frost is likely.

A sharp frost can result in even the smallest branches having a sparkling covering of ice.

WHAT IS ABSOLUTE ZERO?

Absolute zero is a theoretical temperature at which particles could no longer move and so there could be no heat. It is calculated as −273.15°C (−459.69°F).

WHAT IS DRY ICE?

Dry ice is frozen carbon dioxide. When it begins to melt, it turns into a gas without becoming a liquid first. The melting dry ice looks like rolling mist and is often used in theatrical shows to give a mysterious effect.

WHAT IS A GLACIER?

When layers of snow build up in a mountainous region, their weight may cause the crystals to freeze together into a massive sheet of ice that is too thick to melt during the summer. This is called a glacier. Often, glaciers move very, very slowly downhill, carving out new valleys as they do so.

WHAT IS BLACK ICE?

If roads are already wet when the temperature drops, the water may freeze into a layer of ice. The layer may be so thin that the road is visible underneath and the ice can hardly be seen. This black ice poses a serious problem for drivers, as they may be quite unaware of the danger before they begin to skid.

WHAT IS PERMAFROST?

In the Arctic and Antarctic Circles, there are seasons, but even in summer it is very cold. However, in the Arctic Circle, the top few centimetres of soil may defrost, and the land becomes tundra: an area where sparse vegetation can grow and flower. Beneath this defrosted layer, there is soil that is always frozen and in which nothing can grow. This is called permafrost.

WHAT IS MEANT BY A BALANCED DIET?

Human beings need a certain amount of food each day to supply them with energy. Almost all foods can supply some energy, but our bodies have other requirements as well. In order to make sure that we are taking in everything we need, we should eat a wide variety of foods, with the correct amounts of carbohydrates, fat and protein. A diet that fulfils these requirements is called a balanced diet.

carbohydrates

protein

fruits and vegetables

dairy foods

Nutritionists recommend that we should eat something from each of these food groups every day. Carbohydrates give us energy. Protein is needed to build and repair cells and to keep our bones, muscles, blood and skin healthy. Fruits and vegetables contain energy and a wide range of essential vitamins and minerals. Dairy foods contain protein and calcium for healthy bones and teeth.

WHERE DOES DIGESTION BEGIN?

DIGESTION begins as soon as we put food in our mouths. Saliva starts to digest the carbohydrates in the food as we chew it. Chewing breaks the food up into small pieces that can pass easily down the oesophagus and into the stomach, where powerful acids begin to digest proteins and kill harmful bacteria. The stomach is not still. Its muscular walls churn the food into a thick, soupy consistency.

Saliva begins to flow when we see or even think about food. Making food look appetizing is a first step towards good digestion.

WHAT ARE VITAMINS?

VITAMINS are chemicals that we need to stay healthy. They are referred to by the letters A, B, C and so on. Some of them are stored in the body but others, such as vitamin C, need to be eaten every day.

WHY WERE SAILORS ONCE GIVEN LIME JUICE TO DRINK?

IN THE DAYS of sailing ships, sailors could be at sea for months on end. Fresh fruits and vegetables, containing vitamin C, could not be kept fresh for long voyages. As a result of a lack of vitamin C, also known as ascorbic acid, sailors developed a condition called scurvy. This distressing condition caused bleeding gums, weakness and dizziness. In the eighteenth century it was discovered that limes could cure these symptoms.

Although ships began to carry limes in the eighteenth century, it was not until the twentieth century that it was understood that citrus fruits contain vitamin C, and that this vitamin is effective against scurvy.

HOW DOES HUMAN DIGESTION WORK?
....

THE FOOD that we eat travels slowly through our bodies, a journey of up to ten metres (nearly eleven yards), taking about two days. As it passes through the various stages of our digestive system, chemicals called enzymes act on the food to make different parts of it useful to the body. Anything that cannot be used is passed out when we go to the toilet.

HOW DOES FOOD MOVE THROUGH THE DIGESTIVE SYSTEM?
....

IT IS NOT GRAVITY that causes food to move through the long tube that is our digestive tract. In fact, even if you stood on your head, food would still move through your oesophagus and intestines. Muscles in the walls of these organs squeeze and release rhythmically to move the partly digested food along.

oesophagus

gall bladder

liver

duodenum

large intestine

ileum

appendix

stomach

small intestine

rectum

fast facts

WHY ARE SOME PEOPLE FATTER THAN OTHERS?
....

If we take in more energy from our food than we use, it is stored as fat. However, people naturally have different body shapes, and two people of very different builds may both be entirely healthy.

WHY IS DIETARY FIBRE IMPORTANT?
....

Dietary fibre is found in the tough parts of seeds, fruits and vegetables that are not broken down and digested. It is useful because it sweeps through the digestive system like a broom, preventing blockages.

WIICH MINERALS DO HUMANS NEED?
....

As well as vitamins, we need tiny amounts of minerals in our food. These include iron, for making red blood cells, and calcium for healthy bones and teeth.

WHY SHOULD BANANAS NOT BE STORED WITH OTHER FRUIT?
....

Ripe bananas give off a gas that causes other fruit to ripen rapidly and then rot.

WHY DO NEWBORN BABIES ONLY DRINK MILK?
....

The best food for a newborn baby is its mother's milk, which contains just the right amounts of the nutrients needed, all in a form that is easily digestible. Babies' digestive systems are not sufficiently developed to deal with other foods until they are about four months old.

WHAT IS AN RDA?
....

RDA stands for Recommended Daily Allowance. It is used to describe the quantity of vitamins and minerals that should be eaten each day to maintain good health.

WHY IS IRON AN IMPORTANT METAL?

Iron is the most widely used of all metals. It is cheap and very strong, so it can be used to make the supports for huge buildings and bridges. The Industrial Revolution would not have been possible without iron to make the machinery used in new factories. Today most iron is made into steel, a metal that can be used for a wider variety of purposes than any other metal on Earth.

WHAT IS SMELTING?

SMELTING is what is known as a reduction reaction. It is a method of extracting iron from iron ore. Iron ore, or haematite, is a rock that contains iron and oxygen. The process of smelting takes place in a blast furnace, where iron ore, limestone and coke (a form of carbon) are heated together while hot air is blasted into the furnace. The carbon in the coke reacts with the oxygen in the air to form carbon monoxide. This is turn takes oxygen from the iron ore, leaving behind iron mixed with a little carbon.

WHERE IS THE BIGGEST IRON MOLECULE IN THE WORLD?

SO IMPORTANT was the metal-working industry of Belgium that a building in Brussels called the Atomium was made in the shape of a molecule of iron – magnified two billion times!

The blast furnace gets its name from the hot air that is blasted into it. The air reacts with the carbon to form carbon monoxide, which reacts with the oxygen in the ore, leaving the iron behind.

Iron ore, coke and limestone are fed into the blast furnace.

The temperature inside the furnace reaches 2000°C (3450°F).

A waste material called slag is produced as the limestone reacts with impurities in the ore.

WHAT IS STEEL?

STEEL IS AN ALLOY of iron and carbon. Iron extracted from iron ore contains about 4% carbon and some other impurities. The carbon makes it hard but weakens it. Removing some of the carbon and other impurities in an oxygen furnace produces steel.

Molten iron and scrap steel are placed in an oxygen furnace called a converter.

A jet of oxygen is blasted into the converter. The oxygen reacts with most of the carbon to form carbon monoxide.

The furnace tips to pour the molten steel into a ladle.

WHAT IS MADE FROM STEEL?

A HUGE RANGE of items can be made from steel, from tiny paperclips to huge girders forming the frames for skyscrapers. One useful property of steel is that it can be recycled and used over and over again.

Alloys of steel, in which steel is combined with other metals, can be very useful. Railway tracks are often made of an alloy of steel and manganese.

Cutlery can be made from stainless steel. Unlike other metals, it will not rust or react with acids in foods.

Most screws, nails, nuts and bolts are made of steel. The thread of a screw can be given a sharp edge that is strong enough to drive through wood and other materials.

The huge cranes that make modern construction possible are made of steel. They are capable of carrying enormous weights, including the steel girders that form the skeleton of many new buildings.

Inside the dome of the Capitol, in Washington DC, there are massive cast-iron girders supporting the stone cladding.

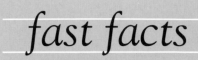
WHO WAS HENRY BESSEMER?

Henry Bessemer was a British scientist who, in 1856, invented a cheap method of extracting most of the carbon from iron ore in a blast furnace. The methods used today are still based on his process.

WHAT IS CAST IRON?

Cast iron is iron that has been poured into a mould while still in a molten state.

WHAT IS STAINLESS STEEL?

Stainless steel contains small amounts of nickel and chromium to make a metal that does not corrode.

WHEN WAS THE IRON AGE?

Although people probably learned how to work iron over 6000 years ago, the period known as the Iron Age relates to the centuries after 1000BC, when the technique of smelting spread throughout Europe.

HOW IS WIRE MADE?

To make wire, rolled steel is pulled through a very small hole in a process called drawing.

WHAT IS MEANT BY FORGING?

Forging is a method of shaping hot steel by pressing it between blocks and rollers.

HOW MUCH CARBON IS LEFT IN STEEL?

Low-carbon steel is more malleable than high-carbon steel, but the latter can be shaped to have a sharp cutting edge, used for the blades of knives and industrial guillotines. All steel contains less than 1.7% carbon.

HOW ARE GREAT INVENTIONS MADE?

An invention is a new method, material or machine that applies theoretical principles to a practical use. That does not mean that the inventor necessarily understands why his invention works! Inventions may be the result of hard work, or luck, or both. Very often, it is the name of the person who popularized the new idea that we remember, not the person who first thought of it.

WHAT DID BENJAMIN FRANKLIN RISK HIS LIFE TO DISCOVER?

IN THE EIGHTEENTH CENTURY, wealthy and influential men often interested themselves in more than one branch of learning. The American Benjamin Franklin was a statesman, printer, author and scientist. He left school at twelve, being the fifteenth child of seventeen, but soon made up for his lack of formal education. As well as his political work, he conducted many experiments concerning electricity. In 1752, he flew a kite in a thunderstorm, attaching a metal key to the damp string. An electrical charge ran down the string and Franklin was able to feel it jump to his finger when he approached the key. From this he concluded that lightning was an electrical spark and in 1753 launched his invention of the lightning conductor.

Inventions such as the Spinning Jenny heralded the arrival of the Industrial Revolution, which brought enormous changes to methods of production and the speed of scientific discovery. Modern industry could not have developed as it has without such beginnings.

WHAT WAS THE SPINNING JENNY?

THE SPINNING JENNY was one of the inventions that revolutionized textile production in the eighteenth century. For thousands of years, spinners were able to produce only one thread at a time, using devices such as spinning wheels. Then in 1764, James Hargreaves, an English weaver, invented a machine that could be operated by one person but spin several threads at the same time.

WHY IS GALILEO REMEMBERED?

GALILEO GALILEI (1564–1642) was an Italian scientist who worked on many mechanical problems but is perhaps best known for his astronomical observations. These supported the ideas developed by Nicholas Copernicus (1473–1543), a Polish scientist. He claimed that rather than the Sun orbiting the Earth, the Earth orbits the Sun. This idea went against the teachings of the Church, so Copernicus did not tell many people about it. Indeed, when Galileo spoke out in its support, he was put on trial and forced to withdraw his claim. Even today, scientific discoveries are not always popular when they go against long-held beliefs.

Aristotle (384–322BC) was a Greek thinker who put forward a theory of the universe in which the stars moved in circles around the Earth. These ideas were held for at least another 1800 years, until the work of Copernicus and Galileo began to show people a different view.

HOW DOES SIR EDMOND HALLEY'S NAME LIVE ON?

SIR EDMOND HALLEY'S name is remembered because he was the first person to predict that the comet he saw in 1682 followed a path that would bring it within sight of the Earth again in 1758. Unfortunately, he was no longer alive at that date to see his prediction come true, but his achievement was recognized and his name attached to the comet ever afterwards. In fact, the comet can be seen from Earth every 75–79 years. Its appearance was first recorded by Chinese astronomers in 240BC. The comet, still an unexpected visitor, also appeared in 1066 and was embroidered onto the Bayeux Tapestry, which records the Norman invasion of England.

A comet is a huge, dirty snowball, perhaps with a nucleus of small pieces of rock. Glowing gas or dust reflecting the Sun's light makes up the comet's "tail".

Hundreds of years ago, news about new products travelled very slowly. Today, advertising is aimed at individual markets and ensures that as many people as possible are aware of what is available.

HOW LONG DOES IT TAKE FOR NEW INVENTIONS TO BECOME WIDELY AVAILABLE?

AT ONE TIME tens or even hundreds of years might have passed between a scientist's discovery of a potentially useful fact or method and its use by a wide range of other people. Nowadays, the process is much quicker. This is partly because research is often very expensive and there is pressure to find a commercial use for an invention to help to pay for new research. Modern methods of mass production and global advertising also mean that new products can become popular very quickly.

WHAT DID JOSEPH PRIESTLEY DISCOVER?

IN 1774, the English chemist Joseph Priestley announced that he had discovered an element within the air. Previously it had been thought that air itself was an element. However, Priestley's achievement is an example of something that happens quite frequently in science. Although Priestley undoubtedly did discover the presence of oxygen, he was not the first to do so. A Swedish chemist called Carl Scheele had discovered it some months before, and it was not until some months later that a French chemist, Antoine Lavoisier, used Priestley's work to explain what oxygen is and its importance in respiration and combustion. He also gave oxygen its name. The sharing of scientific knowledge moves our understanding of the world forward. No one person can put together all the pieces of the jigsaw puzzle.

Joseph Priestley is less well known for the fact that he discovered soda water! This is the basis of most fizzy drinks.

WHAT IS THE BIG BANG THEORY?

The Big Bang theory of the beginning of the universe is based on the discovery made in 1929 by Edwin Hubble that the galaxies of the universe are moving apart. The idea is that this movement is still the result of an enormous explosion (the Big Bang) that began the universe billions of years ago.

WHAT DID GREGOR MENDEL DISCOVER?

Mendel (1822–84) showed how an individual's dominant and recessive characteristics are inherited from its parents. This explained why, for example, two white flowers could produce a pink flower.

WHAT IS ARCHIMEDES SAID TO HAVE DISCOVERED IN HIS BATH?

It is said that Archimedes (287–212BC) jumped out of his bath one day and ran naked through the streets, shouting "Eureka!" ("I've found it!") Whether this story is true or not, Archimedes did find that an object displaces its own weight of water when floating or submerged.

WHEN WERE SPECTACLES FIRST USED?

The first recorded wearing of spectacles to improve sight was in Italy in 1289. No one knows who made this very useful invention, but Ibn-al-Haytham, an Arab physicist, was investigating the properties of lenses as early as AD1000.

WHEN WAS GUNPOWDER FIRST USED?

By 1230, the Chinese were using gunpowder in warfare, making bombs to blow up the walls of towns being attacked.

GLOSSARY

Axis   The imaginary line around which a wheel or planet rotates.

Alloy   A mixture of metals, or of metals and non-metals.

Barcode   A pattern of lines, which represent numbers and can be read by a light pen or scanner using lasers.

Bit   The end piece of a drill that turns or vibrates at high speed to bore into rock, wood or metal.

Characteristic   A distinctive or typical feature of a material or person.

Component   A part of a larger machine or system, such as an electrical or electronic circuit.

Constituent   A part of something, such as one of the elements in a compound.

Deflection   A bend, turn or deviation in a light beam or the path of a moving object.

Dominant   When describing a characteristic shown by a living thing, an inherited feature that is shown although it has only been inherited from one parent. The gene inherited from the other parent that affects this part of the organism is carried, but not shown.

Efficiency   When used of a machine, the amount of useful work done compared with the amount of energy or heat supplied to the machine.

Experiment   A procedure designed to test whether an idea (hypothesis) about why or how something happens is true.

Extraction   Removing a metal or other substance from the mixture of elements in which it is found in nature.

Guillotine   A powerful cutting machine, using a sharp blade, named after a Doctor Guillotin, who recommended using a beheading machine for executions during the French Revolution.

Hologram   A three-dimensional image created using beams of laser light.

Indentation   A cut, notch or hollow in a flat surface or angle.

Lubricant   A substance, usually oil or grease, that is used to reduce friction between moving parts.

Nucleus (nuclei)   The central part of a cell, which controls what it does, or the central part of an atom, containing protons and neutrons.

Ozone   A gas with molecules made of three oxygen atoms, found in a layer of the Earth's atmosphere.

Philosopher   A person who uses reason and argument to discover what is real and true.

Pressure   A force being exerted on an object or material. Atmospheric pressure, for example, is the force exerted by the Earth's atmosphere on the planet and everything on it.

Prism   A shaped material, through which light can pass. A prism usually has a triangular cross-section.

Recessive   A term describing a characteristic that is inherited from one parent but not shown. However, it can be passed on to offspring.

Refraction   The change in direction of a beam of light passing from one material to another, such as from air to water.

Saturation   The condition of a solution when it can dissolve no more of a solute.

Soldering   Joining together metal parts by causing another molten metal to solidify between them.

Supersonic   Moving faster than the speed of sound.

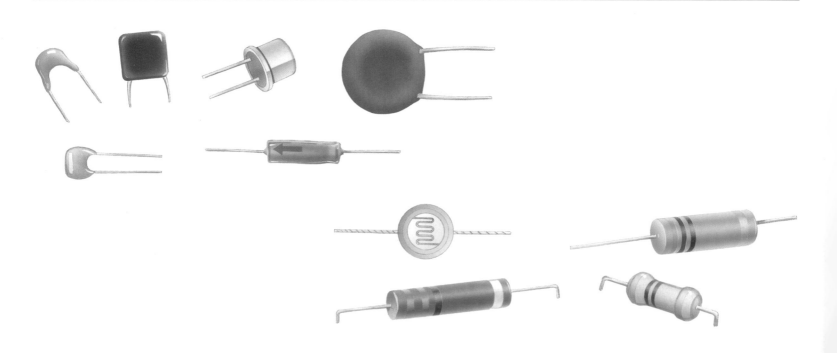

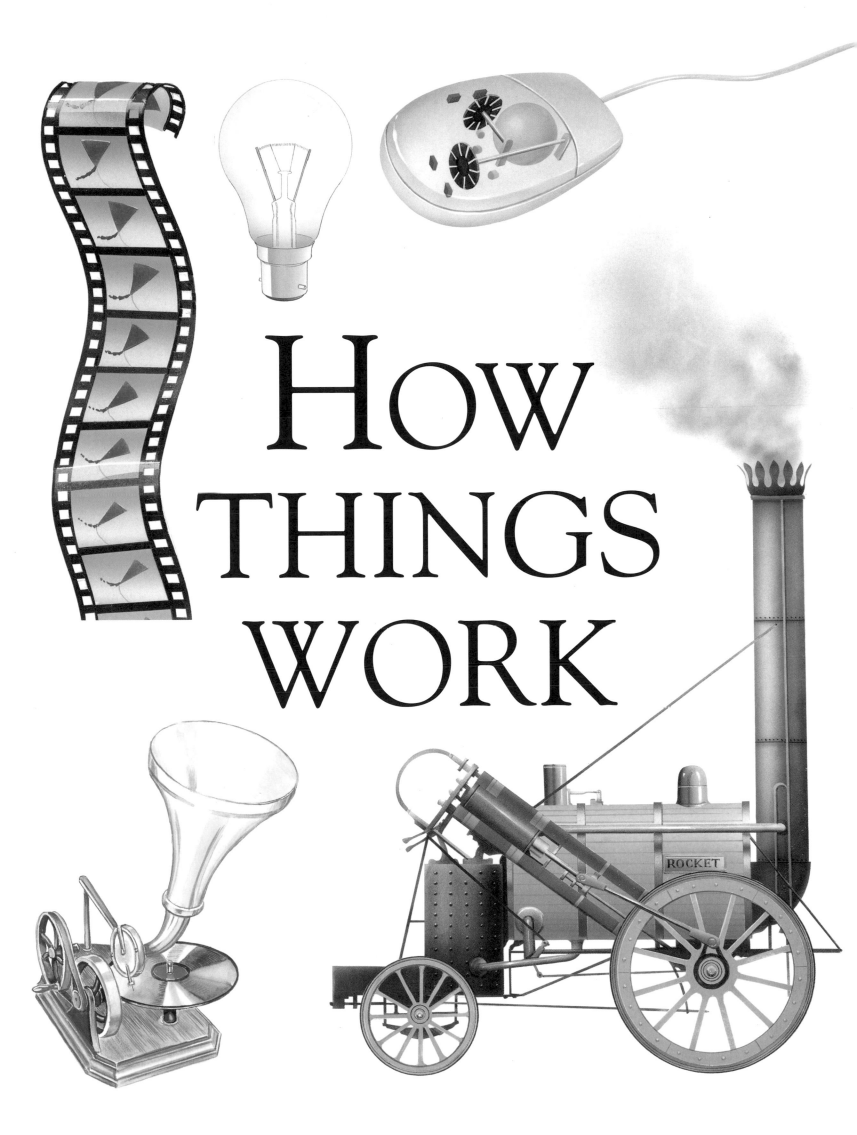

HOW THINGS WORK

WHAT ARE THE SYSTEMS OF THE HUMAN BODY?

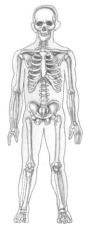

The central nervous system includes the brain and the nerves that carry messages to and from it.

Our bodies are very complicated. It is impossible to think about all the processes that are going on inside them at the same time, so doctors often consider the body as being made up of several different systems, each one with different organs and mechanisms working together to perform particular functions.

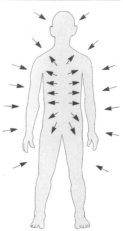

The immune system enables the body to fight off disease and illness and to remain healthy.

The skeletal system is the framework that supports and protects the soft parts of the body.

The muscular system enables the body to move. Muscles contract to cause movement.

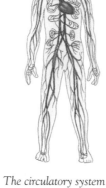

The circulatory system is concerned with the way in which blood flows around the body.

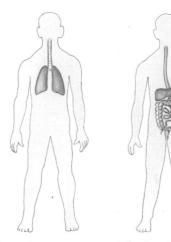

The respiratory system works to supply the body with the oxygen it needs from the air we breathe.

The digestive system enables us to absorb nutrients from what we eat and drink.

The reproductive system differs in males and females, allowing new humans to be born.

HOW DOES THE BRAIN WORK?

THERE IS MUCH that we do not yet know about how the brain works, but we do know that the brain communicates with the rest of the body through a thick cord of nerves running down the middle of the spine and branching off to reach the limbs and internal organs. The nerves are pathways for messages *to* the brain, to inform it about what is happening elsewhere in the body, and *from* the brain to tell the rest of the body how to act. These messages, and the processes happening within the brain, are made up of tiny electrical impulses. By far the largest part of the brain is the cerebrum, which is divided into two halves, called hemispheres. The rest of the brain is made up of the cerebellum, the pons and the medulla, which join together at the top of the spinal cord.

One very important function of the brain is memory, without which we would all be like tiny babies. Repetition seems to help the brain to memorize things. These dancers have probably repeated their actions over and over again.

HOW MUCH FOOD DO WE NEED?

FOOD IS THE FUEL that our bodies need for movement. But we also need some fuel simply to maintain all the parts of our bodies. Individual cells are being renewed all the time. And even if we do not move the *outside* of our bodies at all, there are many parts *inside* that are constantly in motion. How much food we need depends on our size, age, gender and level of activity.

Food energy is measured in kilojoules (kJ) or kilocalories (kcal). Until puberty, boys and girls need the same amount of food energy, but after that boys tend to need more. Of course, every person has different requirements, and a more active person will always require more food than an inactive one.

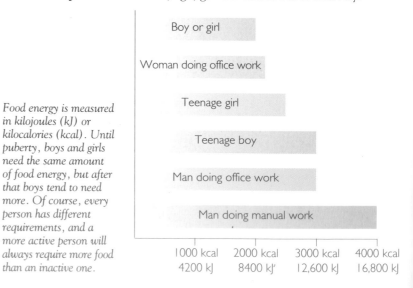

Boy or girl

Woman doing office work

Teenage girl

Teenage boy

Man doing office work

Man doing manual work

| 1000 kcal | 2000 kcal | 3000 kcal | 4000 kcal |
| 4200 kJ | 8400 kJ | 12,600 kJ | 16,800 kJ |

HOW MANY MUSCLES DO WE HAVE?

THERE ARE more than 600 muscles in the human body. Over 100 of these are in our faces, which is why we can have so many different expressions. Although we can perform a great variety of movements, each muscle can only do one thing: contract. That is why muscles often work in pairs, so that one muscle can move a part of the body in one direction, while its partner can move it back again. Perhaps the most important muscle in the human body is the heart, which is contracting and relaxing all the time to pump blood around the body.

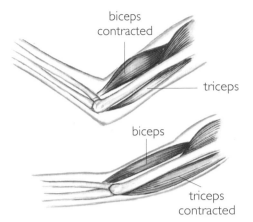

Two muscles work together in our upper arms. When the biceps muscle contracts, the forearm is lifted. When the triceps muscle contracts, the forearm is lowered again.

Once almost everyone did manual work of some kind. It was essential for survival. Human bodies were not designed for the sedentary lives many of us now lead. That is why exercise is important for good health.

HAVE HUMAN BODIES CHANGED THROUGH THE CENTURIES?

OVER MILLIONS OF YEARS, evolution is changing the way humans look. Over a shorter period, improved nutrition and medical discoveries have meant that people in some parts of the world today are generally bigger and stronger than their ancestors. But we are also losing some abilities that no longer seem useful. The smallest toe, for example, can no longer be moved independently by most people. As recently as Roman times, some people may have been able to "prick up their ears", moving them slightly towards sounds as some animals can.

WHAT IS THE DIFFERENCE BETWEEN VEINS AND ARTERIES?

VEINS ARE BLOOD VESSELS that carry blood to the heart, while arteries carry it from the heart. The heart acts as a pump, pushing blood to every part of the body. Adults have between five and six litres (between nine and ten pints) of blood. As well as containing red cells to carry oxygen to the body's organs, blood also plays an important part in fighting infection. White blood cells attack and digest harmful bacteria, while platelets in the blood form clots so that wounds can heal and no further infection can enter the body.

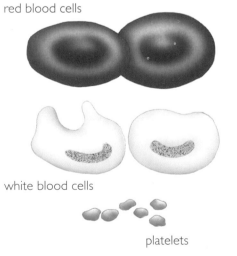

The three kinds of blood cell are carried in a yellowish liquid called plasma. Plasma is 90% water.

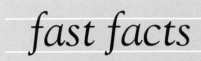

WHICH IS THE MOST WIDELY SPOKEN LANGUAGE?

Languages are living things, changing all the time to meet the needs of their speakers and writers. It is only in the last few hundred years that attempts have been made to standardize the way in which languages are used, so that people using the same language can understand each other as well as possible. In the world today, Mandarin Chinese is the most widely used language, with over a billion speakers. English is next, with around half a billion speakers.

Chinese characters can be very complicated, with up to 26 strokes in each. The Japanese have adapted over two thousand characters to write their language, but they also have two alphabets, one for Japanese words and one for foreign words!

Perhaps the nearest thing we have to a universal language is road signs!

DO ALL LANGUAGES HAVE ALPHABETS?

ALPHABETS consist of letters that represent sounds. By writing different combinations of letters, all the sounds in a language can be represented. The first alphabet was probably developed by the Phoenicians before 1500BC. Even if they use the same letter forms, not all languages have the same number of letters in their alphabets. English, for example, uses 26 letters to write all its sounds, but Italian uses just 21, with j, k, w, x and y seen only in foreign words. However, the most widely spoken language of all, Chinese, does not use an alphabet. Instead, it has over 50,000 characters, each representing a word or part of a word.

ARE ALL LANGUAGES RELATED?

NOT ALL LANGUAGES are related, but they do seem to form related groups. Most languages that were originally European, some of which are now spoken all over the world, are thought to have developed from an ancient and unknown language that linguists know as "Proto Indo-European".

IS THERE A UNIVERSAL LANGUAGE?

MANY PEOPLE have dreamed of a world in which everyone speaks the same language. Some international jobs use one language to avoid dangerous misunderstandings. However, even gestures can be misunderstood, as a shake of the head can mean "yes" in some countries and "no" in others!

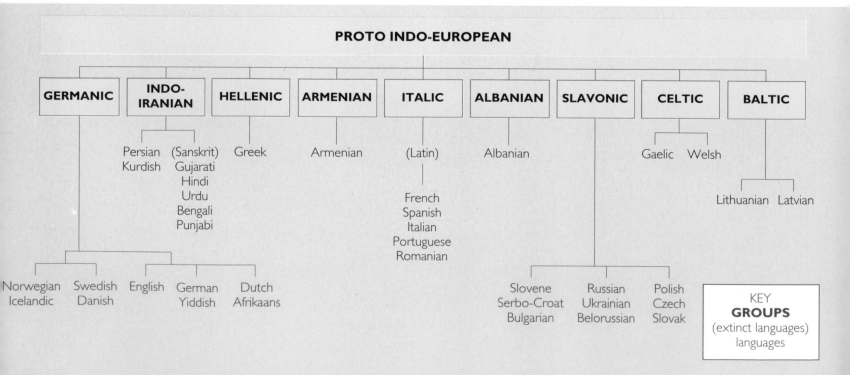

PROTO INDO-EUROPEAN

GERMANIC	INDO-IRANIAN	HELLENIC	ARMENIAN	ITALIC	ALBANIAN	SLAVONIC	CELTIC	BALTIC

Persian
Kurdish

(Sanskrit)
Gujarati
Hindi
Urdu
Bengali
Punjabi

Greek

Armenian

(Latin)

French
Spanish
Italian
Portuguese
Romanian

Albanian

Gaelic   Welsh

Lithuanian   Latvian

Norwegian   Swedish   English   German   Dutch
Icelandic   Danish   Yiddish   Afrikaans

Slovene
Serbo-Croat
Bulgarian

Russian
Ukrainian
Belorussian

Polish
Czech
Slovak

KEY
GROUPS
(extinct languages)
languages

HOW AND WHY ARE NEW WORDS INVENTED?

LANGUAGES grow and change because they need to. New words are invented when new ideas or articles require a name. Usually, new words are based on earlier ones. When the television was invented, the word chosen to describe it was a combination of an ancient Greek word, meaning "far" and a Latin word to do with "seeing". Sometimes a writer takes delight in inventing words. Lewis Carroll wrote a poem about a creature he called the "Jabberwock", for example.

WHAT IS THE ROSETTA STONE?

THIS STONE was found near Rosetta, in Egypt. On it was an inscription, given three times in three different languages. One of the versions was in Greek, which scholars could read. Another version was in ancient Egyptian hieroglyphs, a kind of picture-writing that no one in modern times had been able to decipher. Given the Greek "key", it became possible to read the hieroglyphs on the stone, and later, thousands of other hieroglyphs carved on monuments and buildings.

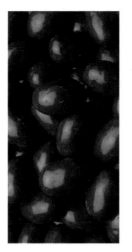

Sometimes a "new" word is simply borrowed from another language. "Chocolate" came into the English language as a version of the word that the Aztecs used to describe a drink made from the cocoa bean. This drink was unknown in Europe until the Spaniards discovered the Aztecs in South America. Once it was known, it had to be named! Borrowing the local name for it was an easy solution.

Until Egyptian hieroglyphs were deciphered, it was not known that most of them represent sounds and syllables, not whole words.

WHEN WAS BRAILLE DEVELOPED?

BRAILLE is a system of writing that uses raised dots, punched into paper or plastic. It enables people with little or no vision to read with their fingers. The system was invented in the first half of the nineteenth century by Louis Braille (1809–52), a Frenchman who had himself been blind since the age of three.

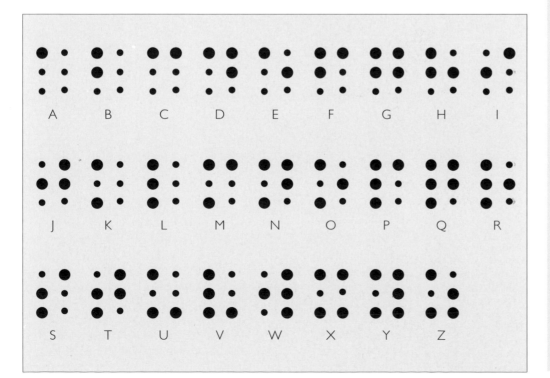

WHAT IS A DIALECT?

A language may have speakers who use different accents, vocabularies and ways of putting words together. Varying forms of the same language are called dialects, especially when they are found in particular regions.

WHICH ARE THE RAREST LANGUAGES?

Usually, when the last person to speak a language dies, the language dies too, even if it has been recorded. Each year, a few languages or dialects disappear for ever. This is specially true at the moment of some native American languages.

CAN ANYONE SPEAK ANY LANGUAGE?

Babies are born with the ability to make the sounds of any language, but as they learn one language, they gradually lose this ability.

WHAT IS ESPERANTO?

Esperanto is a language invented in 1887 by a Polish doctor called Zamenhof. He hoped that it would become a worldwide language.

HOW SOON DO CHILDREN RECOGNIZE THEIR NATIVE LANGUAGE?

Researchers have found that children as young as three months can tell the difference between the language they hear most frequently and other languages or even dialects.

HOW CAN WE TELL HOW ANCIENT LANGUAGES WERE PRONOUNCED?

We cannot be sure how languages of long ago sounded. However, by studying how languages change over time and looking at poetry in the dead languages, it may be possible to make a good guess about how they sounded.

HOW HAVE MODERN COMMUNICATIONS CHANGED OUR LIVES?

Modern communications have affected our lives in numerous ways. Being able to pass information down telephone wires or via satellites means that some people can work from anywhere in the world and still keep in constant touch with their offices. A surgeon in Arizona, via a satellite link, can assist a colleague in Beijing with a complicated operation. News can travel halfway around the world as quickly as it can reach the next town. Perhaps the biggest effect of communications has been to make us all feel that the world is a smaller place, and that we need to be concerned about its future and the futures of people thousands of miles away.

Communication satellites usually circle the Earth in what is called a geostationary orbit. This means that the satellite is always above the same point on the Earth's surface.

HOW MUCH HAS THE SPEED OF COMMUNICATION INCREASED?

ONLY A FEW HUNDRED YEARS ago, the fastest way that a piece of news could travel was to be carried by a person on horseback. Messages sent overseas could only travel as fast as the fastest sailing ship and were at the mercy of the wind and weather. The development of steam locomotives and steamships made it possible for information to move around the world more quickly, but it still had to travel physically from one place to another, as a letter. The breakthrough came with the invention of the electric telegraph and messages in Morse Code. The message was sent down a wire in bursts of electric current. Today, images of written documents, sound recordings or television pictures can be flashed around the globe in less than a second by means of satellites and radio communications.

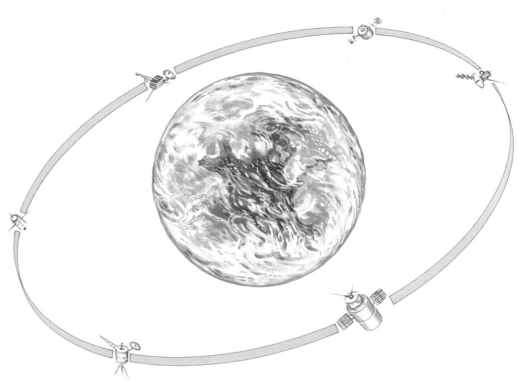

Satellites have different shapes and sizes, depending on the job they have to do. They are launched into orbit around the Earth by rockets. As a result, they are very expensive to put into position. Astronauts are sometimes sent to repair damaged satellites.

HOW DO COMMUNICATION SATELLITES WORK?

THE LAYER of the Earth's atmosphere called the ionosphere can reflect some radio waves back to Earth. This is used for sending messages over fairly short distances, but for messages to travel further across the Earth, the radio signals can be bounced off a satellite, orbiting almost 36,000km (22,000 miles) above the Earth's surface. Several satellites, in different orbits, are required to give coverage over the whole globe, and different satellites are used to reflect signals for different media, such as telephone messages and television pictures.

WHAT IS SEMAPHORE?

SEMAPHORE is a means of signalling using pairs of flags. Different flag positions stand for different letters and numbers. Semaphore signals are useful when the signaller is within sight of the receiver of the message but too far away to call out. It was widely used between ships sailing near each other in the days before ship-to-ship radio.

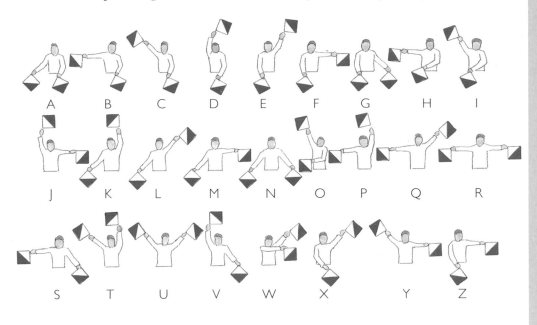

HOW DOES A TELEPHONE WORK?

A TELEPHONE works by sending and receiving electrical signals that represent sounds, including the human voice. When the required number is dialled, a signal passes to the called telephone, causing it to ring, buzz, flash a light, or even vibrate to attract the attention of the person using it. When the telephone is picked up or switched on, a connection is made, and a conversation can take place.

The receiver of the telephone converts the electric current back into sounds by using an electromagnet to make a diaphragm vibrate.

The mouthpiece contains a microphone. Sound vibrations are converted into an electric current which varies as the sounds do.

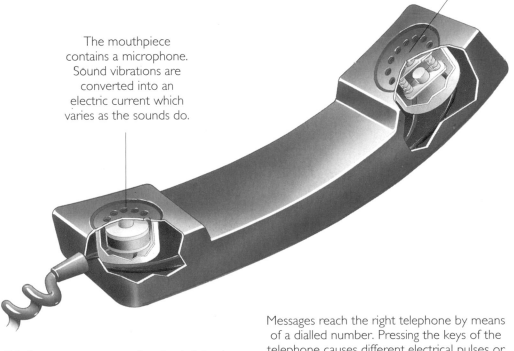

Telephone messages can travel as electrical signals along wires or through the air as radio waves. As signals take time to travel, you may notice a very slight delay in the response of the person being called if they are thousands of miles away.

Messages reach the right telephone by means of a dialled number. Pressing the keys of the telephone causes different electrical pulses or varying tones to pass to electronic equipment at the telephone exchange. This "reads" the pulses or tones and routes the call to the correct area and telephone.

WHY DO SHIPS FLOAT?

Ships float, even if they are made of iron, because their overall density is less than that of the water that supports them. The water displaced (pushed aside) by the hull of the ship pushes back upwards with a force called upthrust or buoyancy. If this is equal to or greater than the force of gravity pulling the ship's mass downwards, the vessel will float. In fact, ships need a certain amount of weight to give them stability in the water, so many of them have hulls weighted with concrete or another kind of ballast. Without it, the ship would bob around on the water like a cork.

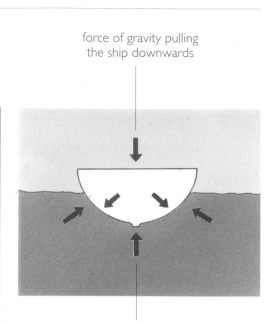

force of gravity pulling the ship downwards

upward force of the displaced water

ARE SHIPS STILL IMPORTANT NOW THAT AIR, ROAD AND RAIL TRAVEL ARE SO MUCH FASTER?

SHIPS are of vital importance to the world's economy. They carry over 90% of the freight that travels around the globe. Although air travel is a quicker way of crossing the oceans, it is very expensive, and weight is always a problem. Ships may be slower, but they can carry enormous loads. Nowadays many loads are carried in large steel containers, which can be stacked on the ship and then lifted by crane directly onto the back of a truck in the port, doing away with the need to pack and unpack cargo at each change of carrier.

Containers protect the goods inside. They can be stored in stacks on the dockside until transferred to a ship, truck or train.

HOW DOES A SUBMARINE SUBMERGE AND SURFACE?

SUBMARINES, unlike most ships, are not always required to float! In order to make a submarine sink beneath the surface, its density must be increased to be greater than that of the water. This is done by taking in water, which fills ballast tanks within the outer hull of the submarine. The amount of water entering can be controlled, so that the vessel sinks slowly. To bring a submarine back to the surface, pumps force the water out of ballast tanks. The submarine's density becomes less than that of the water it is displacing, so it rises.

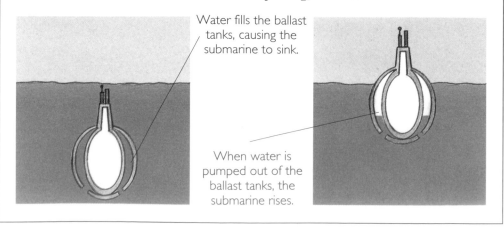

Water fills the ballast tanks, causing the submarine to sink.

When water is pumped out of the ballast tanks, the submarine rises.

WHAT IS A PERISCOPE?

A PERISCOPE is a metal tube that can be extended above the submarine while it is underwater. The tube contains lenses and mirrors, which enable an image of the scene above the surface to be seen below in the submarine. The periscope can swivel, so that a 360° view is obtained.

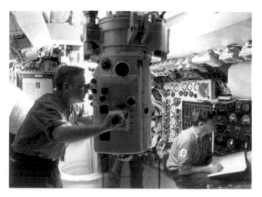

The operator turns the periscope by means of the handles on the side. These fold up when it is not in use, as space is always at a premium in a submarine.

WHY ARE PORT AND STARBOARD SO CALLED?

TRADITIONALLY, the lefthand side of a ship, looking forward, is called the port side, while the righthand side is called the starboard side. The term "starboard" comes from "steerboard". The large oar used to steer early ships was usually on the right. "Port" comes from the fact that ships had to tie up on the left side in port so that their steering oar would not be crushed against the dock.

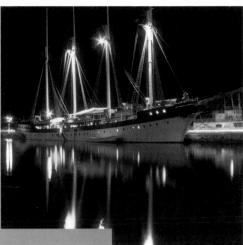

At night, ships show a green light on their starboard side and a red light on their port side.

In a race, it is often the efficiency with which a boat tacks, compared with its competitors, that makes it a winner.

HOW DOES A YACHT TACK?

SAILORS cannot change the direction of the wind, but they are not powerless to change the direction of their sailing boats. By steering a zigzag course, called tacking, they are able to sail in the direction they require. This can be a time-consuming process. It is important that the navigator keeps an accurate check on the boat's position, so that it does not travel too far off course while tacking.

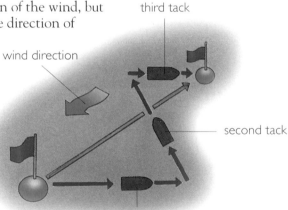

third tack

wind direction

second tack

first tack

WHAT WERE THE FIRST BOATS LIKE?

IT IS LIKELY that the first boats were made of hollowed-out tree trunks. Perhaps early humans saw fallen hollow logs floating along a river and realized that they could carry goods and people. Tree trunks were hollowed using stone axes and fire. A dugout pine canoe, found in the Netherlands, is thought to be at least 8000 years old.

WHICH WAS THE FIRST CAR?

The very first vehicle able to run on the open road was powered by steam. It was a three-wheeled tractor, built in 1769 by a Frenchman, Nicolas Cugnot (1725–1804). However, it was not until the development of the internal combustion engine in the second half of the nineteenth century that motor transport began to be successful. Both Gottlieb Daimler (1834–1900) and Karl Benz (1844–1929) were working on such engines in the 1880s in Germany. It is said that neither knew about the other's work, although they lived less than 100km apart.

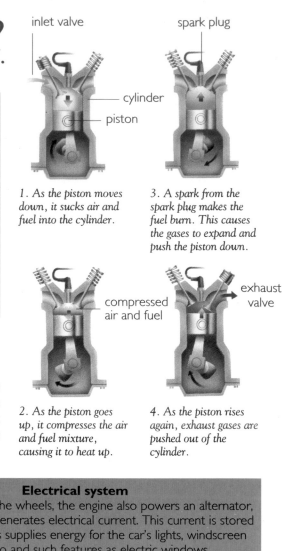

1. As the piston moves down, it sucks air and fuel into the cylinder.

3. A spark from the spark plug makes the fuel burn. This causes the gases to expand and push the piston down.

2. As the piston goes up, it compresses the air and fuel mixture, causing it to heat up.

4. As the piston rises again, exhaust gases are pushed out of the cylinder.

HOW DOES THE INTERNAL COMBUSTION ENGINE WORK?

INTERNAL COMBUSTION ENGINES are usually fuelled by petrol or diesel. This fuel is burnt (combusted) within metal cylinders. The burning fuel causes a piston to move up and down inside each cylinder, and it is this upward and downward movement that is translated into a turning movement by the crankshaft, causing the axles and wheels to turn and the car to move.

WHAT ARE THE MAIN SYSTEMS OF A CAR?

LIKE THE HUMAN BODY, a car can be thought of as having systems with different functions, all working together to make the vehicle operate effectively. The most important systems are shown in the illustration below.

Electrical system
As well as moving the wheels, the engine also powers an alternator, or dynamo, which generates electrical current. This current is stored in the battery. This supplies energy for the car's lights, windscreen wipers, radio and such features as electric windows.

Suspension system
The suspension is a system of springs and shock absorbers that prevents every jolt caused by an uneven road surface being felt by the driver and passengers inside the car.

Transmission system
The transmission system consists of the crankshaft, gears and the differential. This is a system of gears on the axles that allows the wheels to travel at different speeds when going round corners, when the outer wheel travels further than the inner one.

Braking system
Each wheel has a brake unit, connected to the brake pedal by a tube full of brake fluid. Pushing the pedal forces the fluid down the tube, causing a brake shoe to press against a metal disk or drum on the inside of the wheel. Friction causes the wheels to slow and stop.

WHAT IS A CUSTOM CAR?

A CUSTOM CAR is one that has been altered from the manufacturer's original specifications to suit the wishes of its owner. This may involve painting it with extraordinary designs, making the engine more powerful, or even "stretching" it by cutting the entire car in half and inserting additional body parts. Some cars have been made very long indeed by this method. The one below has 26 wheels and contains a swimming pool!

This car was designed by Jay Ohrberg of California, USA. It is over 30m (100ft) long.

HOW DO RACING CAR DRIVERS ACHIEVE HIGH SPEEDS?

FORMULA 1 drivers cannot win races by themselves. Large teams of mechanics and technicians are needed to enable the car to perform well. The driver spends more time testing the car than he does racing, and no aspect of the vehicle is ignored. Even while the car is waiting at the start of a race, special electric heaters are warming the tyres so that they give their best performance. Every second counts in motor racing, so mechanics practise until they can change all four tyres of the car in under three seconds! Controlling the car at high speed puts enormous physical and mental strain on the driver. There is no power steering in Formula 1 cars, so the driver needs great strength and split-second reactions.

Non-professional drivers enjoy competing at many levels of motor racing. Here the actor Paul Newman is preparing to practise for the Daytona 24-hour race.

WHAT IS THE DIFFERENCE BETWEEN A VETERAN CAR AND A VINTAGE CAR?

A VETERAN CAR was made between 1896 and 1903, while a vintage car was built after 1904 and before 1930.

This vintage car is an Austin 7 "Chummy" Tourer, built in 1923.

WHEN WERE SPEED LIMITS INTRODUCED?

Speed limits are almost as old as cars themselves. Early motor vehicles were thought to travel at a dangerous speed, so the first cars in Britain, for example, were required to have a man with a red flag walking in front of them, and had to observe a speed limit of less than 5 miles per hour!

WHAT WAS SPECIAL ABOUT THE MODEL T FORD?

The Model T Ford was the first car to be built on a moving production line. This made the manufacturing process much cheaper and put motor cars within reach of many more people. Henry Ford (1863–1947) began the mass-production of motor cars that continues today.

WHAT IS FOUR-WHEEL DRIVE?

In most modern cars, the engine drives the front wheels of the car. In rear-wheel drive cars, it turns the back axle. In four-wheel drive cars, both axles are driven by the engine, enabling the car to travel powerfully over rough ground.

HOW WILL MOTOR CARS CHANGE IN THE FUTURE?

TWO AREAS of car design have been researched very thoroughly in the past few years. One of these concerns fuel consumption and exhaust gases, as the realization grows that the world's fossil fuels are polluting the atmosphere. The other is safety. It is likely that future cars will be able to prevent some accidents by assessing the distance to an obstacle and taking evasive action without prompting from the driver.

Streamlining helps to save fuel by reducing air resistance. Modern cars tend to have rounded angles and door handles that are flush with the bodywork, as this Chrysler Showcar does.

WHICH WAS THE WORLD'S FIRST PUBLIC RAILWAY?

The first public railway in the world to run a regular service was opened on 27 September 1825. It ran between Stockton and Darlington in the north of England. A steam train called The Locomotion pulled 34 wagons, some of which carried coal, while others were adapted to carry passengers. Both the locomotive and its track were built to the design of George Stephenson (1781–1848). Stephenson's background was in mining engineering. Coal mines had long used tracks to move wagons of coal, and it was with steam engines for these wagons that Stephenson first experimented.

WHAT DO THE NUMBERS BEFORE STEAM TRAIN NAMES MEAN?

STEAM LOCOMOTIVES are described by the arrangement of their leading, driving and trailing wheels. In fact, only the driving wheels are connected to the cylinders that provide the engine's power. So a 2-8-2 has two leading wheels, eight driving wheels and two trailing wheels.

Steam trains are still running scheduled services in some parts of the world. This is a 2-6-2 engine in Sumatra.

WHO INVENTED THE LOCOMOTIVE?

A LOCOMOTIVE is an engine that can travel under its own power, not pulled by horses, for example. But we usually think of it as running on tracks, or tramways, as they were first called. In 1804, Richard Trevithick (1771–1833), an English inventor, designed a train to pull coal wagons in a Welsh colliery. Trevithick was convinced that steam engines had a great future and later travelled to Peru and Costa Rica, where he introduced steam engines into the silver mines.

In 1829, Stephenson built an engine called The Rocket, which won a competition of steam trains called the Rainhill Trials by running at 48km/h (30mph).

fast facts

WHAT WAS THE ORIENT EXPRESS?

Some special trains have gained a romantic image over the years. The Orient Express was a luxurious train running between Paris, France, and Istanbul, Turkey, from 1883. Today, the train still travels over part of this route.

WHAT IS THE LONGEST JOURNEY THAT CAN BE MADE BY TRAIN?

Without changing trains at any point, the longest journey that can be made is 9297km (5777 miles) between Moscow and Vladivostok on the Russian Trans-Siberian line.

WHEN DID RAILWAYS FIRST CROSS THE UNITED STATES?

Railways spread across the world very quickly. In the 1850s, settlers suffered hardship crossing the American continent in wagons. By 1869, the journey could be made by train in relative comfort.

WHAT IS A MONORAIL?

A monorail, as the word suggests, is a railway with only one rail, on which an electric train can run.

WHERE WAS THE FIRST UNDERGROUND RAILWAY BUILT?

THE WORLD'S FIRST city underground railway line was opened in 1863 in London. It was called the Metropolitan.

HOW ARE UNDERGROUND RAILWAYS BUILT UNDER EXISTING CITIES?

BENEATH CITIES are the foundations of large buildings and many pipes carrying water, electricity, gas and telephone cables. Builders have either to tunnel very deeply or to use a technique called "cut-and-cover", which means that they run the railway under existing roads, so that they simply have to dig a huge trench along the road, build the railway, and cover it up again.

WHAT IS THE GAUGE OF A RAILWAY?

THE GAUGE of a railway is the distance between its rails. At one time, the standard gauge in several countries was 1.48m (4ft 10.25in), which was thought to have been the width of Roman chariot tracks. Today, many different gauges are used.

WHAT IS A COWCATCHER?

A COWCATCHER is a V-shaped metal part on the front of a train, designed to push obstacles – including cows! – off the line before the wheels hit them. The American Denver and Rio Grande steam engine below has an example.

HOW DO TRAINS CHANGE TRACKS?

THE INTERSECTIONS that allow a train to move over onto another track are called switches or points. Short pieces of rail are able to move across to bridge the gap between the two tracks, so that the train's wheels cross over as smoothly as possible.

The TGV (Train à Grande Vitesse) of France (left) and the Bullet Train of Japan (below) are two of the fastest trains in the world, aiming to run at 300km/h (186mph) in regular service.

Underground railways help to ease surface congestion in cities around the world. The underground railway in Paris, France, is called the Metro, which is short for Metropolitan, the first underground railway.

HOW DO PLANES FLY?

Aeroplanes fly when two of the four forces acting upon them are greater than the other two. The force of thrust, created by the aeroplane's propellers or jet engines, moves the plane forward. The force of lift is caused by air flowing over the wings. This keeps the plane in the air. The two forces working against thrust and lift are gravity, which pulls the plane towards the Earth, and drag, caused by air resistance, which slows the plane's forward motion.

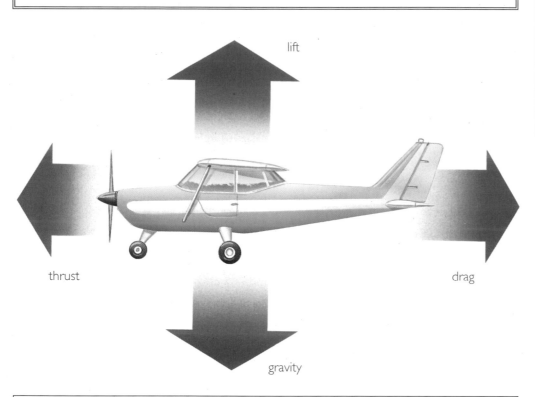

Although they cannot fly in very rough weather, helicopters are extremely useful for rescues at sea, as they can hover over the site of a wreck.

WHY IS A HELICOPTER SO MANOEUVRABLE?

HELICOPTERS have rotor blades above them that are aerofoils. When they turn rapidly, they create lift. The blades are tilted slightly, so that they also provide thrust. The helicopter's tail rotor blades stop the helicopter from spinning and enable it to turn. With this combination of rotors, a helicopter can move in any direction or simply hover. Without long wings, helicopters can manoeuvre in tight places, such as alongside cliff faces, so they are particularly useful for rescue and emergency work.

HOW CAN GLIDERS FLY WITHOUT ENGINES?

GLIDERS are so light that the lift created by their wings can overcome the opposing pull of gravity. However, without engines, gliders cannot take off. There are two widely used methods of launching gliders into the air. They can be catapulted upwards from the ground, or they can be towed up by an aeroplane. The cable between the plane and the glider is then released, and the glider can fly solo. A glider flight is an extraordinary experience, as it is almost silent except for the sound of the wind.

HOW DO AN AEROPLANE'S WINGS CREATE LIFT?

THE SHAPE of all parts of a plane is important, as the more streamlined it is, the less air resistance will cause drag to slow the plane. But the form of the wings is particularly important. The wings of most planes are shaped so that the upper surface is more curved than the lower surface. As the diagram shows, this affects the way in which air moves over them. The air travelling over the upper surface of the wing has further to travel and therefore moves faster than that passing under the wing. This creates an area of lower pressure above the wing, which sucks the wing upwards, creating the force of lift.

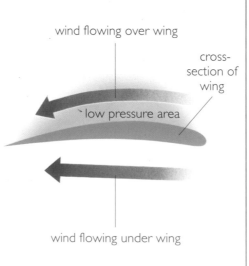

The shape of an aeroplane's wing is called an aerofoil.

HOW DO AIR TRAFFIC CONTROLLERS COMMUNICATE WITH PILOTS?

AIR TRAFFIC CONTROLLERS have screens on which they can see the planes in their sector. It is their job to see that planes are kept safely apart and guided appropriately during take-off and landing. When aeroplanes are near enough, the air traffic controllers can speak to them directly, but they cannot be expected to speak all the languages of international pilots. For this reason, to make communications as safe and clear as possible, all instructions and discussions take place in English all over the world.

Air traffic controllers use an aircraft's registration mark when calling it by radio. As one letter can sound rather like another, words are used instead, each one standing for the letter that begins it.

A Alpha	H Hotel	O Oscar	V Victor
B Bravo	I India	P Papa	W Whisky
C Charlie	J Juliet	Q Quebec	X X-Ray
D Delta	K Kilo	R Romeo	Y Yankee
E Echo	L Lima	S Sierra	Z Zulu
F Foxtrot	M Mike	T Tango	
G Golf	N November	U Uniform	

WHAT IS AN AIRSHIP?

AN AIRSHIP is a cigar-shaped balloon, filled with a gas. Nowadays, this is usually helium, as it cannot catch fire, unlike the hydrogen used in earlier airships. Beneath the balloon, a cabin (often called a gondola) and engines are suspended. In the 1930s, the Germans developed airships called Zeppelins, although the tragic crash of the Hindenburg in the USA in 1937 really spelled the end of the age of the airship.

Today's airships are usually built for publicity purposes rather than as passenger carriers.

This is a 1939 Piper J-3 Cub, flying over Clear Lake, California, USA.

WHICH PLANES CAN LAND ON WATER?

SEAPLANES and flying boats have floats instead of wheels, so that they can land on water. In the 1930s, flying boats were often larger and more luxurious than ordinary aircraft, as they could be made larger without the expense of creating longer runways at airports around the world. Instead, they took off and landed at sea, taxiing in and out of existing harbours.

fast facts

WHICH PLANE CAN AVOID RADAR DETECTION?

Small planes may be able to avoid radar detection by flying very low, but the Northrop B2 Stealth bomber is made of special materials that can absorb radar, while its "flying wing" shape also helps it to avoid detection.

WHEN WAS THE FIRST AEROPLANE FLIGHT?

On 17 December 1903, Orville Wright took off in a plane called the Flyer and travelled 37m (121ft) – only just over half the length of a modern Boeing 747. Orville Wright had designed and built the plane with his brother Wilbur.

WHAT DOES A FLIGHT RECORDER RECORD?

A flight recorder is an electronic recording device contained in a waterproof and fireproof box. It records the plane's speed, height and direction, as well as the conversations of the crew with each other and with ground control. If the plane crashes, the flight recorder can give vital information that will help to save lives in the future.

HOW DO PLANES REFUEL WITHOUT LANDING?

Sometimes planes need to refuel in mid-air. Perhaps they are crossing an ocean or enemy territory. In this case, by very skilful manoeuvring, it is possible for another plane to transfer fuel through a flexible pipe. This is a difficult and potentially dangerous operation.

WHY DOES A ROCKET HAVE STAGES?

A rocket needs enormous power to escape from the Earth's gravity. The velocity required to achieve this is called the escape velocity, which is about 49,000km/h (29,000mph). The rocket's power comes from burning liquid hydrogen and oxygen. Each stage of a rocket is a fuel tank, which is jettisoned when its fuel is used up. After all, carrying an empty fuel tank will only use up more fuel. Only the top stage of the rocket, called the payload, makes the whole journey and brings the crew back to Earth.

A crew of up to eight people has to train for several months to become familiar with the controls in the shuttle's cockpit.

HOW CAN THE SPACE SHUTTLE BE USED OVER AND OVER AGAIN?

AT LIFT-OFF, the space shuttle has two rocket boosters. These are jettisoned when the shuttle reaches a height of 43km (27 miles). The shuttle usually remains in orbit around the Earth for about seven days, although it can continue for 30 days. When it returns to Earth, the shuttle lands on a runway, in a similar way to an ordinary aircraft. The rocket boosters are reattached to it, so that it is ready for another mission.

HOW DO ASTRONAUTS MOVE OUTSIDE THE SHUTTLE?

ASTRONAUTS outside the shuttle are encumbered by a heavy spacesuit, but this is not really a problem in weightless conditions. Controlled movement is more difficult, however. Astronauts wear a unit called a manned manoeuvring unit (MMU) on their backs. This is fuelled by nitrogen and is rechargeable in the shuttle. Several small thrusters allow the astronaut to move in all directions.

WHAT IS THE SPACE SHUTTLE USED FOR?

THE SPACE SHUTTLE has many uses and, because it is reusable, has made it possible to pursue some space activities that would otherwise have been too expensive. It is used to launch satellites and to make repairs to existing satellites. The shuttle can also be used as a laboratory, in which to carry out experiments that are only possible in zero gravity.

CAN ANY HUMAN STRUCTURE BE SEEN FROM SPACE?

THE GREAT WALL, which stretches for over 3640km (2150 miles) across China, is the only human structure that can be seen from space.

HOW DOES A SPACESUIT WORK?

A SPACESUIT is all that stands between an astronaut on a space walk and the emptiness of space. It must supply all his or her needs. There is no breathable atmosphere in space, so a spacesuit supplies oxygen to the astronaut.

Within the helmet, headphones and a microphone enable the astronaut to communicate with crew members and mission control.

A specially treated dark visor protects the astronaut's eyes from the glare of the Sun, while lights can illuminate dark areas.

A camera may be fixed to the astronaut's shoulder, so that other crew members and the ground crew can watch what is being done.

All the joins in the spacesuit must be absolutely airtight. Inside, the spacesuit is pressurized, like a deep-sea diver's suit.

The temperature, pressure and oxygen levels inside the suit are monitored by a control pack on the astronaut's front or back.

Under the outer suit, a body suit contains pipes through which cool liquid flows to protect the astronaut from the heat of the Sun.

The visor and outer layer of the spacesuit must be tough enough not to be torn or cracked by tiny meteorites that may bounce off the astronaut.

Suits are made of artificial materials that offer maximum protection, such as nylon, Kevlar and Dacron.

The astronaut is completely sealed within his or her suit, so urine is collected inside for disposal later!

On Earth, a spacesuit can be as difficult to walk in as a suit of armour, but in the weightlessness of space, the pull of gravity is not a consideration.

fast facts

HOW DO ASTRONAUTS SLEEP IN ZERO GRAVITY?

In order to prevent themselves floating around as they sleep, astronauts have to strap themselves down. Of course, it is important that everything else in the cabin is also firmly fixed.

WHO WAS THE FIRST PERSON IN SPACE?

The Russian cosmonaut Yuri Alekseyevich Gagarin was the first person to travel into space on 12 April 1961 in *Vostok 1*.

WHAT WAS THE SPACE RACE?

In the 1960s and 70s, both the USA and the USSR were investing considerable resources in space exploration at a time when tension between the two countries was high. Their endeavours to outdo each other in outer space were known as the space race. Today, Russian cosmonauts and American astronauts work together on international projects.

WHAT HAPPENS TO SPACE PROBES WHEN THEIR TASK IS DONE?

Most space probes are sent out with a particular job in mind, such as taking photographs or testing the atmosphere of a certain planet. But when this is done, those that have not landed on a planet's surface simply travel on through space. The American probe *Pioneer 10*, for example, sent to Jupiter on 2 March 1972, was still sending back signals from outside our Solar System 25 years later.

WHO WAS THE FIRST MAN ON THE MOON?

Neil Armstrong became the first man to step onto the Moon on 20 July 1969.

WHO WERE THE FIRST GREAT ROAD-BUILDERS?

From the earliest times, humans and animals have created track-ways along well-used routes, but it was the Romans who were the first to set about road-building in a systematic manner. The Roman Empire stretched from North Africa to Scotland. In order to govern successfully, the occupying forces needed to be able to reach trouble spots quickly. Roman roads were built so that armies could march rapidly for hundreds of miles.

Medieval bridges often used arches for support and had shops built along them to catch the passing trade of travellers who had no option but to cross the bridge.

An arch bridge uses the strength of an arch for support, although the roadway itself is usually straight.

A top level of paving stones gave a smooth surface for carts and marching armies.

Roman roads were made in layers. First the route was cleared of large stones and boulders. Then the bed of the road was levelled with sand.

The Romans tried to build straight roads as far as possible. Straight roads were easier to march along and reduced the risk of ambush, as the view was clear in both directions.

Rubble and crushed stone were rammed down on top of the sand.

Drainage ditches beside the road kept it dry.

A bascule bridge has two sections that can be opened so that shipping can pass through.

Suspension bridges have towers from which steel cables stretch to support the bridge beneath.

WHAT ARE THE DIFFERENT KINDS OF BRIDGES?

THE EARLIEST BRIDGES were probably tree trunks across streams or flat slabs of rock. Gradually, people learned to span wider rivers and ravines by supporting the bridge in the middle. Since then, engineers have devised ways of spanning very wide distances.

Beam bridges usually have fairly short spans. Today they are often supported by concrete piers.

WHEN WAS THE HEYDAY OF CANAL-BUILDING?

FOR THOUSANDS OF YEARS, people have transported heavy goods along waterways. The first canals were probably built to join existing navigable rivers. In the fifteenth century, the Aztec city of Tenochtitlan had a sophisticated series of canals, providing transport for goods and people. Venice, in Italy, although a smaller city, was also built on a system of canals rather than roads. However, the golden age of canal-building probably came with the Industrial Revolution, when there was an enormous need for cheap and easy ways to carry the goods made in factories to the nearest port. Canal boats, powered at first by a horse on the towpath and later by coal-fired steam engines, could carry enormous loads much more conveniently than horsedrawn carts on bumpy roads.

In England, barges and narrowboats were often brightly painted with patterns and scenes from life on the canals.

HOW DO CANALS CLIMB HILLS?

WATER, left to its own devices, always flows from its highest point to its lowest, until the two points are on the same level. If a canal sloped as it climbed a hill, its water would simply flow to the bottom. One solution is to bore a tunnel through the hill, so that the canal can continue on a level course, but sometimes this is too costly or geologically impossible. Building locks can solve this problem.

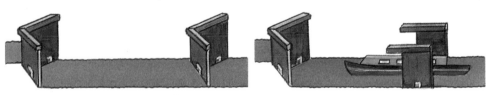

A lock consists of two gates across the canal, with mechanisms for opening them on the towpath.

To climb to a higher level of the canal, a boat enters the first lock gate, which is closed behind it.

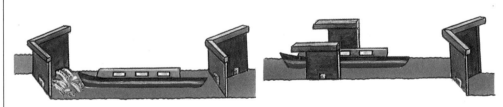

Paddles in the second lock gate are opened so that water can flow in, gradually raising the level of water in the lock.

When the water ahead is level with that in the lock, the gates are opened and the boat can move on.

ARE ROAD SIGNS INTERNATIONAL?

ALTHOUGH ROAD SIGNS do differ across the world, many rely on pictures and symbols rather than words. These are often faster for the motorist to recognize, and avoid some language problems for international travellers.

Whatever language a traveller understands, this sign is very clear.

HOW IS PAPER MADE?

Paper is made from plant fibres. These are very tiny cellulose tubes that make up the stem or leaves of a plant. The fibres are mixed with water and then poured onto a mesh, so that the water can drain through, leaving the fibres behind. The mat of fibres is rolled and dried until it becomes a strong sheet of paper. Although traditionally paper was made by hand, today it is usually made in one large machine, which takes in the water and fibres at one end and produces reels of paper at the other end.

HOW ARE DIFFERENT PAPERS DESCRIBED?

THERE is no such thing as good or bad paper, just paper that is good or bad for a particular job. Blotting paper needs to be able to absorb ink, for example, while paper for printing must let the ink sit on the surface, so that the printing is crisp and clear. Most paper is described firstly by weight. Paper for a children's picture book might weigh 150 grams per square metre. It is said to be 150gsm paper.

The mixture of water and fibres is called stock. It enters the machine through a pipe.

The stock flows into a breast or flow box. This pours the liquid evenly onto a mesh called the wire. Water drains out through the wire and is collected below.

Heated rollers called drying cylinders help to dry the paper.

A couch roll transfers the wet mat of fibres to a felt blanket, which supports it until it becomes drier.

Calender rolls smooth the surface of the paper.

Press rolls squeeze more water out of the mat of paper.

WHAT DOES A DANDY ROLL DO?

A DANDY ROLL has raised patterns on it. As it presses onto the wet paper at the end of the wire, it leaves impressions called watermarks. If you hold a piece of paper up to the light, you may see a pattern or wording left by a dandy roll.

Coatings may be applied to the paper by a size press.

The paper is wound onto a huge reel.

fast facts

HOW CAN YOU MEASURE A PAPER'S OPACITY?

Nowadays a computer can test how opaque paper is (how difficult it is to see through it). A simpler test is to draw a letter in thick black ink on a piece of paper and then place sheets of the paper to be tested on top of it until the letter can no longer be seen. The fewer sheets needed, the more opaque the paper.

HOW IS PAPER RECYCLED?

It is easy to recycle paper. Old paper is soaked in water and put into a giant liquidizer, to blend it into stock. This is poured into the paper-making machine in the usual way.

WHAT IS PAPIER MÂCHÉ?

Papier mâché is French for "torn paper". Paper is torn or cut into small pieces. These are then pasted in layers over a mould. When the glue and the paper are dry, the mould can be removed and the article decorated. Bowls, boxes and even furniture can be made like this.

WHAT IS THE GRAIN OF A PIECE OF PAPER?

If you try to tear an article out of a newspaper, you will find that it tears in quite a straight line in one direction but not in the other. That is because the movement of the wire causes the fibres to settle in one direction, giving the paper a grain. When paper is printed, it is important that the direction of the grain is known, or the pages will buckle.

WHO INVENTED THE FIRST PAPERMAKING MACHINE?

Louis Robert, a Frenchman, invented a papermaking machine in 1799. Four years later, the Fourdrinier brothers in London developed the idea. Papermaking machines are still called Fourdrinier machines today.

WHAT KIND OF PLANT FIBRE IS USED TO MAKE PAPER?

NOWADAYS most paper is made from specially grown trees. These trees are usually softwoods, grown in the cooler parts of the world where little else can thrive. Fir, pine, spruce, larch and cedar trees are all used. The trees do not have to be very tall or straight, as they do for timber. Almost all parts of the tree, except the bark, can be ground up into fibres for papermaking.

Felled trees are heavy. Where possible, the trunks are floated down a river to the sawmill, where they are ground up into fibres.

HOW IS STRONG CARDBOARD MADE?

CARDBOARD is really just very thick paper. The machine that makes it is slightly different because the card is not wound onto a reel at the end, but cut up into sheets. For making strong, light boxes, corrugated cardboard is often used. This has paper pressed into a ridged shape sandwiched between two outer sheets.

WHERE WAS PAPER FIRST MADE?

PAPER WAS FIRST MADE 2000 years ago in China. It was made from pulped rags and old fishing nets, drained on a sieve made of bamboo! Paper may not immediately seem to be an ideal building material, but it is light and cheap, and allows a certain amount of light to pass through it. It is ideal for use with bamboo, which is also very light. Paper has been used in China and Japan for centuries to make screens and internal sliding walls in houses. Although these are not soundproof, they are very attractive and easily replaced if damaged.

CAN PAPER ONLY BE MADE FROM WOOD FIBRES?

PAPER can be made from almost any kind of plant fibre. In some parts of the world, banana stalks and sugar-cane stems made fine, strong paper. On the whole, the longer the fibres, the stronger the paper.

Paper money is folded, pushed into wallets and pockets, and passed from hand to hand. It needs to be very strong. A special paper is made that may contain cotton fibres (which come from cotton plants) or linen fibres (from flax plants).

WHEN WAS PRINTING INVENTED?

Printing – producing identical copies of a picture or piece of writing by pressing an inked block onto a surface – was introduced by the Chinese over a thousand years ago. However, the breakthrough of movable type, which meant that a new block could be made up from existing pieces of type, without having to carve it from scratch, was developed in 1438 by Johannes Gutenberg, in Germany. This was still a fairly slow, manual method, although much faster than the alternative of writing documents out by hand. It was not until the invention of steam and, later, electrical machinery to power the presses that documents could be printed rapidly on a large scale.

HOW MANY COLOURS ARE USED IN COLOUR PRINTING?

HOWEVER COLOURFUL a page in a book may be, it is probably made up of only four colours. Tiny dots of yellow, blue, red and black inks are used to print the page. The dots are so small that they cannot usually be seen with the naked eye. Instead, they "mix" visually to form all the colours on the final page.

WHAT IS REGISTRATION?

THE PAGE to be printed passes between inked rollers or plates four times, each time with a different coloured ink being used. In order to make sure that the final image is clear and sharp, the four printings must line up exactly on top of each other. This is known as registration. Registration marks, at the corners of a page, help the printer to position the images accurately. You may have seen a strip of coloured shapes on the edge of a printed food packet. These also enable the printer to see at a glance if the four printings have been properly positioned.

Registration marks normally fall outside the main printed area. When the pages are trimmed to their final size, the marks are cut off.

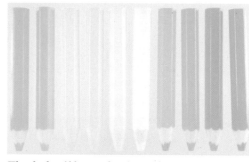

A photograph is scanned to separate the image into a piece of film for each of the four "process" colours.

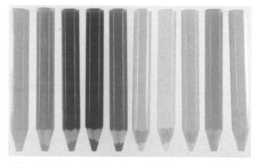

The shade of blue used in four-colour printing is called cyan.

The red ink is a pinkish colour called magenta. Brighter reds are created when magenta is added to yellow.

Black ink gives a deeper black than mixing the three other colours and gives crisper black type.

When the four colour separations are printed one on top of the other, a full-colour picture is produced.

HOW ARE DIFFERENT TONES OF COLOUR PRINTED?

SOME PRINTED IMAGES use one solid colour. These words are printed in solid black ink, for example. The dots are so close together that no background colour shows through. Using increasingly widely spaced dots creates the impression of paler tones of grey.

100% cyan   50% cyan   30% cyan   10% cyan

The tone of a colour being printed is described by the percentage of paper that is covered with ink.

WHAT IS A TYPEFACE?

A TYPEFACE is an alphabet that has been specially designed for printing. It can usually be used in a variety of sizes and styles. The typeface chosen has a huge effect on how a printed page looks. Some typefaces are designed to be easy to read. Others are meant to catch the eye in headings and titles. Today, computers make it easy to manipulate type, **stretching it** or squashing it, for example, to create special effects. It is also easy to adapt typefaces or create your own. Each set of letters, numbers and symbols in a typeface is called a font.

WHY CAN THE NUMBER OF PAGES IN A BOOK USUALLY BE DIVIDED EXACTLY BY 16?

PAGES IN A BOOK are not printed one by one. They are printed on huge sheets of paper that then pass through another machine to be folded. When the book is bound (put into its cover), the edges of the pages are cut on a guillotine. A piece of paper folded in half creates four pages. Larger sheets of paper are folded to make 16, 32 or even 64 pages.

HOW IS A HARDBACK BOOK COVER MADE?

GLUEING, sewing or stapling pages together and placing them within a cover is called binding. Several pieces of card and paper are required to bind a hardback book. It is also possible to add bookmark ribbons and little pieces of fabric called headbands at the top and bottom of the spine (back) of the book.

Pieces of card are glued to a printed cover paper, the edges of which are folded over.

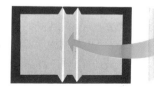

The book block is placed in the cover (or case).

Endpapers – the first and last pages of the book block or separate pieces of paper – are glued down to hold the book block in place.

WHY ARE THE EVEN-NUMBERED PAGES OF A BOOK ALWAYS ON THE LEFT?

Any leaf of a book has two sides (two pages). The first lefthand page of a book is the second side of the first righthand page. If that is page 1, then its other side must be page 2, and every other lefthand page in the book will have an even number.

WHAT DO RECTO AND VERSO MEAN?

A recto page is the righthand page of a book, wherever it is opened. If that page is turned, its other side is known as the verso. So this is a recto page, and page 152 is its verso.

WHAT IS A SERIF?

Some typefaces, such as this one, have little strokes, called serifs, at the ends of some letters. The typeface used in this book for labels to pictures has no strokes and is called a sans serif (without serifs) typeface.

WHAT ARE PROOFS?

Before thousands of copies of a book or magazine are printed, the publisher needs to be sure that everything is right. A few copies of the pages, called proofs, are printed on a special press so that they can be checked before a larger press gets to work on the bulk of the copies.

WHAT IS A CO-EDITION?

Printing presses are massive machines. It takes a long time to get them ready to print, and that time has to be paid for. The more copies that are printed, the cheaper each one is, as the cost of making ready the machine is divided between them. By changing the black plate halfway through a job, a version of the pages in another language can be printed, without the cost of making the presses ready again. This is called a co-edition.

WHAT IS A TEXTILE?

The word "textile" may be used to describe any woven material, or, more broadly, any cloth. Most fabrics are made from threads. These may be looped or passed under and over each other to create a firm cloth, or they may simply be matted together to form a kind of felt. There are thousands of different kinds of textile, each with its own properties and uses.

WHERE DO FIBRES FOR TEXTILES COME FROM?

AT ONE TIME, fibres for textiles came from either plants or animals. The former included cotton from the cotton plant and linen from flax, but also coarser fibres for rope, sacking and matting, such as hemp, jute, sisal and even coconut fibres. Animal-based fibres have been spun from the coats of sheep, goats, camels, llamas and, by real enthusiasts, dogs! Nowadays, there are also artificial fibres, spun from mixtures of chemicals. By mixing different fibres together, it is possible to make fabrics for every purpose.

Spun threads are twisted together for strength, forming yarn of different thicknesses.

WHAT IS SPINNING?

THREADS from plants and animals are usually not more than a few centimetres long. To make a long, strong thread for weaving or knitting, they must be spun. A carding machine combs the fibres so that they are all lying in the same direction and form a loose rope. This rope is then gently drawn out into a thinner thread and twisted into yarn.

These loose ropes of cotton fibres are called slivers. They will gradually be pulled into a thinner rope, called roving, before being twisted into thread. Years ago, this process was done by hand, using a spinning wheel.

HOW ARE THREADS AND TEXTILES COLOURED?

SUBSTANCES called dyes are used to colour threads and textiles. In the past, natural dyes were used, made mainly from plants. Onion skins, for example, give a soft, reddish colour. Most natural dyes fade gradually when washed or exposed to light, which can be very attractive. Many people like the faded colour of denim jeans, for example, dyed with a natural plant-based dye called indigo. Modern chemical dyes do not fade so easily. They give strong, bright colours. Either skeins of thread or finished fabrics may be dyed by passing them through a dye bath, then fixing the dye with other chemicals and drying the result.

Dyed thread may be wound onto small reels for sewing at home, or huge reels for use on powerful industrial weaving, knitting or sewing machines.

WHAT IS THE DIFFERENCE BETWEEN KNITTING AND WEAVING?

BOTH KNITTING AND WEAVING are methods of making threads into cloth, but knitting involves looping one long thread together, while weaving usually involves passing threads lying in one direction over and under threads lying at right angles to them.

In handweaving, the loom holds the lengthways threads (warp), while the weaver passes a shuttle, carrying the crossways thread (weft) between them. The finished fabric cannot be wider than the weaver's outstretched arms.

Threads in woven fabrics can be crisscrossed in hundreds of different ways to add texture to the cloth.

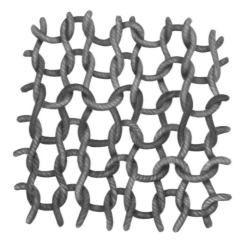

It is not only woollen jumpers that are knitted. The fabric that T-shirts are made from is knitted cotton.

HOW ARE FABRICS PATTERNED?

THERE ARE TWO main ways of patterning fabrics. By using coloured threads in the knitting or weaving, patterns can be made in the fabric itself. This is a very easy way to create stripes and checks, and it is quite cheap to use lots of colours, so the resulting fabric can be very bright. Another method of patterning fabric is to print it, using special dyes. This may be done by big rollers or by squeezing dye through patterned screens. Since only one colour can be printed at a time, each additional colour adds to the cost.

When threads of different colours pass under and over each other, it is as if the colours mix. Here black and cream threads combine to make a grey colour.

WHAT IS SILK MADE FROM?

NATURAL SILK is spun as a thread by silk-worms. They use it to form a cocoon. Unlike other natural threads, the silk-worm's thread is very long – up to one kilometre (0.62 miles). Traditionally made in Asia, silk was such a sought-after textile that the route from Europe to the East became known as the Great Silk Road.

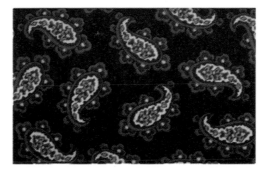

The curved shapes on this printed fabric are described as paisley, after a town in Scotland, although this was originally an Indian design.

HOW LONG DOES IT TAKE TO SHEAR A SHEEP?

IN 1957, a New Zealander sheared a sheep in just 47 seconds!

Expert shearers can remove the fleece from hundreds of sheep in a day.

WHO WAS THE FIRST PHOTOGRAPHER?

The first person to take a photograph was a Frenchman, Joseph Nicéphore Niepce, in 1822. However, as is often the case with new inventions, many other scientists had been experimenting with light, lenses and light-sensitive chemicals. Working with Niepce was a man called Louis Daguerre, who later improved on Niepce's process. Some early photographs were called daguerreotypes.

HOW DOES A CAMERA WORK?

A CAMERA is a lightproof box containing light-sensitive film. To take a picture, the photographer presses a button to open a shutter and let light pass through the aperture, a hole in the front of the camera. The camera's lens focuses the light so that it forms a sharp image on the photographic film, just as the lenses in our eyes focus the light onto our retinas. Then the shutter closes again so that no more light reaches the film. The whole process usually takes just a fraction of a second.

viewer

sprocket holes guide the film through the camera

lens

image focused on light-sensitive film

mirror

When the camera is not in use, a lens cap stops dirt and grit from getting onto the lens.

HOW IS FILM DEVELOPED?

AFTER AN IMAGE has been recorded on light-sensitive film in a camera, the film is moved along, so that the next photograph will be taken on a fresh piece of film. No more light must hit the exposed film until it is developed, or the picture would be spoiled. When all the photographs on a roll of film have been taken, the film is wound into its case, which is lightproof. The development process then takes place in a darkroom, or in a specially made machine.

The film is taken out of its case and immersed in a chemical solution that develops the image.

After rinsing, the film is bathed in more chemicals to fix the image onto the film.

A final rinse and the film is dried. The image is negative: dark areas look light and vice versa.

HOW ARE FILMS PRINTED?

PRINTING converts the negative image of the film into a positive image on paper. Light is shone through the film onto light-sensitive paper. Passing the light through lenses makes the image larger. The print is then developed and fixed just as the film was.

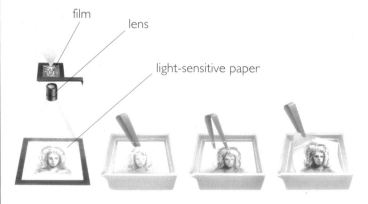
film

lens

light-sensitive paper

HOW CAN PHOTOGRAPHS BE MADE TO MOVE?

MOVING PICTURES, or movies, do not really have moving images at all. They are simply a series of still photographs, shown rapidly one after the other. Our brains are not able to distinguish the individual images at that speed, so we see what appears to be a moving picture.

HOW CAN LENSES CHANGE OUR VIEW?

THE WAY in which we see the world has been greatly influenced by photography. We are used to seeing printed images that we could never see with our naked eyes, either because they happen too fast, or because a special camera lens has allowed an extraordinary view to be taken.

Macrophotography is a way of photographing very small objects by using special macro lenses. Used for both still and moving pictures, macrophotography has transformed our knowledge of the way that tiny living things, such as insects, behave.

These Chicago skyscrapers do not really lean so alarmingly, but by using a special lens, the photographer has been able to emphasize the way in which the massive buildings tower over the church in the foreground of the picture.

Once only wealthy people could have pictures of themselves, painted by an artist. Now most people have family photographs. Before photography, we could only see mirror images of ourselves in a looking glass. Now we can see ourselves as others see us.

fast facts

WHERE DOES THE WORD "CINEMA" COME FROM?

"Cinema" (or "kinema" as it was originally) comes from a Greek word meaning "movement".

WHY DO CARRIAGE WHEELS APPEAR TO GO BACKWARDS IN MOVIES?

As the carriage moves forward, the spokes of its wheels go round, but a movie is just a series of still pictures. Because we cannot distinguish between the different spokes, it can appear that the same spoke is seen in a slightly earlier position each time, when in fact it is simply another spoke that has moved forward that is being seen.

HOW DOES COLOUR FILM WORK?

Colour film has three layers, each sensitive to blue, green or red light. When colour film is processed, the layers are coloured with yellow, magenta and cyan dyes to produce the full-colour image.

WHAT IS A POLAROID CAMERA?

A Polaroid camera uses special film that can develop itself. When the picture has been taken, chemicals are released onto the film, and the final image appears within a minute.

WHICH WAS THE FIRST MOVIE TO HAVE ITS OWN SOUND TRACK?

Full-length movies were silent until 1927, when *The Jazz Singer* was released by Warner Brothers.

WHERE IS BOLLYWOOD?

Just as the movie industry of the United States is based in Hollywood, California, the thriving movie industry of India is centred on Bombay, nicknamed "Bollywood".

WHEN WERE RADIO WAVES FIRST USED TO SEND A MESSAGE?

Although several scientists, including Heinrich Hertz, experimented with sending and receiving radio waves, the first person to patent a useful system for using them to send signals through the air was an Italian engineer called Gugliemo Marconi (1874–1937) in 1896. He created enormous publicity for his work by claiming to have sent the first radio signal across the Atlantic in 1901. Today there is disagreement about whether such a signal was received, but Marconi was right that sending radio messages between Europe and the Americas was possible, and his work encouraged the enthusiasm for and development of radio communications that continues to this day. As Marconi's messages did not pass through wires, the system was known as wireless telegraphy.

A	• —	S	• • •
B	— • • •	T	—
C	— • — •	U	• • —
D	— • •	V	• • • —
E	•	W	• — —
F	• • — •	X	— • • —
G	— — •	Y	— • — —
H	• • • •	Z	— — • •
I	• •		
J	• — — —	1	• — — — —
K	— • —	2	• • — — —
L	• — • •	3	• • • — —
M	— —	4	• • • • —
N	— •	5	• • • • •
O	— — —	6	— • • • •
P	• — — •	7	— — • • •
Q	— — • —	8	— — — • •
R	• — •	9	— — — — •

WHY WAS MORSE CODE INVENTED?

MORSE CODE was ideal for sending messages by telegraph because it used only two kinds of signal: a long one, called a dash, and a short one, called a dot. By sending long and short bursts of radio waves along a wire, a transmitter could send a clear message. Samuel Morse (1791–1872) was an American engineer who invented a practical magnetic telegraph. His invention was more or less ignored on both sides of the Atlantic, until, in 1843, the United States government allotted 30,000 dollars for a telegraph line between Washington and Baltimore. Morse invented Morse Code for use on his telegraph, which became very successful.

WHY HAVE RADIO MESSAGES BEEN BEAMED INTO SPACE?

NO ONE KNOWS if we are alone in the universe. In order to try to make contact with other intelligent life forms in our galaxy, some laboratories regularly send radio signals out into space. In fact, distant constellations do emit radio waves, but so far they do not seem to have been transmitted intentionally by living creatures. Scientists watch for a regular pattern of signals that might indicate a living transmitter.

WHAT ARE TELECOMMUNICATIONS?

TELECOMMUNICATIONS include sending and receiving messages by radio, television, telephone and fax. They began when the telegraph used electrical pulses, sent down a wire, to send information. Radio waves, electricity, or light can carry telecommunications. As well as a method of carrying the message, telecommunications also require a transmitter, to send the signals, and a receiver.

Modern telecommunications make it possible for people all over the world to make contact with each other, however remote their locations.

HOW DOES A TELEVISION SHOW PICTURES?

TELEVISION TECHNOLOGY uses electric signals through cables or ultra-high frequency (UHF) radio waves to transmit pictures and sound to a television set, which acts as a receiver. The signals come into the television through a cable or an aerial. The picture signals are divided into three – one each for red, green and blue. In the television, there is an electron gun for each colour, which fires electron beams (also known as cathode rays) onto the screen. The screen is covered with chemicals called phosphors. The electron beams scan rapidly across the screen, causing tiny dots of phosphors to glow red, green and blue. Viewed with normal vision, from a distance, the dots blur into a full-colour picture.

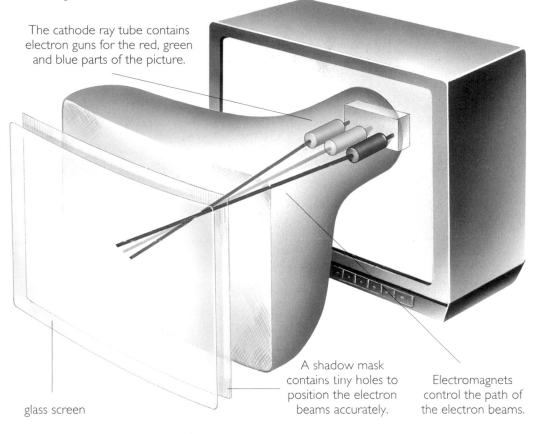

The cathode ray tube contains electron guns for the red, green and blue parts of the picture.

glass screen

A shadow mask contains tiny holes to position the electron beams accurately.

Electromagnets control the path of the electron beams.

HOW CAN RADIOS HELP NATURALISTS?

BY PUTTING COLLARS with radio transmitters onto wild animals, naturalists have been able to track their movements, night and day, adding enormously to our knowledge of animal behaviour. The collars do not interfere with the animals' normal lives. As well as learning about animal migrations and hunting patterns, naturalists are also able to discover more about the life span of animals in the wild, which may differ enormously from that of those kept in zoos and wildlife parks.

Polar bears can be fiercely protective of their young, and the conditions of the Arctic in winter make it difficult for naturalists to follow their movements. A harmless tranquillizer is used to send the animal to sleep while a transmitting collar is fitted.

HOW DOES A VIDEO RECORDER WORK?

A VIDEO RECORDER stores television sound and pictures on a magnetic tape. It receives the electric signal that comes through a cable or aerial into the machine, then records it on tape in much the same way as a tape recorder does, although the video recorder makes diagonal tracks so that more information can be held on the tape. A record–replay head in the video recorder enables the information on tape to be sent to a television set.

CAN SENDERS OF MORSE CODE BE ANONYMOUS?

Of course, the receiver of a message in Morse Code may be thousands of miles away from its sender, so he or she may not be sure who is pressing the Morse key. But when sending Morse manually, everyone has his or her own style and rhythm. An experienced Morse receiver can often recognize the sender by the way the message is sent, just as we may recognize the sender of a letter by his or her handwriting.

HOW DO RADIO WAVES ACT AS BABYSITTERS?

Many parents with small children use baby alarms. These transmit radio signals of the sounds a child makes to a receiving radio in another room or even a nearby home. They can help to reassure a parent that a child is still sleeping while they are out of hearing range.

WHAT IS CLOSED-CIRCUIT TELEVISION?

Closed-circuit television, which is most commonly used for security purposes, is a system in which the television pictures travel directly from the camera taking them to a screen. This does not mean that they cannot be stored. The pictures can be captured on videotape in the normal way.

Videotape has many uses in sport. For example, it may be used for an "action replay", to check what really happened in a fast-moving sport. Athletes are also able to study videotape in order to see where they are making errors and so improve their technique.

WHAT WAS THE EARLIEST SOUND RECORDING?

In 1877, the American inventor Thomas Edison (1847–1931) experimented with a machine called a "phonograph", which converted sound vibrations into grooves on a cylinder covered with tinfoil. A sharp needle, called a stylus, was attached to a diaphragm at the narrow end of a large horn. When sound waves travelled into the horn, they made the diaphragm vibrate, causing the needle to move up and down, and cutting a groove of varying depth in the tinfoil. If this process was reversed, so that the needle was made to run over the grooves, it caused the diaphragm to vibrate. Vibrations passed through the horn, pushing air in front of them, to reach the listener's ear as sound. Later, wax-coated cylinders were used instead of tinfoil, to give a better result.

HOW DOES A CASSETTE TAPE RECORD AND PLAY?

DISCS were the main method of recording and playing music for the first half of the twentieth century, but sound recording on steel tape was used in the 1930s by radio stations. In 1935, two German companies developed a strong plastic tape, which had a layer of iron oxide on the surface. This invention eventually made it possible for smaller, domestic tape recorders to come into use. In 1963, Philips introduced something they called a "compact cassette", which contained a thin tape within a plastic case. This was much lighter and more convenient for home use.

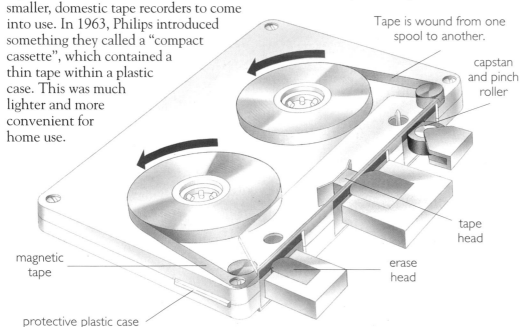

Tape is wound from one spool to another.

capstan and pinch roller

tape head

magnetic tape

erase head

protective plastic case

On blank magnetic tape, the magnetized particles are all facing in the same direction. Electrical signals created by recorded sounds cause the magnetized particles to move into patterns that match the sound signal. When the tape is played, the head "reads" the magnetized particles and creates electrical signals to match them, which are relayed to a loudspeaker to be played. In order to wipe the recording from the tape, all that needs to happen is for the tape to be passed through a strong magnetic field, which lines up the magnetized particles once more.

WHO INVENTED THE GRAMOPHONE?

In 1888, the German-American inventor Emile Berliner (1851–1929) invented a system of sound recording that could be mass produced. He devised a flat disc, called a gramophone record. On the disc, a groove ran in a spiral from the outer edge of the disc to the centre. Side-to-side, rather than up-and-down movements of the stylus recorded and played the sound vibrations. Once one disc had been made, it could be used as a mould to make a metal die, which could then stamp out exact copies of the disc in large numbers.

In the second half of the twentieth century, magnetic tape has been an important storage medium for sound and computerized information. Today compact discs and other recording methods are taking over.

HOW DOES A COMPACT DISC WORK?

A COMPACT DISC (CD) has a plastic surface on which sounds are stored in binary code as very small holes, called pits, and flat areas, called lands. These can be "read" by a laser beam. The laser beam scans across the surface of the disc. When the light falls on a pit, it is scattered, but when it falls on a land, it is reflected back to a light-sensitive detector. This in turn causes a pulse of current to pass to a loudspeaker, which converts it back into sound.

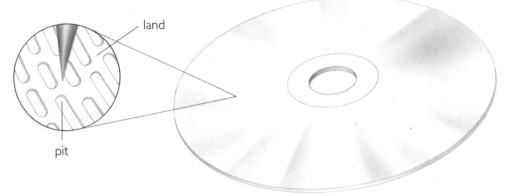

land

pit

As the laser scans the disc, a motor spins the CD round. CDs can be used to store words and pictures as well as sounds. The photographs in this book were stored on compact discs before being used.

HOW DO MICROPHONES WORK?

INSIDE A MICROPHONE is a metal disc, called a diaphragm. When a sound wave hits the sensitive diaphragm, it makes it vibrate at the same frequency. This causes a wire coil, beneath the diaphragm, to move up and down. As the coil comes near to a magnet below, it creates a pulse of electric current in the wire. The pattern of these pulses matches the pattern of the sound wave. The pulses can be sent along a wire to a loudspeaker, to be turned back into sound, or they can be recorded on a tape or compact disc.

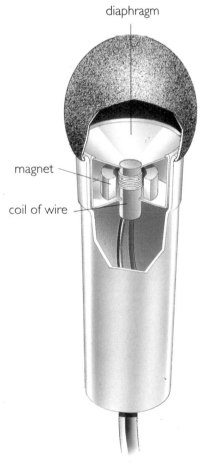

diaphragm

magnet

coil of wire

Microphones and loudspeakers make it possible for huge numbers of people to hear speakers or performers at public events. For actors and singers, very small microphones can now be attached to their faces, near their cheekbones, so that the audience cannot see them at all.

WHY DID SINGERS ONCE PERFORM IN CAVES?

We do not hear our own voices as others hear them, because the sounds pass through flesh and bone to reach our ears. Today singers can hear recordings of their voices, but before sound recording, the only way they could judge their own singing was to perform in a cave and listen to the echo!

HOW CAN RECORDINGS HELP HISTORIANS?

Written records give historians lots of useful information, but do not tell the whole story. Recordings of the voices of ordinary people, recalling their own views and memories, give vivid pictures of the past. Imagine how interesting it would be to hear people from five hundred years ago speaking. In four hundred years time, that will be possible!

WHAT IS SAMPLING?

Sampling involves recording different sounds and then using digital technology to manipulate them, changing pitch, volume, tone and tempo to create special effects.

Face microphones are very useful in musical theatre, where actors have to sing and dance at the same time.

HOW DOES A LOUDSPEAKER PRODUCE SOUND?

A LOUDSPEAKER works like a reversed microphone. Electric current flows into a coil of wire, turning it into an electromagnet. This attracts the coil to another magnet inside the loudspeaker, causing the coil to vibrate. This vibrates a diaphragm at the same frequency as the original sound, pushing air in front of it to carry the sound to the ears of the listeners. Many loudspeakers can be connected together, so that sound is heard all around a large outdoor or indoor space.

DID EARLY BUILDERS HAVE PLANS TO FOLLOW?

For thousands of years, people have been building homes, temples and monuments, but until only a few centuries ago, they had no proper plans to follow before building began. They based their work on tried and tested methods, estimating how strongly walls had to be built to support the floors above and the roof. Of course, many buildings collapsed or subsided, but others are still standing to this day, a tribute to the skill of builders in times past.

HOW WERE THE PYRAMIDS BUILT?

THE EGYPTIANS were building massive pyramids almost 5000 years ago. We are still not sure how they achieved this without the mechanical lifting and cutting equipment that we have today, but the answer must be that they used huge numbers of slaves to shape and haul the enormous stones with which they built. Recently, scientists have calculated that as many as 10,000 slaves were probably needed to work on these structures.

WHAT ARE THE EARLIEST BUILDINGS KNOWN?

THE EARLIEST HUMAN HOMES that we know of are caves. We know that they were inhabited because paintings have been found on the walls, but these homes were not built – they were made by nature, not human beings. The earliest mud and wooden shelters and huts have not survived intact, but from about 2700BC people began to build some of the huge stone structures that have survived to this day. Apart from the Egyptian pyramids, one of the earliest was the circle of stones known as Stonehenge, in England. It is not known exactly what this was for, but it probably had religious significance. Throughout history, religion has spurred builders to create many of the largest and most impressive buildings ever seen.

DO ALL HUMAN SOCIETIES BUILD HOMES?

WHEN PREHISTORIC PEOPLES began to farm, they built settlements. However, some peoples preferred to continue to move about in search of food, following a nomadic lifestyle. Nomads do not need settled homes, but they do need shelter from the weather, so many of them carry tents made of skins or woven fabric. Tents are light to carry and can be put up very quickly.

Some Native Americans made shelters from skins and sticks. A hole in the top let out smoke.

HOW HAVE BUILDING STYLES DEVELOPED THROUGH HISTORY?

ALTHOUGH many traditional building styles are still in use, the appearance of buildings and the way in which they are built changes as outside influences are brought to bear on their architects and builders. Naturally, buildings are based on shapes that give the strongest structures: rectangles, cylinders, triangles and domes. In the search for new forms, architects have often looked back to the past. In the fourteenth century in Italy, for example, designers rediscovered the architecture of ancient Rome and neo-classical ("new" classical) buildings in the subsequent centuries were built all over the world, especially where a building was meant to embody power, learning and dignity. New buildings today still combine recent ideas with traditional motifs.

Doric column   Ionic column   Corinthian column

Classical styles of architecture were divided into orders, of which the Doric, Ionic and Corinthian were three that may still frequently be seen on large houses, churches and public buildings.

fast facts

WHICH ARE THE BEST BUILDING MATERIALS?

On the whole, building materials are not better than one another. Some are simply more suitable in some situations and for some purposes than others. Traditionally, people have built with the materials nearest to hand, using wood in forest areas, mud in dry areas, and bricks where there was clay to make them. The towering structures built today require modern building materials, such as reinforced steel, concrete and glass.

HOW IS CONCRETE REINFORCED?

Used since the 1850s, reinforced concrete has metal bars or wires embedded in it for extra strength.

WHAT WAS A ZIGGURAT?

Ruins of ziggurats can still be seen. They were ancient Mesopotamian stepped towers, with temples on top.

WHAT DO AN ARCHITECT'S PLANS SHOW?

AN ARCHITECT'S plans give all the information needed to build the structure shown. The plans show the materials to be used, how they fit together, and all the measurements necessary to complete the building. Plans usually show several elevations (different views) of the structure, including a floor plan and a plan of each side of the building. Nowadays, computers are increasingly used to draw up plans. They can provide lists of the materials and equipment needed as the plans are drawn, and work out costings.

IS CONCRETE A NEW BUILDING MATERIAL?

CONCRETE is a mixture of sand, water and cement, a powder made of lime and clay. Far from being a new material, concrete was used by the Romans in the first century AD to build the dome of the Pantheon in Rome.

HOW ARE SKYSCRAPERS BUILT?

SKYSCRAPERS have a frame, usually made of steel or concrete, to support the floors and walls, which are attached to the frame. The frame is rather like the skeleton inside a human body. It is not designed to be completely rigid, but to sway a little in high winds, thus reducing the force of the wind upon the structure.

WHAT ARE CERAMICS?

*Ceramics are objects made of materials that are permanently
hardened by being heated. Usually, the word is used to mean articles
made of various forms of clay. Sticky clay is dug from the Earth and
needs to have impurities, such as stones, removed before it can be
used. The clay may be naturally red, yellow, grey or almost white,
but can be coloured before shaping or covered with a coloured glaze.*

WHAT CAN BE MADE FROM CLAY?

CLAY CAN BE USED to make a huge variety of ceramic articles,
from tiny electronic components to bricks and baths. It is a
good insulator and, when covered with a glaze, is completely
waterproof. Unlike many metals, glazed clay is unreactive, so
that acidic foods will not stain it, and exposure to water and the
air will not tarnish or corrode it.

HOW ARE CLAY ARTICLES SHAPED?

CLAY CAN BE SHAPED when it is wet by
squeezing it between the fingers,
"throwing" it on a potter's wheel, or
pushing it into a mould. Before using any
of these methods, the potter must make
sure that there are no air bubbles in the
clay. If there are, the air will expand
when the clay is baked, and the article
may explode, breaking other items in the
kiln as well. However ceramic articles are
produced, they are made a little larger
than the finished product needs to be, as
they shrink slightly when baked.

*A potter's wheel consists of a turntable, powered by a
treadle or motor. The clay is placed (or "thrown")
into the middle of the wheel and shaped with wet
hands or tools as it turns. A skilled potter can make a
perfectly symmetrical pot in this way.*

*Mass-produced items are usually produced by
moulding. A machine called a jolley pushes a piece of
clay into a mug-shaped mould. Then a profiling tool
presses round inside to push the clay against the sides
of the mould and leave the inside of the mug empty.
The handle is added later.*

WHY ARE CERAMICS BAKED?

CERAMICS are baked to make them hard and waterproof. Until they are baked (fired), ceramics can be mixed with water again to form clay. Firing is done in a large oven called a kiln. In large ceramics factories, the kilns are heated all the time. They are like long tunnels, through which ceramics move slowly on trolleys in a never-ending process. The first firing that a clay article receives is called a biscuit firing. It makes the article hard and brittle, but it is still porous. Water can be absorbed by it.

Pots for plants grown outside need to be chosen carefully if the gardener lives in an area that has frosts in the winter. If the pots are too porous, they will absorb a lot of water. If this freezes, it will expand and crack the pot.

This Chinese bowl has intricate patterns painted onto it in coloured glazes. In English, some kinds of pottery are often called "china". This is because fine pottery was first imported from China.

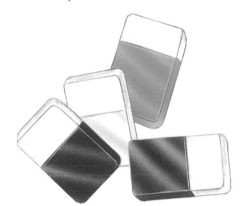

Glazes often change colour in the kiln, so test pieces of clay, dipped in glaze, are fired to make sure that the colour will come out as required.

HOW IS POTTERY DECORATED?

THERE ARE MANY WAYS of decorating pots. They can be dipped in a glaze, made of tiny particles of glass in a liquid, and fired for a second time. The glassy covering melts onto the pottery, making it completely waterproof. Pottery can also be decorated after glazing, with transfers, hand-painted designs, or by screen-printing. It may then be fired for a third time to fix the decoration.

WHAT IS SLIP?

SLIP IS A MIXTURE of clay and water, forming a thick liquid. It can be used as a kind of glue to stick a handle onto a cup when both are "leather hard" (hard enough to handle but still soft enough to cut with a knife). Slip can also be poured into plaster moulds to form intricate shapes. The plaster absorbs water from the slip, causing it to dry on the outside first. If the rest of the slip is poured away, hollow vessels and ornaments can be made.

WHY ARE THERE UNGLAZED PARTS ON THE UNDERSIDE OF A CERAMIC OBJECT?

IN THE HEAT of the kiln, glaze would fuse with the shelf that the object stands on, so glaze is carefully wiped from the base of the object before it is fired.

WHAT IS GLASS MADE OF?

Glass is an extraordinarily useful material. The substances from which it is made are easy to find and very cheap. Glass is mainly melted, cooled sand, but other ingredients are added, such as sodium carbonate (soda ash) and limestone. Although it appears solid to us, glass is in fact a liquid, flowing incredibly slowly. When windows that are hundreds of years old are measured, they are found to be slightly thicker at the bottom than at the top, as the glass very gradually flows downwards.

Coloured glass is made by adding metallic oxides, such as iron, copper, manganese and chromium.

HOW IS PLATE GLASS MADE?

PLATE GLASS is thick, good quality glass made in huge sheets for shop windows. Its very smooth surface is made by floating the molten glass onto a bath of molten tin. Tin melts at a lower temperature than glass, so the glass begins to set on the tin and is then passed over rollers as it finishes cooling. The larger the bath of molten tin, the larger the glass that can be made.

HOW IS GLASS CUT?

HARDENED METAL BLADES can cut glass but are easily blunted. More often, glass is cut with the hardest natural substance known   a diamond. If a furrow is made in glass with a diamond, it will usually break cleanly when pressure is applied to it.

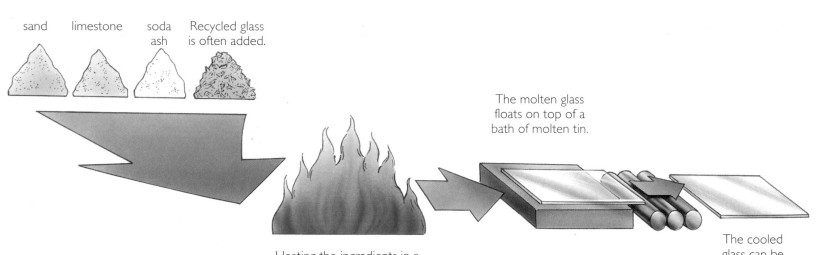

sand limestone soda ash Recycled glass is often added.

The molten glass floats on top of a bath of molten tin.

Heating the ingredients in a furnace makes molten glass.

The cooled glass can be cut into smaller sheets.

HOW IS GLASS BLOWN?

GLASSBLOWERS dip a long tube into molten glass, then blow air into it as it cools, causing the glass to form a bubble. While it is still very warm, this bubble can be shaped, cut with shears, or added to other glass shapes. A slightly different method is used when glassware is made by machine. Then, lumps of hot glass are placed in a mould and air is blown in to force the glass to the sides of the mould. With both methods, the glass can be engraved, or sandblasted to give it a rough texture, after it has cooled.

Sweden is famous for its handblown glass. Here the glassblower is positioning molten glass to be shaped.

The more air that is blown into the glass, the thinner it becomes. Very delicate objects can be made.

HOW ARE STAINED GLASS WINDOWS MADE?

SINCE MEDIEVAL TIMES, glorious decorative windows have been made by joining small pieces of coloured and painted glass together with lead strips. The lead is soft and easy to bend but strong enough to hold the glass.

Stained glass has been popular for centuries. In the days when most people could not read, the stained glass in Christian churches told biblical stories in a way that the congregation could understand. It also meant that no one could look out of the window during lengthy sermons!

HOW WERE WINDOWS MADE BEFORE GLASS WAS WIDELY AVAILABLE?

WINDOWS have three main purposes: to let light into a building, to allow ventilation, and to allow the occupants to see out. Although glass has been made for thousands of years, it is only comparatively recently that techniques have been developed for making large sheets of glass for windows. Before that, although small sheets of glass were available, they were expensive. Small windows were sometimes covered with thin panels of horn. Although this could not be seen through, it did let in a certain amount of light and kept out cold winds.

Buildings dating from the sixteenth century or earlier usually have very small windows, in which little panes of glass can be fitted into wooden frames. Strips of lead may be used to hold them in place.

HOW ARE MIRRORS MADE?

MIRRORS are made by coating the back of a sheet of glass with an alloy of mercury and another metal. This means that light does not pass through the glass, but is bounced back to give a reflection.

As mirrors show us ourselves, they have often been thought of as slightly mysterious, as in the story of Snow White.

This castle has very small windows so that there are few entrances for enemy arrows and bullets. A narrow slit was all that was necessary for the castle's inhabitants to fire on attackers outside. In any case, large windows would have been terribly draughty.

Nowadays we are used to seeing entire buildings covered with glass, but vehicles need windows too. This boat allows tourists an uninterrupted view of Paris, as it travels down the River Seine in France.

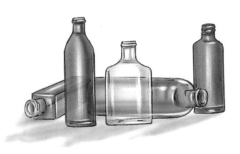

WHY DO WE COOK FOOD?

There are several reasons why food is cooked. Most obvious is the fact that cooking makes food hot! In cold weather, hot food is especially warming and comforting. Cooking also alters the flavour and texture of food. Heat causes chemical reactions to take place, altering the way that the food tastes and feels in our mouths. Because of these chemical reactions, cooking may also make food easier to digest. Finally, cooking can make food safer to eat by killing bacteria within it.

Preservatives extend the life of foods, so that bacteria do not cause them to deteriorate within days or even hours.

HOW DOES YEAST WORK?

YEAST is a single-celled living organism that digests starches and gives off carbon dioxide gas in the process. Bread can be made light and airy by mixing yeast into the flour and water that make up bread dough. The dough is then left to rise in a warm place. The warmth encourages the yeast to give off tiny bubbles of carbon dioxide, which are trapped within the elastic dough. When the dough is put into the oven, some water evaporates from the flour mixture, and the dough becomes firmer, with the tiny bubbles trapped within it.

In a bakery, huge machines mix and knead the dough. Different kinds of flour are used to make different breads, while flavourings, fats and other ingredients may also be added.

Flavourings and flavour enhancers can intensify natural flavours or provide a cheaper way to flavour food.

WHAT MAKES A CAKE RISE?

IN ORDER for a cake to rise and become light and spongy, air has to be trapped inside the mixture, just as it does in bread. Instead of yeast, most cakes contain a raising agent, such as bicarbonate of soda. When it is heated with flour and liquid, chemical reactions take place to produce little bubbles of carbon dioxide, which are then trapped in the mixture as it becomes firm. Another way of incorporating air into cakes is to whisk eggs before adding them to the mixture. The air is trapped in the egg mixture, which becomes firm as it cooks. This method is used in cakes that do not contain fat.

Uncooked cake mixture is a very thick liquid. As it cooks, bubbles form in it, and it expands. This expansion causes the mixture to move upwards (rise) as the baking tin prevents it from expanding in any other direction. As the cake cooks, it becomes solid, taking on the shape of the container in which it is cooked.

Colourings make foods and drinks more enticing. They may replace the colour lost when food is cooked.

Emulsifiers enable fats to be suspended in tiny globules in liquids.

WHY ARE CHEMICALS ADDED TO FOOD?

WHEN WE READ the lists of ingredients on food packaging, they sometimes sound more like a chemistry lesson than a recipe! Nowadays, food safety regulations and the demand of consumers for products with a reliable taste and texture mean that many different additives are found in some foods.

HOW CAN FOODS BE PRESERVED WITHOUT FREEZING?

BACTERIA that cause food to go bad need certain conditions in which to grow. If they are deprived of those conditions, they may die or be unable to reproduce themselves. One thing that bacteria need is water, so drying foods can help to preserve them. Bacteria cannot reproduce at temperatures below 6°C (39°F) or above 37°C (98°F), so making them hot or cold can prevent them from being active. Canning preserves food by sealing it into a can and then heating it to a high temperature, killing off the bacteria inside. As no more bacteria can enter the can, the food is safe for a long time, until the can is opened. High concentrations of salt or sugar prevent bacteria from being able to use available water, as can acids, so foods such as pickles and preserves are cooked and stored in brine (a mixture of salt and water), vinegar or sugar.

WHAT ARE THE BASIC FOOD FLAVOURS?

MOST OF US can recognize hundreds of different flavours if tested blindfold, but food technologists see these as mixtures of four basic flavours: sweetness, sourness, bitterness and saltiness. Flavour receptors on different parts of the tongue are best at sensing these flavours. You can test this for yourself with a little sugar for sweetness, salt for saltiness, vinegar for sourness and squeezed lemon peel for bitterness, but hold your nose as you test so that aromas do not affect your judgment.

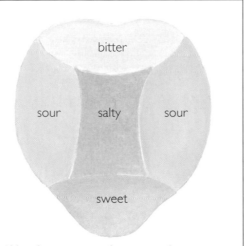

Although our tongues take in taste information, it is our brains that process it.

HOW DOES PACKAGING HELP TO PRESERVE FOOD?

THE MAIN WAY in which packaging helps to preserve food is by preventing bacteria from contaminating its contents, but modern packaging is very sophisticated. Some foods are vacuum packed, so that plastic wrappings exclude any air from the product. Other kinds of packaging are designed to trap gases such as oxygen, nitrogen and carbon dioxide. Mixtures of these help to preserve different foods and to give them a pleasant appearance. Meats, for example, can be kept pink and fresh-looking. Sometimes you will see that meat looks browner where it touches the packaging. This is because the gases cannot reach it at this point. As these are gases that we breathe in every day, they are perfectly safe.

fast facts

DOES FREEZING PREVENT FOODS FROM GOING BAD?

Freezing does not kill the bacteria that cause food to spoil, but it does slow them down so that they are unable to multiply. That means that when a food is defrosted, it will continue to deteriorate at the same rate it would have done if it had not been frozen.

WHAT IS EXTRUSION?

Extrusion is a means of shaping foods by squeezing a mixture through a nozzle and then cooking it quickly so that it retains the shape. Breakfast cereals shaped like hoops or stars are made like this, as is spaghetti and other pasta shapes.

WHAT IS IRRADIATION?

Irradiation is a way of killing the bacteria in food by bombarding it with gamma rays.

WHAT DID LOUIS PASTEUR INVENT?

This French chemist invented a way of making milk safe by heating it. It is not boiled, which would change the flavour, but kept at a high temperature for several minutes. This process is now known as pasteurization.

WHY DO FOODS SOMETIMES SEEM TASTELESS IF YOU HAVE A COLD?

Although we do taste food with the sensitive areas of our tongues, we also use our sense of smell a great deal. Some "flavours" are really aromas. When we have a cold, our sense of smell can be affected, which in turn affects the way our food tastes.

Today's food packaging is often brightly coloured to encourage consumers to buy. But packages also have important nutritional information and a date by which the food should be eaten, while it is still fresh.

WHAT ARE FOSSIL FUELS?

Fossil fuels, which include coal, oil and natural gas, were formed millions of years ago when prehistoric plants and animals died, and their decaying bodies, pressed under layers of rock and earth, became fossilized. Life as we know it would not be possible without fossil fuels. Not only are they burned to supply heat and energy to homes and industry, but by forming the fuel for power stations, they also supply most of the electricity we use. In addition, fossil fuels can be processed to produce many other useful materials, including plastics, dyes and bitumen.

On land, oil is brought up to the surface by a pump called a nodding donkey. It gets its name from the upward and downward motion of its "head".

HOW IS OIL MINED?

THE ROCKS in which deposits of crude (unrefined) oil are found may be hundreds of metres beneath the soil or the sea bed. In either case, a shaft must be drilled down to the deposits. On land, the drill can be set up on a steel structure called a derrick. At sea, a drilling platform is needed. This may have legs that stand on the sea bed or, in very deep water, the drilling platform may float on the surface. Floating platforms must still be anchored firmly to the sea bed so that they can withstand high winds and tempestuous seas.

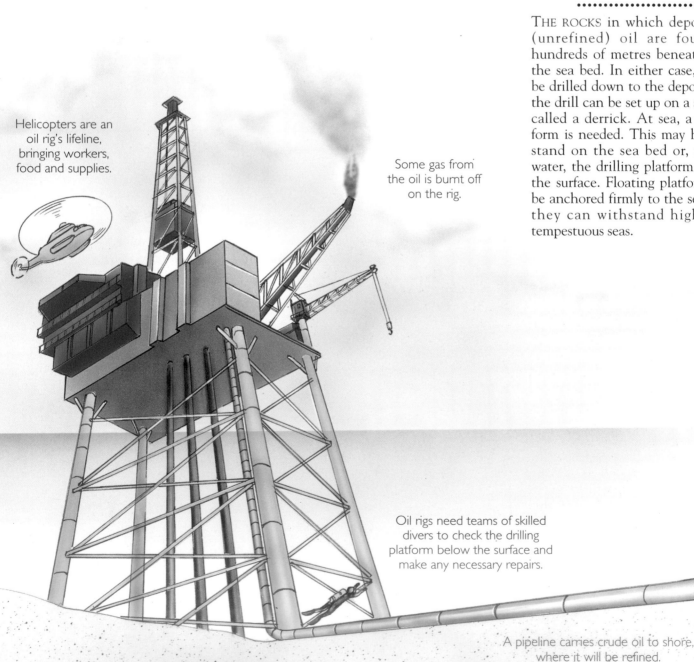

Helicopters are an oil rig's lifeline, bringing workers, food and supplies.

Some gas from the oil is burnt off on the rig.

Oil rigs need teams of skilled divers to check the drilling platform below the surface and make any necessary repairs.

A pipeline carries crude oil to shore, where it will be refined.

HOW IS OIL REFINED?

CRUDE OIL is refined in a process known as fractional distillation. The oil is heated to about 350°C (660°F) and its vapour is piped into a round column, about 50m (165ft) high. Inside the column, there are perforated trays at different levels. The vapour cools as it rises up the column. Different substances within the crude oil condense at different temperatures (and therefore different levels). They are called fractions.

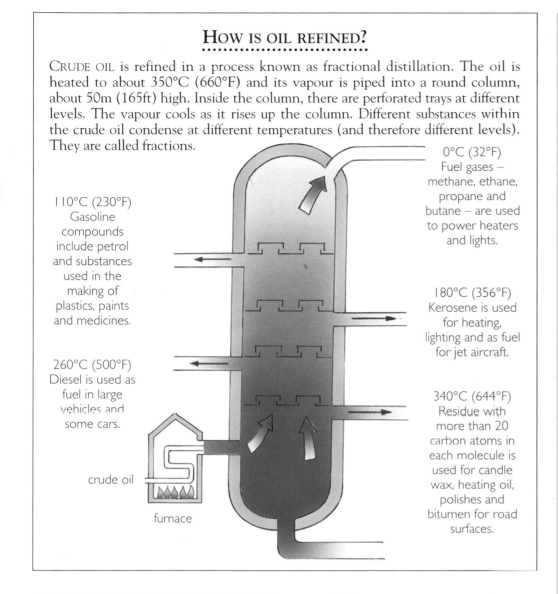

110°C (230°F)
Gasoline compounds include petrol and substances used in the making of plastics, paints and medicines.

260°C (500°F)
Diesel is used as fuel in large vehicles and some cars.

crude oil

furnace

0°C (32°F)
Fuel gases – methane, ethane, propane and butane – are used to power heaters and lights.

180°C (356°F)
Kerosene is used for heating, lighting and as fuel for jet aircraft.

340°C (644°F)
Residue with more than 20 carbon atoms in each molecule is used for candle wax, heating oil, polishes and bitumen for road surfaces.

WHAT IS CRACKING?

CATALYTIC CRACKING is another method of refining crude oil. By applying pressure and heat to some of the heavier fractions obtained by distillation, lighter, more useful fractions are produced.

In an oil refinery, crude oil is separated into usable compounds. By mixing these with other substances and treating them in various ways, literally thousands of useful materials can be made.

WHAT IS PEAT?

PEAT IS partly carbonized vegetable matter, which has decomposed in water. If placed under enormous pressure for millions of years, peat would become coal. Although it does not give off as much heat as coal or oil does when burned, peat is still a useful fuel in some parts of the world, where it is dug from peatbogs. Peat has also been much prized by gardeners for improving the condition of soil.

Peat has been a traditional Irish fuel for centuries. Nowadays, conservationists are concerned that too much digging of peatbogs is destroying the environment that they provide, so alternative fuels and soil conditioners are recommended.

fast facts

HOW IS OIL FOUND?

Geologists know what kinds of rocks are likely to contain or cover oil deposits. When they find a likely area, on land or at sea, test drilling is carried out to find out if there is oil beneath the surface.

WHAT ARE THE DIFFERENT KINDS OF COAL?

Coal is found in three forms. Lignite, or brown coal, provides the least heat, as it contains less carbon and more water than the other two kinds, which are bituminous coal and anthracite.

HOW ARE OIL RIG FIRES EXTINGUISHED?

If the gas gushing from an oil well is ignited, the fire burns far too fiercely to be put out with water or normal fire extinguishers. Instead, firefighters use a special crane to position an explosive device in the flames. It seems strange to fight a fire with an explosion, but when the explosion occurs, it takes the surrounding oxygen, temporarily depriving the fire and putting it out.

WHY WERE CANARIES TAKEN INTO MINES?

Traditionally, in British mines, a canary in a cage was taken down to the coal face with the miners. The small birds were very sensitive to the dangerous gases that might build up in the shafts. If the canary died suddenly, miners knew that they must run for their lives. Now, the practice seems cruel, but it did save many human lives.

WHAT WAS A DAVY LAMP?

In deep mines, lamps were needed, but naked flames might cause an explosion. In 1815, Humphry Davy invented a safety lamp with a wire mesh around the flame, so that gases would not be ignited.

WHICH MINERALS ARE OBTAINED BY MINING?

Strictly speaking, all "minerals" are obtained by mining, as that is one meaning of the word, although it is sometimes used to refer to other inorganic substances. Mining usually involves digging in the Earth's crust, although a few minerals, such as gold, sometimes come to the surface naturally and are found in rivers or on the seashore. Metals, precious and semi-precious stones, and minerals such as sulphur and salt are all obtained by mining.

Rocks found beneath the Earth's surface have many uses in industry. Others, such as malachite, are used for decoration.

WHERE ARE THE WORLD'S MOST IMPORTANT MINING AREAS?

FOR MINING to be economical, minerals need to be found in high concentrations. Sometimes they occur in seams. These are layers of minerals or mineral ores occurring between other rocks. In different parts of the world, rocks dating from various periods of the Earth's history are nearest the surface. This gives mineralogists their first clue as to the minerals that may be found within them.

IS WATER USEFUL IN MINING?

IN DEEP MINES, water can pose a great danger, undermining layers of rock and causing collapses and flooding, but other types of mining use water to great advantage. Sulphur, for example, can be mined in an unusual process using water. Three pipes of different sizes, one inside another, are drilled into the sulphur reserves. Then extremely hot water, under pressure, is pumped down the outer pipe. This melts the sulphur. Compressed air is then pumped down the central pipe, causing the melted sulphur to move up the middle pipe to the surface. This system was developed by an American engineer, Herman Frasch (1851–1914).

KEY
☐ precious metals, such as gold, platinum and silver
◇ precious stones, such as diamonds
○ base metals, such as copper, lead, mercury, tin and zinc
■ light metals, such as aluminium, lithium and titanium
▽ rare metals, such as uranium
⊙ iron, chromium, cobalt, manganese and nickel
▲ industrial minerals, such as asbestos, china clay, mica and talc
△ chemicals, such as borax, nitrates, phosphate, potash, salt and sulphur

CAN MINERALS BE OBTAINED FROM PLACES OTHER THAN THE EARTH'S CRUST?

FOR PRACTICAL PURPOSES, the Earth's crust is the only source of minerals. There are, of course, huge amounts of minerals in the Earth's core and in space, but at the moment it is not possible for us to reach and use them.

Despite modern safety regulations, mining is still a dangerous occupation. However, opencast mines are less hazardous than deep-shaft mines, where miners have to work hundreds of metres below the surface.

WHAT IS OPENCAST MINING?

OPENCAST MINES are used when the deposit lies near the surface. Overlying earth and rock can be moved by machine or washed away with water. Although opencast mining is cheaper than digging deep mines, some people feel that the environmental costs of it are high, as large areas of land are laid bare and wildlife destroyed. Nowadays great attention is often paid to landscaping the area after an opencast mine has been abandoned. Many are made into parks or wildlife refuges. Planting the areas also helps to stabilize heaps of spoil.

COULD THE EARTH'S MINERALS BE USED UP?

ALTHOUGH there are enormous reserves of iron and aluminium in the Earth's crust, other metals, such as tin, lead, silver, zinc, mercury and platinum are not so plentiful. Some further sources of such metals are known, but at present it would prove too expensive to reach them. As with other non-renewable resources, it is important that we recycle metals or use other materials where possible.

HOW DO UNDERGROUND MINES OPERATE?

DEEP DEPOSITS are reached by driving a shaft vertically into the ground. Miners descend the shaft in a lift. An air shaft takes fresh air down into the mine, where poisonous gases may accumulate. Trucks carry the mined material to a freight lift, which brings them to the surface. Trucks may also be used to take miners to the nearest deposits. Drift mines are dug where the deposit lies in an outcrop of rock near the surface. The seam can be mined directly from the surface, which is often on the slope of a hill.

WHAT IS A CARAT?

A carat is a unit of weight for precious stones, equivalent to 200 milligrams (0.007oz). It is also used as a measure of purity of gold. Pure gold is 24 carats.

WHICH IS THE LARGEST DIAMOND EVER FOUND?

A diamond called the *Cullinan* was found in 1905 at the Premier Diamond Mine, in South Africa. It weighed 3106 carats and was cut into 106 polished diamonds.

HOW DEEP IS THE DEEPEST MINE?

A gold mine at Carltonville, in South Africa, has reached a depth of 3581m (11,749ft).

WHICH ARE THE MOST COMMON MINERALS IN THE EARTH'S CRUST?

Aluminium, in the form of the ore bauxite, is the most common mineral in the Earth's crust, followed by iron and magnesium.

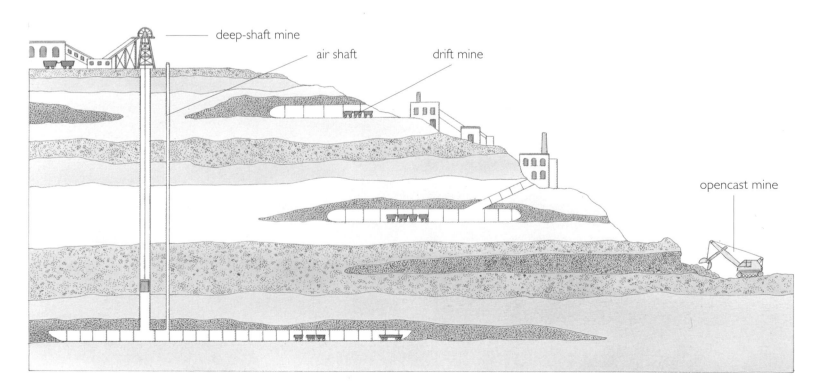

deep-shaft mine

air shaft   drift mine

opencast mine

HOW ARE MODERN MAPS MADE?

A map is similar to an aerial view of the Earth. The landscape is shown as though you are looking down on it, so that the relation of one place to another is clear. But maps are much more than simply bird's-eye views. A great deal of information about the names of places and what they are like can be given in words, numbers and symbols. Although maps are more than aerial snapshots, surveying by plane or satellite has helped mapmakers considerably. Surveying on the ground is time-consuming and may be difficult in remote places. Computer-controlled aerial surveying can give very accurate results and show overall changes in such features as vegetation and coastlines much more clearly than traditional methods.

An aerial view can show roads, rivers, buildings and vegetation, but it cannot tell you the name of a street or the height of a hill. This information has to be added to maps by the mapmakers themselves, known as cartographers.

WHAT IS A PROJECTION?

GLOBES can represent the Earth in miniature, with features shown in a true relationship to each other, but they are not practical to put in your pocket for an afternoon walk. Paper maps are much easier to use, but an adjustment needs to be made in order to show a curved land surface on a flat map. The adjustment chosen is called a projection. Several different projections can be used, depending on the purpose of the map.

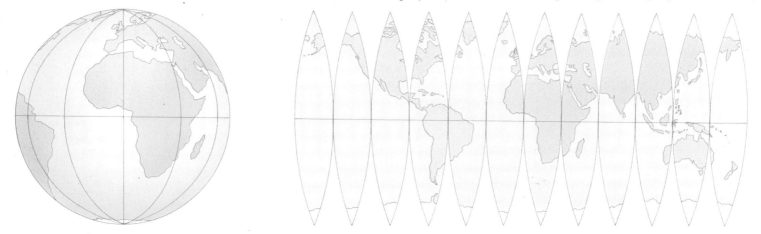

In order to flatten out the Earth's surface, it can be thought of as being divided into segments, like peeling an orange. But that leaves gaps at the top and bottom that make the map impossible to use.

WHO WAS GERARDUS MERCATOR?

GERHARD KREMER (1512–94) was called Gerardus Mercator, meaning merchant, because he made maps for merchants travelling from country to country. In 1569, he made a world map using a projection that has come to be known as Mercator's projection. It is a map that seems familiar to us, but in fact it makes countries at the far north and south of the globe appear much larger than they really are.

This map is based on Mercator's projection, but it does not look very much like the map that he produced in 1569. For one thing, Mercator had no idea of the existence of Australia or New Zealand.

This map of the world is based on Peters' projection. In the 1970s, Arno Peters devised a projection that gave each land mass its true area, but to do so he had to distort the shapes of the oceans and continents.

SCALE : 1:10,000

WHAT IS A KEY?

A MAP must be as easy to read as possible, which means that symbols and colours can often give more information than words. A key explains what the symbols and colours mean, as the one on the right does for the map above.

KEY

▬▬	motorway
───	railway
▬▬	main road
	canal
	built-up area

WHAT IS THE SCALE OF A MAP?

MAPS ARE MADE for many purposes. The details that an airline pilot needs to see, for example, are very different from those needed by a person following a local footpath. In addition to the actual content of the map, it needs to be drawn to an appropriate scale. That means that a distance on the map will need to be multiplied by a certain figure to find the distance on the ground itself. On a scale of 1:10,000, for example, one millimetre on the map will be equivalent to 10,000 millimetres (or 10 metres) in real life. The scale of the map above is shown on the map itself.

Many leisure maps for walkers and cyclists are drawn at a scale of 1:50,000.

WHAT IS AN ASTRAL MAP?

An astral map is a map of the stars and other heavenly bodies. Astral maps are usually made from the viewpoint of Earth, but still present difficulties as they do not represent a definite surface as maps of the Earth do. The stars are millions and millions of kilometres apart but are shown on maps as though they were merely distant in two dimensions, not three.

WHAT USE ARE OUT-OF-DATE MAPS?

Out-of-date maps are not much use for finding your way today, but they are extremely interesting to historians, who can tell a great deal about the knowledge and interests of the people who made them. Medieval maps of the world, for example, show how much of the Earth was known to European mapmakers at that time. Huge areas of Africa and Asia are left blank, while the Americas and Australasia are not present at all.

WHAT IS A THEODOLITE?

A theodolite is an instrument used by surveyors and mapmakers. It measures horizontal and vertical angles, enabling surveyors to chart the distance between features of the landscape and their relative positions above sea-level.

WHAT IS ORIENTEERING?

Orienteering is a sport that combines map-reading and running. Competitors follow a cross-country course, reaching checkpoints as quickly as possible by using a map. At each checkpoint, there is a rubber stamp, which runners use to show that they have completed all parts of the course.

HOW IS FITNESS MEASURED?

Fitness is the physical condition of an individual. When considered in terms of sports and other physical activity, it is often thought of as having four aspects: endurance, strength, flexibility and speed. Sports differ in the degree to which each of these factors is important. For example, weightlifting requires enormous strength, while a sprinter needs the greatest possible speed. The four aspects of fitness are measured in different ways, but one general way of measuring fitness is to see how the heart responds to physical activity. During exertion, the rate at which the heart beats increases, as it pumps more oxygenated blood around the body. How quickly the heart rate returns to normal after exercise is one way to assess how fit someone is and how exercise is improving their fitness.

Modern exercise bicycles have computers that can give instant readings of the time and distance pedalled and monitor the exerciser's heart rate.

HOW CAN TRAINING IMPROVE PERFORMANCE?

TRAINING improves performance by building up endurance, strength, flexibility and speed. This is done by improving the techniques used in a particular sport, strengthening the muscles used, improving athletes' understanding of how their bodies are performing and giving them confidence to try even harder. There are lots of training methods, and variety can help to prevent boredom setting in.

Decathlon

100m, 400m and 1500m races

long jump

shot put

high jump

110m hurdles

discus

pole vault

javelin

Modern pentathlon

fencing

freestyle swimming

pistol shooting

cross-country running

riding

Triathlon

swimming 3.8km

cycling 180km

running 42.2km

Many people use weight training to increase their strength. Lifting light weights and repeating the exercise a specified number of times builds muscle strength without creating bulk.

WHAT ARE MULTI-DISCIPLINARY SPORTING EVENTS?

SOME ATHLETES do not specialize in just one sport but maintain a very high standard at several. For them, multi-disciplinary sports, in which points are awarded for performance in a variety of events, are ideal. Some of the most popular are shown above.

HOW ARE RACES ON A CIRCULAR TRACK MADE FAIR?

WHEN ATHLETES are running a circuit, those on the inside tracks have to run less far than those on the outside. In order to ensure that everyone runs the same distance, the start is staggered, so that those on the inside appear to start much further back than those on the outside. It is not until the final straight that it is really possible to see who is winning. Longer races often start from a simple curved line. Athletes break out of their lanes quite quickly and each runs as close to the inside of the track as possible.

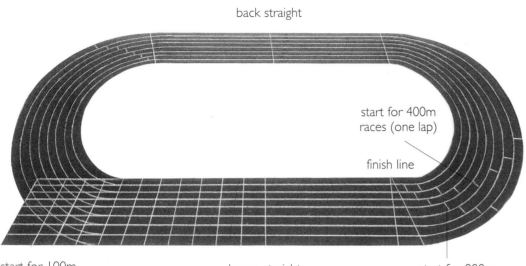

back straight

start for 400m
races (one lap)

finish line

start for 100m
races

home straight

start for 800m
races (two laps)

WHAT ARE THE PARALYMPICS?

IN 1960, in Rome, Italy, the first Paralympics were held. These are Olympic Games for athletes with disabilities. They are now held after each Olympic Games, often on the same site, and give disabled athletes from all over the world an opportunity to compete against each other.

Athletes at the Paralympics train just as hard as their Olympic colleagues. Wheelchairs are specially built for various sports, including track and field events.

WHEN WERE THE MODERN OLYMPIC GAMES INTRODUCED?

THE ANCIENT GREEKS held sporting contests over 2000 years ago. In 1896, a Frenchman called Baron Pierre de Coubertin prompted the revival of the Olympic Games. The first modern Olympics were held in Athens, Greece, in honour of their origin. Since then they have been held every four years, except in wartime, in cities all over the globe.

The Olympic flame is a symbol of the Olympic spirit of striving to do one's best. Before each Olympic Games, a series of runners carries the flame from Greece to the site of the Games, where it is used to light the main flame at the opening ceremony.

WHAT IS A PLASTIC?

Plastics are polymers, which means that they are made of lots of small molecules joined together to form larger molecules in the form of long chains. Polymers can be manufactured from crude oil, natural gas, or coal. They include artificial fibres and many kinds of plastic. Plastics are extremely useful because they are extraordinarily versatile. They are easy to shape and colour. They can be made into rigid objects or thin, pliable sheets. Some plastics are heatproof, while others melt at low temperatures.

WHAT CAN BE MADE FROM PLASTIC?

ALMOST ANYTHING can be made from plastic! Plastic packaging keeps food fresh and protects it from bacteria. A plastic coating, called Teflon, can prevent food from sticking to cooking pans. Plastic can be elastic, like the skin of a balloon, or very rigid and reinforced with other fibres, as in a protective helmet. Plastic can also be a good insulator. A plastic sleeve on electrical wiring protects the wires from corrosion and the user from electric shocks. Polystyrene packaging can help to keep take-away food warm. Plastic can be dyed in bright colours or completely transparent, to make spectacles and contact lenses. Without plastics, there would be less music in our lives, with no cassette tapes, compact discs or even old-fashioned records.

HOW IS PLASTIC SHAPED?

PLASTIC may be shaped in various ways. It can be extruded (pushed through a nozzle when liquid) to form sheets, tubes and fibres. Molten plastic can be poured into moulds. Vacuum forming is a way of making complicated plastic shapes. A sheet of warm plastic is placed over a mould, then the air is sucked from under it so that the sheet is pulled firmly against the sides of the mould. When the plastic is cooled, it retains the mould's shape. Disposable cups are often made in this way.

WHAT IS THE DIFFERENCE BETWEEN THERMOPLASTICS AND THERMOSETS?

SOME PLASTICS, such as polythene, can be melted and reshaped over and over again. These plastics are recyclable and are called thermoplastics. Other plastics are more resistant to heat and cannot be melted and reshaped. They are known as thermosets. Plastic kitchen worksurfaces and the hard plastic casings around some electrical goods are made from thermosets.

Many inexpensive plastic products are made from fairly flexible thermoplastics, such as polythene. This can be formed in thin sheets or moulded.

The plastic casing of this glue gun is made from thermoset plastic. It needs to be rigid and to resist the heat generated inside it.

ARE THERE ANY NATURAL POLYMERS?

STARCH, rubber, wool, silk and hair are all natural polymers. Their molecular structure, under the right conditions, makes them strong and flexible.

The sap of rubber trees is a white, milky substance called latex. It is collected by cutting the bark and allowing the latex to run into a cup underneath. When heated and treated, the latex solidifies into rubber.

HOW HAVE PLASTICS CHANGED OUR LIVES?

PLASTIC MATERIALS can be shaped very efficiently by machines, so plastic objects are cheaply made in great numbers. Some people think that this has contributed to the "disposable society", where we are inclined to throw something away when it is worn or broken, instead of trying to mend it, as would have happened in the past. They warn, too, that most plastics do not easily decay, so our thrown-away food cartons and shopping bags will remain to pollute the planet for years to come. However, plastics have also brought great benefits, playing a part in so many aspects of our lives that it is difficult now to imagine the world without them.

It was a natural polymer, rubber, that was used to make the first truly waterproof clothing, when Scottish chemist Charles Macintosh (1766–1843) sandwiched a layer of rubber between two pieces of cloth. Today, many different waterproof materials are made from polymers, using plastic coatings and artificial fibres.

Once tennis equipment was made entirely of natural materials: wood, cat gut, rubber and wool. Now synthetic polymers may be used to make the racket frame, strings and tennis balls.

WHO BUILT THE FIRST COMPUTER?

In the early 1830s, an English inventor called Charles Babbage (1792–1871) designed the first programmable computer and began to build it. In fact, he never finished, as the machine was extremely complicated! This computer was entirely mechanical. Over a hundred years had to pass before the electronic components that are used today were invented.

WHAT ARE THE MAIN PARTS OF A COMPUTER?

THE CENTRAL PROCESSING UNIT (CPU) is the "brain" of a computer, where its calculations take place. It is contained within a larger processing unit. In order to give instructions to the computer, input devices, such as a keyboard, stylus, mouse, or joystick, are needed. The monitor enables the user to see data on a screen. Many other machines, called peripherals, can also be connected to the computer. They include printers, scanners and modems.

HOW IS INFORMATION STORED IN A COMPUTER?

INSIDE A COMPUTER is a "hard disk", which is able to store information (data) even when the machine is turned off. But there are also two other kinds of storage in a computer. ROM (read-only memory) stores the instructions that tell the computer how to start working when it is first switched on. RAM (random-access memory) stores data that is in use. To make sure that data is permanently stored, it must be "saved" on the hard disk before the computer is switched off.

monitor

central processing unit (CPU)

keyboard

mouse

WHAT IS THE DIFFERENCE BETWEEN HARDWARE AND SOFTWARE?

THE HARDWARE of a computer consists of all the parts described above: the machine itself and any other machinery that is attached to it. But a computer by itself is simply a collection of components. In order to do anything at all, it must be programmed (given a set of instructions). Programs are what is known as software. They are written in a code that a computer can "understand" and act upon. The codes in which programs are written are sometimes called languages.

floppy disk   compact disc   cassette   optical disk

10MB   230 MB   230

An enormous amount of data can be stored in a computer's memory, but as a back-up and so that data can be shared between machines, several different portable storage devices are used.

HOW DOES A MOUSE WORK?

A MOUSE is a device for giving the computer information (an input device). When the mouse is pushed around on a mat, a pointer on the computer's screen is moved, indicating how data needs to be changed, moved or processed. Tiny beams of light inside the mouse shine through slotted wheels. The ball of the the mouse moves as it is pushed across the mat, and the beams of light are interrupted in a way that tells the computer the direction that the mouse is moving.

Slotted wheels send information on the mouse's position to the computer.

mouse ball

WHAT IS INSIDE THE PROCESSING UNIT OF A COMPUTER?

INSIDE the processing unit of a computer are collections of integrated circuits (microchips) and other components, usually positioned on circuit boards. There are also slots for floppy disks and CDs to be inserted, a "hard disk" on which data is stored, and perhaps devices such as fans to keep the components cool. Portable computers also have space for a battery, which can be recharged.

Many computers have what are known as expansion slots. Special circuit boards can be inserted into these to increase the computer's power or allow it to perform a particular function.

WHAT IS A PIXEL?

A PIXEL is a tiny dot of colour, which, together with millions of other dots, makes up a picture on a computer or television screen. It is short for "picture element".

fast facts

WHAT DOES CAD STAND FOR?

CAD stands for "computer aided design". There are very few areas of manufacturing and production that do not now call on computers to help with designing new products and improving existing ones.

WHAT DOES THE WORD "COMPUTER" MEAN?

A computer is simply something that can "compute", or calculate. Although today computers can be used for much more than simple calculations, all their functions are based on mathematics.

WHAT IS PROCESSING?

Processing is anything that the computer does to data. It could include sorting it, changing the way it looks, performing calculations on it, or any number of other activities.

WHAT IS A MODEM?

A modem is a device that links a computer to a telephone line or other communication system. It enables information to be shared between computers directly or via the Internet, which is a huge "net" of computer connections stretching across the world.

HOW DO COMPUTERS TODAY DIFFER FROM THE FIRST ELECTRONIC ONES ?

Early computers took up whole rooms, which were filled with machinery and spools of whirring magnetic tape. Today, a personal computer (PC) can sit on top of a desk, yet offers many times more power than those huge machines. Today's computers are much faster and have huge memories compared with their ancestors. They are also able to handle pictures and even video footage in a way that was impossible even a few years ago.

HOW DOES AN ELECTRIC MOTOR WORK?

An electric motor uses a current and a magnetic field to create motion. A specially shaped coil of wire, called an armature, is positioned between the poles of a permanent magnet. When an electric current is fed into the wire, the coil becomes a magnet too and forces of attraction and repulsion between it and the permanent magnet cause the armature to move around its axis. A device called a commutator then reverses the current, so that the armature's magnetic poles are reversed and it turns through 180 degrees. If the current is continually reversed, the armature is always turning on its axis. It is this motion that can be used to drive a huge number of machines, such as washing machines, hairdriers and food processors.

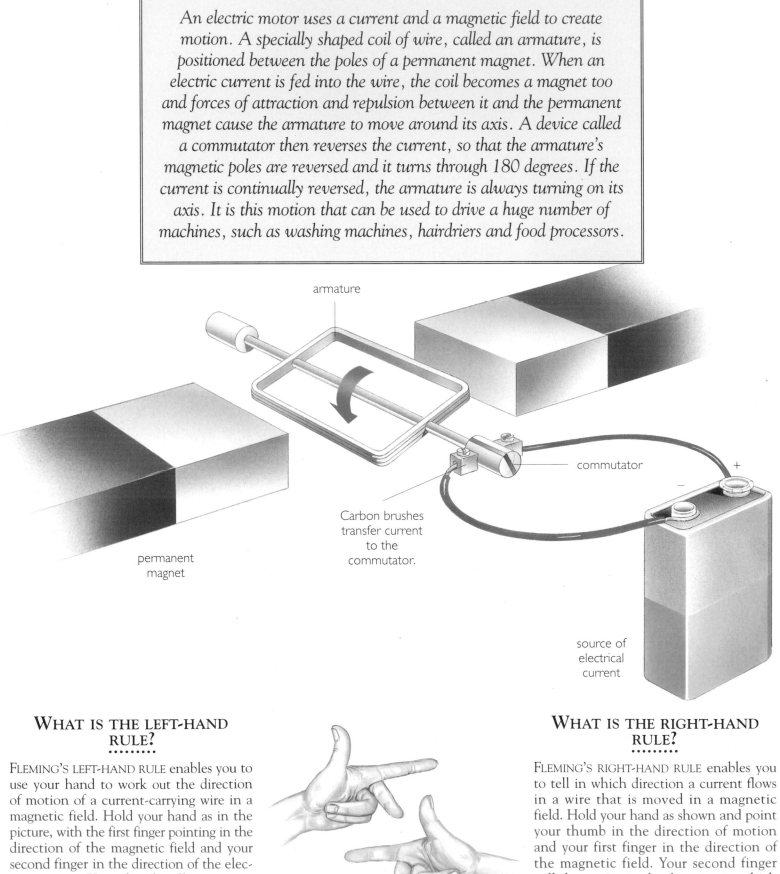

armature

commutator

Carbon brushes transfer current to the commutator.

permanent magnet

source of electrical current

+

−

WHAT IS THE LEFT-HAND RULE?

FLEMING'S LEFT-HAND RULE enables you to use your hand to work out the direction of motion of a current-carrying wire in a magnetic field. Hold your hand as in the picture, with the first finger pointing in the direction of the magnetic field and your second finger in the direction of the electric current. Your thumb will now point in the direction of motion of the wire.

WHAT IS THE RIGHT-HAND RULE?

FLEMING'S RIGHT-HAND RULE enables you to tell in which direction a current flows in a wire that is moved in a magnetic field. Hold your hand as shown and point your thumb in the direction of motion and your first finger in the direction of the magnetic field. Your second finger will then point in the direction in which current flows in the wire.

HOW DOES AN ELECTRIC LIGHT WORK?

INSIDE many electric light bulbs is a wire called a filament, made of tungsten. When current is passed through the wire, it glows white hot, giving off light and some heat. As the oxygen has been removed from the bulb, combustion cannot take place, so the wire does not burn out immediately.

sealed glass bulb

filament

metal contacts through which current can flow

WILL ELECTRICALLY POWERED VEHICLES EVER BE POSSIBLE?

ELECTRICALLY POWERED VEHICLES have been in use for many years! Powering motor cars with electricity does present certain problems, as batteries are heavy and a car's energy requirement is high. This means that the distance an electric car can travel before it is recharged may be too low for many uses. In hot countries, engineers have experimented quite successfully with supplementing a car's battery power with solar power, using solar panels on the roof of the car.

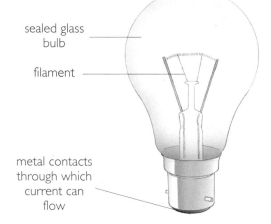

Where vehicles can obtain electrical energy from a fixed wire or track, there is no problem about electrical supply. Electrically powered trains, such as the French train shown above, are the fastest in the world.

We are used to thinking of small domestic electric light bulbs, but in some situations a great deal more light is needed. Some lighthouses have their own generators, which must be kept working all the time if the light is not to fail.

Specially designed electrically powered wheelchairs and vehicles enable disabled people to move about at the same speed as pedestrians.

WHAT IS A GENERATOR?

A GENERATOR is a machine that produces electrical current by moving a wire in a magnetic field. Energy is needed to move the wire. This may come from steam, wind, moving water, or, in the case of the small generator called a dynamo that may be found on some bicycles, from the movement of human legs! Dynamos produce just enough electrical energy to power the lights of a bicycle, but this energy is not stored. If the cyclist stops pedalling, the lights dim and go out.

fast facts

WHO BUILT THE FIRST ELECTRIC MOTOR?

The first electric motor was based on the work of Michael Faraday (1791–1867), an English physicist. Not only was he the first to show how current and a magnetic field could produce motion, but he also discovered the principle of the generator.

WHAT IS ALTERNATING CURRENT?

Alternating current is electrical current that continually changes direction. This happens many times in a second.

WHAT IS DIRECT CURRENT?

Direct current is electrical current that flows in only one direction.

HOW DOES A FUSE WORK?

A fuse is a short piece of wire, often sealed in a plastic and metal casing, that forms the weakest link in a circuit. If the current in the circuit becomes too high, the fuse wire will melt, breaking the circuit.

WHAT IS A SOLENOID?

A solenoid is another name for a coil of wire in which an electromagnetic field is created when a current passes through it.

The windmills of a wind farm can power generators to produce electricity for hundreds of homes.

WHAT IS ARABLE FARMING?

Arable farming is the growing and harvesting of crops, particularly where the ground is ploughed between harvests, as the term comes from the Latin word for ploughing. Arable farming is of enormous importance to the world's population, since most of us rely on grains or vegetables for our staple foods.

WHICH ARE THE WORLD'S MOST WIDELY GROWN CROPS?

Wheat is the most widely grown crop, as its various hybrids can grow in a variety of soils and climates. Apart from some grains kept for seed, harvested wheat is ground into flour to make bread, pasta and baked goods.

Rice is the main food for over half the world's population, largely in Asia and South America. Up to three crops of rice per year can be harvested from the same well-watered land. Rice needs a growing-season temperature of over 21°C (70°F).

Maize, or corn, originated from the Americas but is now grown in all warm parts of the world. It is used for human food, as a vegetable, and in the form of maize flour and breakfast cereals. It is also milled and fed to animals.

WHICH CROPS ARE NOT GROWN FOR FOOD?

NOT ALL CROPS are grown for human or animal food. Cotton, flax and jute are grown to be made into fabric. Esparto grass may be cultivated for the manufacture of rope and paper. Tobacco is grown for smoking, while bamboo canes have hundreds of varied uses.

Other non-food crops, such as lavender, are grown for the perfume and cosmetics industries.

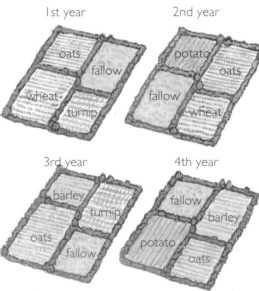

A typical four-year rotation is shown here. During fallow years, grass or clover was grown. The latter was particularly good for restoring nitrogen to the soil.

WHAT WAS THE AGRICULTURAL REVOLUTION?

IN EUROPE in the Middle Ages, large fields were often divided into strips, with individuals farming their strip as intensively as possible. Since little was understood about the nutrients that plants need and the use of fertilizers, the soil in these strips soon became exhausted, with poorer and poorer yields resulting. The Agricultural Revolution was a change in farming practice that took place gradually during the eighteenth century. The technique of resting ground for a year (leaving it fallow) and rotating crops, so that the same crop was not grown year after year on the same plot, was tested and found to improve harvests. A two-year rotation, and later three- and four-year rotations came to be widely practised.

WHICH ARE THE MOST COMMONLY FARMED ANIMALS?

LIVESTOCK is farmed chiefly to supply foods such as meat, eggs and milk, but also for leather, fur and wool. Animal by-products may also include glue, gelatin and fertilizer. The most commonly farmed animals in the world today are shown below.

Cattle are found all over the world, reared for meat, milk and as draught animals. Cows remain in milk for up to 10 months after the birth of a calf. Different breeds of cattle are suited to almost all climates.

Bred for meat, eggs and feathers, poultry may be chickens, turkeys, ducks or geese. Recently, ostriches have also been farmed. Poultry are often reared indoors for all of their comparatively short lives.

Sheep are kept for meat, milk and wool. They can survive on poorer pasture than cattle. Huge numbers of sheep are raised in Australia and New Zealand, where vast areas of land are given over to them.

There are very few parts of the pig that cannot be used as meat, leather, bristles or fat. Traditionally allowed to roam in woodland, they are now kept in purpose-built huts and intensively farmed.

HOW CAN FISH BE FARMED?

FISHING in the open seas is expensive, dangerous and increasingly difficult as some fish stocks diminish. Fish farming involves using lakes, rivers and netted-off coastal areas to raise fish that can be harvested more easily. Freshwater fish and shellfish have been most successfully farmed in this way. Many deep-sea fish require conditions that are impossible to recreate in managed waters.

The oceans are so immense that it seems impossible that they could be over-fished, but modern fishing boats are like huge floating factories. They can be at sea for weeks, processing and freezing on board the fish that they literally scoop from the sea. The latest ultrasonic aids help in finding shoals of fish.

HOW HAS MACHINERY CHANGED FARMING?

MACHINERY has made it possible for the work of a dozen farm workers to be done twice as quickly by one worker. There are fewer people working on the land in developed countries than ever before. Machinery exacts a price from the environment as well, as hedges and ditches are removed to allow larger machines to work the enormous fields. Crops have been bred for the machine age, too. They need to ripen together, not over a period of time, so that machinery can harvest them in one operation.

There are still many parts of the world where traditional farming methods are used, but the use of machinery is increasing year by year.

WHAT IS FACTORY FARMING?

Factory farming is an intensive farming method in which animals are kept in buildings until they are slaughtered. They have little space to move and so need less food energy to bring them to the desired size. While some consumers are glad of the cheaper food that is available from this method, others feel that the quality of life of the animals is unacceptably low.

WHAT IS IRRIGATION?

Irrigation involves bringing water to cultivated land, by means of ditches, reservoirs, pipes or sprayers.

WHAT IS HYDROPONICS?

Hydroponics is a way of growing food crops in gravel or polythene. All the nutrients they need are dissolved in water, which is pumped directly to their roots.

WHICH CROP TAKES LONGEST TO GROW?

Trees, grown for timber and paper-making, may need to grow for 50 or 60 years before they are harvested.

WHAT IS PASTORALISM?

Pastoralism is another term for livestock farming, although strictly speaking it does not include factory farming.

WHO WAS HIPPOCRATES?

*Hippocrates is often described as "the father of modern medicine".
He was a Greek doctor, living in the fourth and fifth centuries BC,
who taught that a doctor's first duty is to his or her patient and that
the aim must at all times be to try to do good rather than harm.
When they qualify, many modern doctors take the Hippocratic
Oath, promising to follow these principles throughout their careers.*

The anaesthetist usually sits at the patient's head, monitoring breathing and heart rate.

Nurses pass instruments to the surgeons. They also make sure that no instruments are left inside the patient by mistake!

Those in the operating theatre wear sterile clothing and cover their noses, mouths and hair to prevent bacteria infecting the open wound.

Sterile drapes cover the patient except for the area where the operation is taking place.

WHAT WAS THE EARLIEST OPERATION?

ARCHAEOLOGISTS have found skulls, dating from at least 10,000 years ago, that have holes drilled into them. Because bone has begun to grow around the holes, they were clearly made while the person was still alive. It is believed that this technique, called trepanning, was the first operation. It was probably done to relieve headaches or to let out evil spirits that were thought to be trapped inside the patient's head.

WHEN WAS ANAESTHESIA FIRST USED?

ANAESTHESIA prevents pain signals from being received by the brain, so that the pain is not felt by the patient. Hundreds of years ago there were few ways to relieve a patient's pain during surgery. Alcohol might be used, but it was not very effective. It was not until the nineteenth century that anaesthetic drugs began to be widely used. The first operation to be performed using a general anaesthetic was by an American surgeon, Crawford Long, in 1842.

fast facts

WHAT IS ACUPUNCTURE?

Acupuncture is an ancient Chinese technique for improving or maintaining health by pushing needles into certain points in the body.

WHAT IS ENDOSCOPY?

Endoscopy is a way of looking inside the body without major surgery. An instrument called an endoscope is inserted into the body through a small hole. Inside it, optical fibres enable the doctor to see internal organs through an eyepiece or on a screen. Endoscopy also enables some operations to be performed using a technique called keyhole surgery, in which only a small incision needs to be made, as the endoscope enables the surgeon to manipulate instruments inside the patient.

HOW DID JOSEPH LISTER HELP TO SAVE LIVES?

Joseph Lister (1827–1912) was an English chemist who introduced the first widely-used antiseptic. By spraying the operating theatre with carbolic acid, he was able to kill harmful bacteria and reduce the infection of wounds dramatically.

WHEN WAS THE FIRST HEART TRANSPLANT?

In 1967, the South African surgeon Christiaan Barnard performed the first transplantation of a heart from a person who had recently died into the body of a man with terminal heart disease. The recipient lived for 18 days. Since then, many patients have lived for years following successful surgery, and the transplantation of other organs, such as kidneys and lungs, is routinely undertaken.

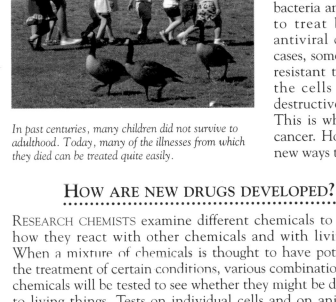

In past centuries, many children did not survive to adulthood. Today, many of the illnesses from which they died can be treated quite easily.

HOW ARE NEW DRUGS DEVELOPED?

RESEARCH CHEMISTS examine different chemicals to find out how they react with other chemicals and with living cells. When a mixture of chemicals is thought to have potential in the treatment of certain conditions, various combinations of the chemicals will be tested to see whether they might be dangerous to living things. Tests on individual cells and on animals are made before human beings are given the new drug. Many people think that drug-testing on animals is wrong, but others feel that this is the best way to make sure that drugs are safe. Trials of the drug, in which some patients are given a placebo (a drug with no active ingredients), are carried out to assess the drug's effectiveness. It is usually only after many years of testing and monitoring that the drug is released for use by doctors.

HOW DO VACCINATIONS WORK?

IN 1796, an English doctor called Edward Jenner (1749–1823) gave the first vaccination. He realized that milkmaids who caught cowpox did not catch the very dangerous disease of smallpox. By injecting the cowpox virus into a child, he was able to vaccinate him against the more serious disease. As the body fights the virus, antibodies are formed in the blood that prevent further infections or infection by some similar viruses. Today, huge vaccination programmes ensure that most children are protected against a range of diseases.

WHAT CAUSES ILLNESS?

UNDERSTANDING the cause of an illness can often help a doctor to bring a patient back to good health or to suggest ways to prevent the illness from recurring or affecting other people. Illness may be caused by an accident, which physically affects part of the body, or it may be brought about by tiny organisms such as bacteria and viruses. Antibiotics are used to treat bacterial infections, while antiviral drugs attack viruses. In both cases, some disease-causing organisms are resistant to drug therapy. Occasionally, the cells of the body seem to act in destructive ways for no obvious reason. This is what happens in some forms of cancer. However, researchers are finding new ways to combat disease all the time.

Drugs in powder form may be pressed into tablets or contained in capsules that dissolve in the stomach. To help pharmacists and patients to distinguish between drugs, they are shaped and coloured in different ways.

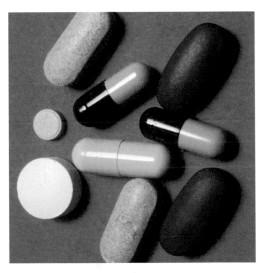

Vaccinations are given with hypodermic needles. These are manufactured in sterile conditions and packaged so that bacteria cannot contaminate them.

GLOSSARY

Aerial A wire or rod that is used to transmit or receive radio waves.

Ballast Heavy material placed in the hull of a boat or ship to increase its stability.

Book block The pages of a book, sewn or glued together, before the cover is put onto them.

By-product A secondary product, resulting from a process mainly designed to extract or manufacture another product.

Cockpit The place in the fuselage of a plane in which the pilot sits.

Diaphragm A thin disc or sheet used to separate two areas. The diaphragm is usually designed to vibrate or move up and down when the pressure on one side of it is higher than on the other.

Die An engraved stamp used for decorating coins and other objects, or a hollow mould for shaping metal or plastic items.

Fuselage The body of an aeroplane.

Gender Whether a plant or animal is male or female.

Incision A cut, such as that made by a surgeon to open the skin for an operation.

Leaf (of a book) The two sides of a page.

Mica Any one of several minerals made of aluminium silicate or other silicates with a layered structure.

Organ Part of the body of an animal or plant that performs a particular function. The lungs, for example, are organs of respiration. The stomach is an organ of digestion.

Piston A disc or cylinder of metal, wood or plastic that fits closely within a tube and is able to move up and down within it. Pistons create motion in steam and petrol engines.

Receptor In a living body, a receptor is an organ that is able to sense aspects of the outside world, such as light, heat, aromas and flavours.

Repulsion The act of repelling: pushing something back or away.

Reservoir A tank or lake in which large amounts of liquid, especially water, can be stored.

Scanner A device that can gather information about an image by passing a beam of light across it. Scanners are used to separate colour pictures into four films for printing, and to store an image digitally so that it can be processed and output by a computer.

Spoil Earth, rocks and minerals brought to the surface during mining but not needed for further processing. Spoil may often be seen piled in heaps near mines and quarries.

Surveying Determining the nature of a piece of land by measuring distances and angles. Surveys are needed before a new building is constructed and for making maps or finding new deposits of minerals.

Talc A form of magnesium silicate used, in powdered form, as a lubricant between moving parts or to stop two surfaces from sticking together.

Tempo The speed of a piece of music, and sometimes its characteristic rhythm as well.

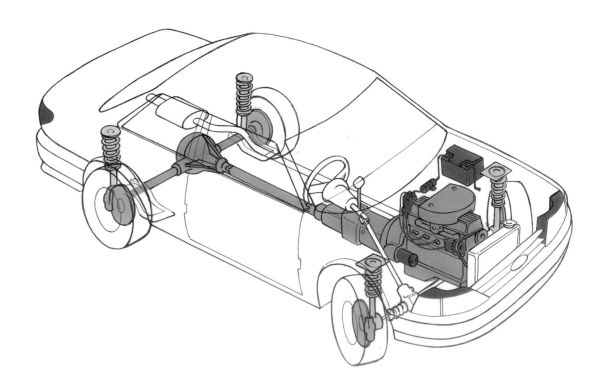

INDEX